SOA Patterns with BizTalk Server 2009

Implement SOA strategies for BizTalk Server solutions

Richard Seroter

PUBLISHING

BIRMINGHAM - MUMBAI

SOA Patterns with BizTalk Server 2009
Implement SOA strategies for BizTalk Server solutions

First published: April 2009

Production Reference: 1200409

Published by Packt Publishing Ltd.
32 Lincoln Road
Olton
Birmingham, B27 6PA, UK.

ISBN 978-1-847195-00-5

www.packtpub.com

Cover Image by Vinayak Chittar (vinayak.chittar@gmail.com)

Credits

Author
Richard Seroter

Reviewers
Charles Young
Ewan Fairweather
Zach Bonham

Acquisition Editor
James Lumsden

Development Editors
Nikhil Bangera
Siddharth Mangrole

Technical Editor
Gagandeep Singh

Indexer
Rekha Nair

Production Editorial Manager
Abhijeet Deobhakta

Editorial Team Leader
Akshara Aware

Project Team Leader
Lata Basantani

Project Coordinator
Neelkanth Mehta

Proofreader
Camille Guy

Production Coordinator
Shantanu Zagade

Cover Work
Shantanu Zagade

About the author

Richard Seroter is a solutions architect for an industry-leading biotechnology company, a Microsoft MVP for BizTalk Server, and a Microsoft Connected Systems Advisor. He has spent the majority of his career consulting with customers as they planned and implemented their enterprise software solutions. Richard worked first for two global IT consulting firms, which gave him exposure to a diverse range of industries, technologies, and business challenges. Richard then joined Microsoft as a SOA/BPM technology specialist where his sole objective was to educate and collaborate with customers as they considered, designed, and architected BizTalk solutions. One of those customers liked him enough to bring him onboard full time as an architect after they committed to using BizTalk Server as their enterprise service bus. Once the BizTalk environment was successfully established, Richard transitioned into a solutions architect role where he now helps identify enterprise best practices and applies good architectural principles to a wide set of IT initiatives.

Richard maintains a semi-popular blog of his exploits, pitfalls, and musings with BizTalk Server and enterprise architecture at http://seroter.wordpress.com.

First off, I need to thank my exceptional technical reviewers and editors for doing such a fine job. Charles Young, Zach Bonham, and Ewan Fairweather all made significant contributions in their role as technical reviewers and this book is of a higher caliber as a result of their insight and wisdom. Tim Wieman also took time to review the book content and his real-world perspective was a welcome addition. I have to thank James Lumsden, Neelkanth Mehta, Nikhil Bangera, Gagandeep Singh and the whole top notch team from Packt Publishing for doing such a seamless job shepherding this book from inception through delivery.

I'd have been much worse off in this endeavor without the assistance from Microsoft. Thanks to Richard Hughes and Emil Velinov for acting as facilitators to the Microsoft technical team and efficiently routing my questions to the appropriate individual. These capable Microsofties include Dmitri Ossipov, David Stucki, John Taylor, Sarathy Sakshi, and Rong Yu.

I'm thankful every day that I work with some of the brightest and most creative technologists that you'll ever come across. They have contributed greatly to my architectural maturity and helped me (unwittingly or not!) craft many of the patterns that you'll find in this book. These people include my peerless manager Nancy Lehrer and colleagues Fred Stann, Ian Sutcliffe, Chris Allen, Simon Chatwin, Jaydev Thakkar, Elizabeth Waldorf, Felix Rabinovich, Aki Hayashi, and Victor Fehlberg.

Finally, I had wondered before I wrote this book why everyone always thanks their families in a book's "acknowledgements" section. Now I know. I couldn't have gotten this task done without the support of my wife Amy and son Noah. Actually, Noah's too young to have put up a real fight, but he's a trooper nonetheless. Thanks you two for putting up with the late weeknights and stolen weekends. Hopefully my book residuals are enough to take us all to a nice dinner.

About the reviewers

Charles Young has more than twenty years' experience of software architecture, design, and implementation, and has worked on numerous projects as a developer, trainer, and consultant. He works as a Principal Consultant at Solidsoft, a UK-based company specializing in integration, workflow, and business process management on the Microsoft platform. Charles has wide experience of applying BizTalk Server, WCF, and WF to real-world problems. He has blogged extensively on the use of BizTalk Server and Business Rules, and is a regular speaker at architectural conferences and seminars.

Ewan Fairweather has worked for Microsoft for four years. He currently works as a Program Manager in the BizTalk Product Group on the Customer Advisory Team (CAT). The BizTalk CAT is responsible for improving customer experience with BizTalk through: defining and delivering the enterprise services that the product requires, providing prescriptive guidance on best practices to all customers, and improving future versions of the product through customer feedback and key learnings.

Prior to this, Ewan spent over three years working for Microsoft UK in the Premier Field Engineering team. In this role he worked with enterprise customers, helping them to maintain and optimize their BizTalk applications. This involved providing both proactive and reactive onsite assistance within the UK and the rest of Europe. Ewan has also worked in a dedicated capacity on some of the world's largest BizTalk deployments, predominantly within financial services.

Ewan co-authored the successful Professional BizTalk Server 2006 book and has written many whitepapers for Microsoft including the Microsoft BizTalk Server Performance Optimization guide which is available on Microsoft's MSDN website. Prior to joining Microsoft Ewan worked as a Cisco Certified Academy Instructor (CCAI) for a regional training organization delivering advanced routing and networking courses. Ewan holds a first class honors Bachelor of Science degree in Computing with Management from the University of Leeds. Outside of work, Ewan's hobbies include reading, taking part in as many sports as possible, and regularly going to the gym.

Zach Bonham is a software developer working primarily with Microsoft's connected systems technology. Zach is active in the Dallas/Fort Worth user group community and is a member of Microsoft's Connected Technologies Advisor Group. You can catch up with Zach at http://zachbonham.blogspot.com.

I would like to thank Richard Seroter for taking the time to write this book as well as for his contributions to the online community. I would also like to thank Ray Crager for being the "smartest man alive" and a great teacher. There are an incredible number of BizTalk community members who need to be thanked, too many to list here, but you know who you are! Finally, I would like to thank my wife, Sally, and our two children for their love and support.

Table of Contents

Preface

Repeat after me: SOA is something you do, not something you buy.

-David Linthicum

That may seem an odd quote to use when beginning a book about employing a particular product to facilitate the implementation of a service-oriented architecture (SOA). However, I think it sets the tone for what I'd like to accomplish here.

There are countless books available on service-oriented architecture, and nearly as many independent definitions of what SOA actually is. Is it about web services, event-driven design, enterprise architecture, reusability, or maybe just a retread of existing object-oriented design? Depending on whom you ask, any of those preceding themes would be deemed correct. If you're looking to implement a SOA, you would find numerous vendors who claim to offer "SOA in a box" where becoming service oriented is as straightforward as installing a product. However, I prefer to define SOA as an *architectural discipline based on loosely-coupled, autonomous chunks of business functionality, which can be used to construct composite applications.* There are plenty of vital characteristics that can be teased out of that definition, but the most important point is that building a successful SOA requires an enterprise commitment and a particular way of thinking about software design, which cannot be achieved by simply hitching your wagon to the SOA product de jour.

That said, a service-oriented architecture cannot be implemented using only high-minded strategies recorded with paper and pencil. It requires a technology solution that can realize the goals and vision of the business architecture. In this book, we're going to specifically investigate how to design and build service-oriented solutions using BizTalk Server 2009 as the host platform. The crop of high quality BizTalk Server books currently available all admirably cover the entire suite of capabilities which make up the product. And BizTalk by nature has many built-in service-oriented concepts such as loose coupling and message-oriented design, which are discussed in the existing books on hand. However, there is no book currently available that specifically looks at how to map service-oriented principles and patterns to the BizTalk product. That's where this book fits in.

One might look at Windows Workflow Foundation (WF) and Windows Communication Foundation (WCF) and ask why it matters to keep talking about BizTalk Server. Aren't these exciting technologies shepherding in a new era of Microsoft-based enterprise software design that makes a messaging bus like BizTalk obsolete? Fair question. Today, WF and WCF are foundational platform technologies on which future Microsoft applications will be built upon. They are both excellent at servicing particular problem areas around unified communication and workflow. BizTalk Server is Microsoft's enterprise class product, which enables process integration across disparate entities (such as organizations, platforms, applications) through a robust event-driven infrastructure that provides durable messaging, load balancing, and reliability. Similarly, while one can build a portal solution on top of Microsoft Internet Information Services (IIS) and ASP.NET technologies, the premier, complete portal offering from Microsoft is the SharePoint Server. I can attempt to build my own messaging solution using WCF and WF, but trying to design, build, and test such a solution takes me away from my primary goal of helping my organization solve business problems.

What about the upcoming "Oslo" wave of products from Microsoft, which include the "Dublin" server, "Oslo" repository, and modeling toolset? The "Dublin" server, which fits into IIS and provides a powerful host for WCF and WF applications, solves specific problems around hosting and managing WCF and WF solutions. It is not a replacement of BizTalk Server and serves a different purpose. The "Oslo" modeling platform offers a compelling way to visualize solutions and construct rich models which can turn into actual applications. It is meant to solve problems around overall application design and does not provide any sort of infrastructure for actually running applications.

Take a look at Chapter 12 for more about these upcoming technologies.

Much has been written about the business aspect of SOA and achieving enterprise momentum for designing software in a service oriented fashion. If you are looking at how to engage your CEO or business stakeholders and expound on the virtues of SOA, this book is not your best resource.

You will find that this book is a technical resource for folks looking to implement service-oriented patterns while exposing new services or consuming existing ones. We will take a deep look at how BizTalk Server works with the new WCF service model. We will also see how to take advantage of the BizTalk engine to build asynchronous processes and reusable orchestrations.

This book, at its core, is an explanation of how to construct flexible solutions that are built for change.

Is BizTalk Server the only product that can help you reach a service-oriented nirvana? Of course not. You can very successfully build a SOA without using BizTalk Server, or any single product, for that matter. In fact, your SOA strategy should NOT be dependent on a single vendor or product, but rather support an ecosystem of service enabled platforms. This protects you from future change, while encouraging general SOA patterns that are not product-specific.

That said, I plan to show you that BizTalk Server is an excellent platform for advancing your service-oriented architecture and creating new opportunities for making your environment more agile and flexible. As we work together through the examples in this book, I hope that you'll be able to visualize exactly how to utilize BizTalk Server in the most efficient manner within your organization's IT environment.

What this book covers

This book is put together in a way that encourages you to follow along and build up your comfort level and knowledge as we progress from chapter to chapter. Throughout this book, I will make use of simple pharmaceutical scenarios to demonstrate key concepts. This industry is where I spend my time nowadays, and the demos that we build should have a common theme. That said, if you have no experience in the pharmaceutical industry, there's nothing to worry about. The examples we work through will involve basic "patient" and "drug evaluation trials" scenarios that are easily understood and don't distract from the underlying technology message.

Chapters 1–3 are designed to introduce you to BizTalk and WCF and show you how to build a BizTalk services solution from scratch. This will help you keep up with the brisk pace of the later chapters. Chapters 4–12 build upon this knowledge and help you design and apply increasingly complex patterns and scenarios.

In *Chapter 1*, we will look at what exactly BizTalk Server is, review the core architecture of the application, and show how to build an end-to-end solution.

WCF is still a relatively new technology and many BizTalk customers are still comfortably using the classic ASP.NET web services framework. However, the future of the communication subsystem of Microsoft products is WCF, and it's an important technology to understand. In *Chapter 2*, we take a look at what problem WCF is attempting to solve, and how to actually build and host WCF services.

After having a solid foundation on BizTalk and WCF, we will look at how to actually use services in the BizTalk environment. In *Chapter 3*, we build a number of common scenarios using BizTalk and WCF services.

By *Chapter 4*, you will be comfortable with how BizTalk and WCF work, and how to build BizTalk solutions that take advantage of services. At this point it's crucial to investigate exactly what a service-oriented BizTalk solution looks like. What types of services should I expose? How can I exchange messages through the BizTalk bus? We'll answer these questions and much more at this stage of the book.

A critical part of the technology portion of your service design is the contract definition. What are you sharing with the outside world? In addition to the contract, the actual transportation channel is a vital selection for your service. In *Chapter 5*, we will look at building service-oriented contracts and how to effectively work with BizTalk's service endpoints.

BizTalk relies upon asynchronous communication, and in *Chapter 6*, we will look at how to take advantage of asynchronous messaging to build robust service-oriented solutions. We'll also cover the tricky concept of providing acknowledgements or results to clients that call services in a fire-and-forget fashion.

You can use BizTalk orchestration to design new service logic or, build new composite applications based on existing services that have been discovered. In *Chapter 7*, we will look at how to build reusable orchestrations, accommodate transactions, and work with service aggregation.

It's hard to build for change but it's a fact of life for every IT department. Fiddling with a service contract is a delicate operation, and in *Chapter 8*, we will investigate the options for minimizing the impact of service modifications.

BizTalk Server 2009 offers a brand new WCF-based SQL Server adapter. In *Chapter 9*, we will investigate common usage patterns for polling data and updating data.

Microsoft's UDDI Services have moved from being part of Windows Server to now being included only with BizTalk Server 2009. In *Chapter 10*, we will take a look at how to use the UDDI server to register and resolve services.

Microsoft's Enterprise Service Bus Guidance is a key part of a service-oriented BizTalk solution and in *Chapter 11*, we will dig through the various components and build a series of examples.

The Microsoft team responsible for BizTalk Server has an array of offerings on the upcoming slate. In *Chapter 12*, we will take a look at the role of .NET Services, what "Dublin" is, what's in store from "Oslo", and where BizTalk is heading in the future.

Who this book is for

There are multiple target audiences for this book. First off, I'm writing this book as a resource for *developers* who have been tasked with building service-oriented BizTalk Server solutions. Developers will be able to use this book to implement common patterns to design services in way that fosters reuse and encourages flexibility. When developers are tasked with using BizTalk to consume existing services, they can also use this book to review strategies and considerations they need to take into account.

This book is also targeted at *architects*, who are responsible for envisioning an enterprise solution and implementing the software blueprint. We will cover a variety of ways to use BizTalk in a service-oriented fashion that will help architects decide the best way to distribute the system processing.

As I mentioned earlier, this book is not a pure tutorial on BizTalk Server or WCF. So, I'll expect that you are somewhat familiar with BizTalk Server 2006 development, and have seen a WCF service in action before.

Also, I'll be spending plenty of time using Visual Studio.NET to demonstrate development tasks, so it would be useful if you have used Microsoft's development environment in the past.

That said, I will be providing a brief overview of both BizTalk Server and WCF, so if you are new to either, or both, I'd like to think that you will still find this book a valuable resource in your library.

Conventions

In this book, you will find a number of styles of text that distinguish between different kinds of information. Here are some examples of these styles, and an explanation of their meaning.

Code words in text are shown as follows: "The next thing to do is to delete the `Address` node."

A block of code will be set as follows:

```
[XmlElementAttribute("FailureScreen", typeof(FailureScreen)]
[XmlElementAttribute("StandardScreen", typeof(StandardScreen)]
    public object Item {
      get {
        return this.itemField;
      }
      set {
    this.itemField = value;
  }
}
```

When we wish to draw your attention to a particular part of a code block, the relevant lines or items will be shown in bold:

```
public bool BuyThisBook(int copies)
{
  if(copies <=2)
  {
    //inserted new code here
    PlaceOrder(copies + 2);
  }
}
```

New terms and **important words** are shown in bold. Words that you see on the screen, in menus or dialog boxes for example, appear in our text like this: "clicking the **Next** button moves you to the next screen".

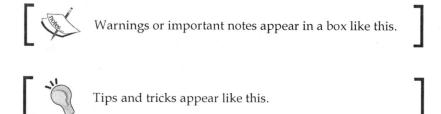

Warnings or important notes appear in a box like this.

Tips and tricks appear like this.

Reader feedback

Feedback from our readers is always welcome. Let us know what you think about this book—what you liked or may have disliked. Reader feedback is important for us to develop titles that you really get the most out of.

To send us general feedback, simply drop an email to feedback@packtpub.com, and mention the book title in the subject of your message.

If there is a book that you need and would like to see us publish, please send us a note in the **SUGGEST A TITLE** form on www.packtpub.com or email suggest@packtpub.com.

If there is a topic that you have expertise in and you are interested in either writing or contributing to a book, see our author guide on www.packtpub.com/authors.

Customer support

Now that you are the proud owner of a Packt book, we have a number of things to help you to get the most from your purchase.

Downloading the example code for the book

Visit `http://www.packtpub.com/files/code/5005_Code.zip` to directly download the example code.

The downloadable files contain instructions on how to use them.

Errata

Although we have taken every care to ensure the accuracy of our contents, mistakes do happen. If you find a mistake in one of our books—maybe a mistake in text or code—we would be grateful if you would report this to us. By doing so, you can save other readers from frustration, and help us to improve subsequent versions of this book. If you find any errata, please report them by visiting `http://www.packtpub.com/support`, selecting your book, clicking on the **let us know** link, and entering the details of your errata. Once your errata are verified, your submission will be accepted and the errata added to any list of existing errata. Any existing errata can be viewed by selecting your title from `http://www.packtpub.com/support`.

Piracy

Piracy of copyright material on the Internet is an ongoing problem across all media. At Packt, we take the protection of our copyright and licenses very seriously. If you come across any illegal copies of our works in any form on the Internet, please provide us with the location address or website name immediately so that we can pursue a remedy.

Please contact us at `copyright@packtpub.com` with a link to the suspected pirated material.

We appreciate your help in protecting our authors, and our ability to bring you valuable content.

Questions

You can contact us at `questions@packtpub.com` if you are having a problem with any aspect of the book, and we will do our best to address it.

Building BizTalk Server 2009 Applications

1

Creativity is the power to connect the seemingly unconnected.
-William Plomer

Let's begin our journey by investigating what BizTalk Server actually is, why to use it, and how to craft a running application. This chapter will be a refresher on BizTalk Server for those of you who have some familiarity with the product.

In this chapter, you will learn:

- How to articulate BizTalk Server, when to use it, and how it works
- To outline the role of BizTalk schemas, maps, and orchestrations
- BizTalk messaging configurations

What is BizTalk Server?

So what exactly is BizTalk Server, and why should you care about it? In a nutshell, Microsoft BizTalk Server 2009 uses adapter technology to connect disparate entities and enable the integration of data, events, processes, and services. An **entity** may be an application, department, or even an altogether different organization that you need to be able to share information with. A software adapter is typically used when we need to establish communication between two components that do not natively collaborate. BizTalk Server adapters are built with a common framework which results in system integration done through configuration, not coding.

Traditionally, BizTalk Server has solved problems in three areas. First, BizTalk Server acts as an **Enterprise Application Integration (EAI)** server that connects applications that are natively incapable of talking to each other. The applications may have incompatible platforms, data structure formats, or security models. For example, when a new employee is hired, the employee data in the human resources application needs to be sent to the payroll application so that the new employee receives his/her paycheck on time. Nothing prevents you from writing the code necessary to connect these disparate applications with a point-to-point solution. However, using such a strategy often leads to an application landscape that looks like this:

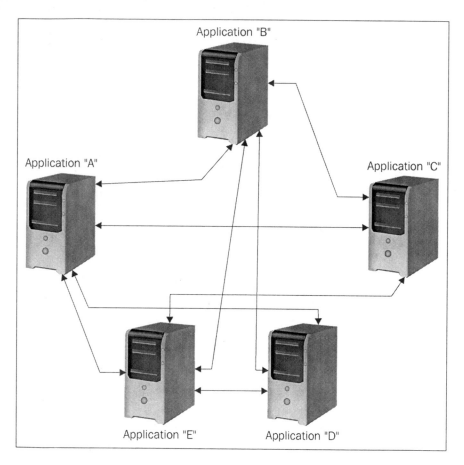

Many organizations choose to insert a communication broker between these applications as shown in following figure.

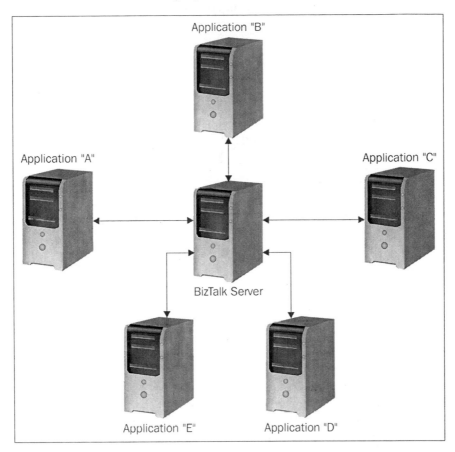

Some of the benefits that you would realize from such an architectural choice include:

- Loose coupling of applications where one does not have a physical dependency on the other
- Durable infrastructure that can guarantee delivery, and queue messages during destination system downtime
- Centralized management of system integration endpoints
- Message flow control such as in-order delivery
- Insight into cross-functional business processes through business activity monitoring

BizTalk Server solves a second problem by filling the role of **business-to-business (B2B)** broker that facilitates communication across different organizations. BizTalk supports B2B scenarios by offering Internet-friendly adapters, industry-standard EDI message schemas, and robust support for both channel- and message-based security.

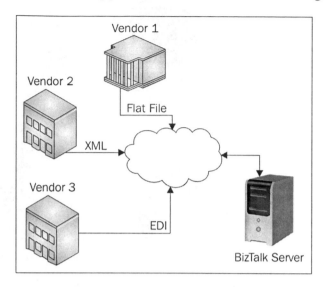

The third broad area that BizTalk Server excels in is **Business Process Automation (BPA)**. BPA is all about taking historically manual workflow procedures and turning them into executable processes. For example, consider the organization that typically receives a new order via email and the sales agent manually checks inventory levels prior to inserting the order into the Fulfillment System. If inventory is too low, then the sales agent has to initiate an order with their supplier and watch out for the response so that the Inventory System can be updated. What problems are inevitable in this scenario?

- Poor scalability when the number of orders increase
- Lack of visibility into the status of orders and supplier requests
- Multiple instances of redundant data entry, ripe for mistakes

By deciding to automate this scenario, the company can reduce human error while streamlining communications between applications and organizations.

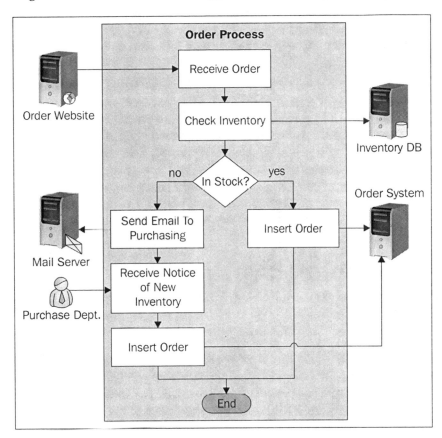

What's one thing all of these BizTalk Server cases have in common? They all depend on the real-time interchange and processing of discrete messages in an event-driven fashion. This partially explains why BizTalk Server is such a strong tool within a service-oriented architecture. We'll investigate many of BizTalk's service-oriented capabilities in later chapters, but it's important to note that the functionality that exists to support three top-level scenarios above (EAI, B2B, and BPM) nicely fits into a service-oriented mindset. Concepts such as schema-first design, loose coupling, and reusability are soaked into the fabric of BizTalk Server.

Critical point

BizTalk Server should be targeted for solutions that exchange real-time messages as opposed to Extract Transform Load (ETL) products that excel at bulky, batch-oriented exchanges between data stores.

BizTalk Server 2009 is the 6th release of the product, the first release being BizTalk Server 2000. Back in those days, developers had access to four native adapters (file system, MSMQ, HTTP, and SMTP); development was done in a series of different tools, and the underlying engine had some fairly tight coupling between components. Since then, the entire product was rebuilt and reengineered for .NET and a myriad of new services and features have become part of the BizTalk Server suite. The application continues to evolve and take greater advantage of the features of the Microsoft product stack, while still being the most interoperable and platform-neutral offering that Microsoft has ever produced.

BizTalk architecture

So how does BizTalk Server actually work? BizTalk Server at its core is an event-processing engine, based on a conventional publish-subscribe pattern. Wikipedia defines the publish-subscribe pattern as:

> *An asynchronous messaging paradigm where senders (publishers) of messages are not programmed to send their messages to specific receivers (subscribers). Rather, published messages are characterized into classes, without knowledge of what (if any) subscribers there may be. Subscribers express interest in one or more classes, and only receive messages that are of interest, without knowledge of what (if any) publishers there are.*

Critical point

This pattern enforces a natural loose coupling and provides more scalability than an engine that requires a tight connection between receivers and senders. In the first release of BizTalk Server, the product DID have tightly coupled messaging components, but thankfully the engine was completely redesigned for BizTalk Server 2004.

Once a message is received by a BizTalk adapter, it runs through any necessary pre-processing (such as decoding) in BizTalk **pipelines,** before being subjected to data transformation via BizTalk **maps,** and finally being published to a central database called the **MessageBox**. Then, parties which have a corresponding subscription for that message can consume it as they see fit. While introducing a bit of unavoidable latency, the MessageBox database makes up for that by providing us with durability, reliability, and scalability. For instance, if one of our subscriber systems is offline for maintenance, outbound messages are not lost, but rather the MessageBox makes sure to queue messages until the subscriber is ready to receive them. Worried about a large flood of inbound messages that steal processing threads away from other BizTalk activities—no problem! The MessageBox makes sure that each and every message finds its way to its targeted subscriber, even if it must wait until the flood of inbound messages subside.

There are really two ways to look at the way BizTalk is structured. The first is the traditional EAI view, which sees BizTalk receiving messages, and routing them to the next system for consumption. The flow is very linear and BizTalk is seen as a broker between two applications.

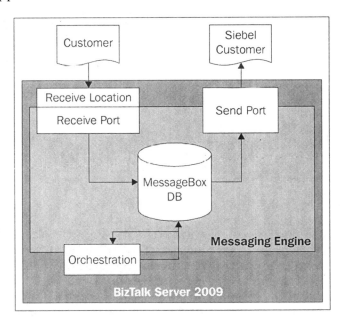

However, the other way to consider BizTalk, and the focus of this book, is as a service bus, with numerous input/output channels that process messages in a very dynamic way. That is, instead of visualizing the data flow as a straight path through BizTalk to a destination system, consider BizTalk exposing services as on-ramps to a variety of destinations. Messages published to BizTalk Server may fan out to dozens of subscribers, who have no interest in what the publishing application actually was. Instead of thinking about BizTalk as a simple connector of systems, think of BizTalk as a message bus which coordinates a symphony of events between endpoints.

This concept, first introduced to me by the incomparable Charles Young (`http://geekswithblogs.net/cyoung/`), is an exciting way to exploit BizTalk's engine in this modern world of service-orientation. In the diagram below, I've shown how the central BizTalk bus has receiver services hanging off of it, and has a multitude of distinct subscriber services that are activated by relevant messages reaching the bus.

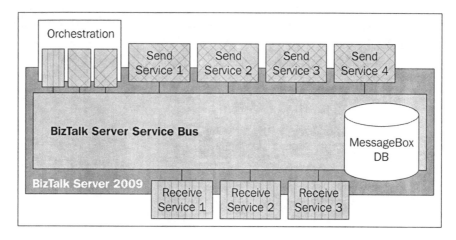

If the *on-ramp* concept is a bit abstract to understand, consider a simple analogy. In designing the transportation for a city, it would be foolish of me to create distinct roads between each and every destination. The design and maintenance of such a project would be lunacy. I would be smart to design a shared highway with on and off ramps, which enable people to use a common route to get between the numerous locations around town. As new destinations in the city emerge, the entire highway (or road system) doesn't need to undergo changes, but rather, only a new entrance/exit point needs to be appended to the existing shared infrastructure.

What exactly is a **message** anyway? A message is data processed through BizTalk Server's messaging engine, whether that data is transported as an XML document, a delimited flat file, or a Microsoft Word document. The message content may contain a command (for example `InsertCustomer`), a document (for example `Invoice`), or an event (for example `VendorAdded`). A message has a set of properties associated with it. First and foremost, a message may have a *type* associated with it which uniquely defines it within the messaging bus. The type is typically comprised of the XML namespace and the root node name (for example `http://CompanyA. Purchasing#PurchaseOrder`). The message type is much like the class object in an object-oriented programming language; it uniquely identifies entities by their properties. The other critical attribute of a message in BizTalk Server is the property bag called the **message context**. The message context is a set of name/value properties that stays attached to the message as long as it remains within BizTalk Server. These context values include metadata about the transport used to publish the message, and attributes of the message itself. Properties in the message context that are visible to the BizTalk engine, and therefore available for routing decisions, are called **promoted properties**.

How does a message actually get into BizTalk Server? A **receive location** is configured for the actual endpoint that receives messages. The receive location uses a particular adapter, which knows how to absorb the inbound message. For instance, a receive location may be configured to use the FILE adapter which polls a particular directory for XML messages. The receive location stores the file path to monitor, while the adapter provides transport connectivity. Upon receipt of a message, the adapter stamps a set of values into the message context. For the FILE adapter, values such as `ReceivedFileName` are added to that message's context property bag. Note that BizTalk has both application adapters such as SQL Server, Oracle, and SAP as well as transport-level adapters such as HTTP, MSMQ, and FILE. The key point is that the adapter configuration user experience is virtually identical regardless of the type of adapter chosen.

Receive locations have a particular **receive pipeline** associated with them. A pipeline is a sequential set of operations that are performed on the inbound message in preparation for being parsed and processed by BizTalk. For instance, I would need a pipeline in order to decrypt, unzip, or validate the XML structure of my inbound message. One of the most critical roles of the pipeline is to identify the type of the inbound message and put the type into the message context as a promoted property. As discussed earlier, a message type is the unique characterization of a message. Think of a receive pipeline as doing all the pre-processing steps necessary for putting the message in its most usable format.

A **receive port** contains one or more receive locations. Receive ports have **XSLT maps** associated with them that are applied to messages prior to publishing them to the MessageBox database. What value does a receive port offer me? It acts as a grouping of receive locations where capabilities such as mapping and data tracking can be applied to any of the receive locations associated with it. It may also act as a container that allows me to publish a single *entity* to BizTalk Server regardless of how it came in, or what it looked like upon receipt. Let's say that my receive port contains three receive locations, which all receive slightly different "invoice" messages from three different external vendors. At the receive port level, I have three maps that take each unrelated message and maps it to a single, common format, before publishing it to BizTalk.

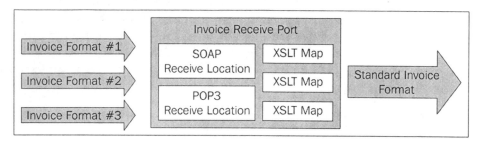

Critical point

By default, all messages pass through BizTalk Server as a stream of bytes, not as an XML message loaded into the server's memory. Therefore, when the message is published to the MessageBox, BizTalk Server has yet to look inside the message unless:

- The receive port had an XSLT map corresponding to the inbound message type
- An XML validation/disassemble/decoding pipeline component was applied to the message.

Note that custom pipeline components may also peek into the message content. If the message has promoted properties associated with it, then the disassembler pipeline component will extract the relevant data nodes from the message and insert them into the message context.

Now that we have a message cleaned up (by the pipeline) and in a final structure (via an XSLT map), it's published to the BizTalk Server MessageBox where message routing can begin. For our purposes, there are two **subscribers** that we care about. The first type of subscriber is a **send port**. A send port is conceptually the inverse of the receive location and is responsible for transporting messages out of the BizTalk bus.

It has not only an adapter reference, adapter configuration settings, and a pipeline (much like the receive location), but it also has the ability to apply XSLT maps to outbound messages. If a send port subscribes to a message, it first applies any XSLT maps to the message, then processes it through a send pipeline, and finally uses the adapter to transmit the message out of BizTalk.

The other subscriber for a published message is a BizTalk **orchestration**. An orchestration is an executable business process, which uses messages to complete operations in a workflow. We'll spend plenty of time working with orchestration subscribers throughout this book.

Setting up new BizTalk projects

What do you need to set up a brand new BizTalk project? First, you will want to have a development environment with Windows Server 2008, IIS 7.0, SQL Server 2008, Visual Studio 2008, and BizTalk Server 2009, installed in that order.

Consider using a standard structure for all of your BizTalk Server solutions. This makes it easier to package and share source code, while also defining a consistent place to store solution artifacts in each project. To build the structure below, I put together a VBScript file, which is available on my blog at: `http://seroter.wordpress.com/2007/03/29/script-for-automatically-creating-biztalk-solution-structure/`.

Note that BizTalk Server 2009 solutions can (and should) be centrally persisted in standard source control applications such as Subversion or Microsoft Team Foundation Server.

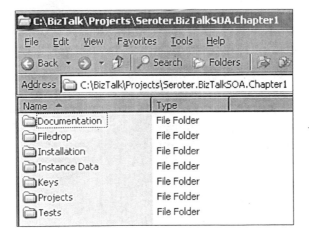

You can tell if you have successfully installed BizTalk Server in your development environment if you are able to see **BizTalk Projects** in the Visual Studio.NET **New Projects** menu option.

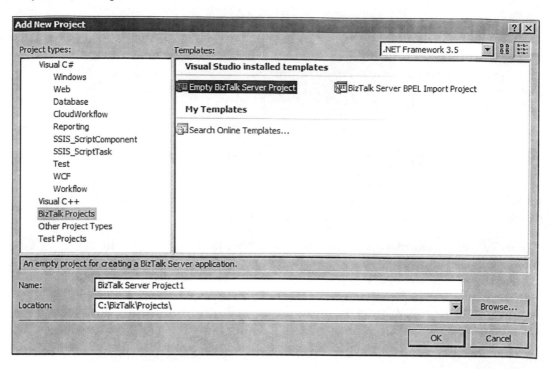

When a new BizTalk Project is added to a Visual Studio.NET solution, you should immediately right-click the project and select the **Properties** option. In BizTalk Server 2009, we can now set properties in the familiar C# project properties pane, instead of the BizTalk-only properties window. The BizTalk project type has been redesigned so that BizTalk projects are now simply specialized C# project types.

The first value that you need to set is under the **Signing** section. You can either point to an existing strong name key, or now in BizTalk Server 2009, generate a new key on the fly. BizTalk Server projects are deployed to the **Global Assembly Cache (GAC)** and must be strong named prior to doing so. After setting the necessary key value, navigate to the BizTalk-specific **Deployment** section, and set the **Application Name** to something meaningful such as **BizTalkSOA**.

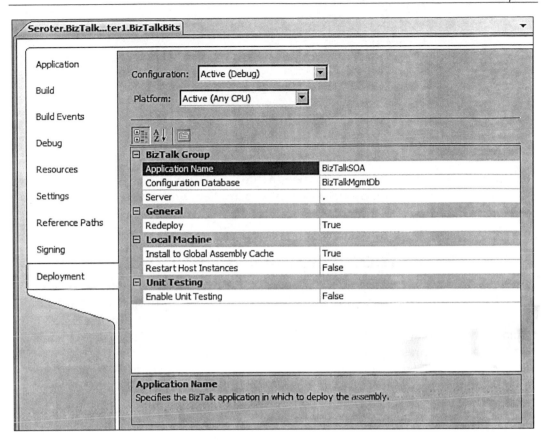

Once you have a project created, the strong name key set, and application name defined, you're ready to start adding development artifacts to your project.

What are BizTalk schemas?

Arguably the building block of any BizTalk Server solution (and general SOA solution) is the data contract, which describes the type of messages that flow through the BizTalk bus. A contract for a message in BizTalk Server is represented using an industry-standard XML Schema Definition (XSD). For a given contract, the XSD spells out the elements, their organizational structure, and their data types. An XSD also defines the expected ordering of nodes, whether or not the node is required, and how many times the node can appear at the particular location in the node tree. Following is an example XSD file:

```
<xs:schema
  xmlns:xs="http://www.w3.org/2001/XMLSchema">
    <xs:element name="Person>
```

```
<xs:complexType>
    <xs:sequence>
        <xs:element name="FirstName" type="xs:string"/>
        <xs:element name="LastName" type="xs:string"/>
        <xs:element name="Age" type="xs:int"/>
    </xs:sequence>
</xs:complexType>
</xs:element>
</xs:schema>
```

Having a strict contract can reduce flexibility but it greatly increases predictability as the message consumer can confidently build an application, which depends on the message being formatted a specific way.

Schema creation and characteristics

While producing completely valid XSD syntax, the BizTalk Schema Editor takes a higher-level approach to defining the schema itself. Specifically, instead of working purely with familiar XML concepts of elements and attributes, the BizTalk Schema Editor advances a simpler model based on records and fields, which is meant to better represent the hierarchical nature of a schema. Do not let this fact mislead you to believe that the BizTalk Schema Editor is just some elementary tool designed to accommodate the drooling masses. In fact, the Editor enables us to graphically construct relatively complex message shapes through a fairly robust set of visual properties and XSD annotations.

There are a multiple ways to create schemas in the BizTalk Schema Editor. These include:

- You can generate a schema from an existing XML file. The BizTalk Editor infers the node names and structure from the provided XML instance. In many integration projects, you start off knowing exactly what the transmission payload looks like. If you are fortunate enough to start your project with a sample XML file already in place, this schema generation mechanism is a big time-saver. However, there are caveats to this strategy. The BizTalk Editor can only build a schema structure based on the nodes that are present in the XML file. If optional nodes were omitted from the instance file, then they will be missing from the schema. Also, the schema will not mark "repeating" structures unless the XML file represents a particular node multiple times. Finally, the generated schema will not try to guess the data type of the node, and will default all nodes to a type of string. Despite these considerations, this method is a fantastic way to establish a head start on schema construction.

- XSD schemas may also be manufactured through the BizTalk adapters. For example, the BizTalk adapters for SQL Server and Oracle will generate XSD schemas based on the database table you are targeting. As we will see shortly, BizTalk Server also generates schemas for services that you wish to consume. Using adapters to harvest metadata and automatically generate schemas is a powerful way to make certain that your messages match the expected system format.

- New schemas can actually be created by importing and including previously created schemas. If XSD complex types are defined in a schema (for example `Address`), then new schemas can be built by mixing and matching existing types. Because these inherited types are merely referenced, not copied, changes to the original content types cascade down to the schemas that reuse them. If you are inclined to design a base set of standard types, then building schemas as compositions of existing types is a very useful way to go.

- Finally, you have the option to roll up your sleeves, and build a new XSD schema from scratch. Now while you can switch to a text editor and literally type out a schema, the BizTalk Editor allows you to graphically build a schema tree from the beginning. Note that because of BizTalk Server's rigorous support for the XSD standard, you can even fashion your XML Schemas in alternate tools like Altova's XML Spy. We will handcraft many of our schemas in the BizTalk Editor for the schemas that we build together in this chapter and throughout the book.

If you're like me, you often sketch the schema layout first, and only later worry about concepts such as data types, repeating nodes, and entry restrictions. By default, each new node is assigned a `string` data type and is assumed to only exist once in a single XML document. Using the BizTalk Server Schema Editor, you can associate a given node with a wide variety of alternate data types such as `dateTime`, `integer`, and `base64Binary`. One thing to remember is that while you may use a more forgiving schema for inbound data, you should be strict in what you send out to other systems. We want to make sure to only produce messages that have clean data and stand little chance of being outright rejected by the target system.

Changing the number of times a particular node can appear in an XML document is as simple as highlighting the target node and setting the **Max Occurs** property. It's also fairly straightforward to set limits on the data allowed within certain nodes. What if we want a **ZipCode** field to only accept a maximum of 10 characters? Or what if the data stored in an **AddressType** node should be constrained to only 3 allowable choices? By default, these options are not visible for a given node. To change that, you can select a node and set the **Derived By** equal to **Restriction**. A flurry of new properties becomes available such as **Maximum Length** or **Enumeration**.

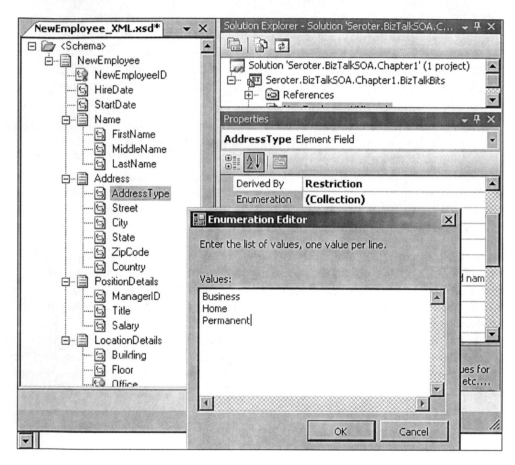

Property schemas

A critical BizTalk schema concept to examine is the **property schema**. Earlier in this chapter, I mentioned the notion of promoted properties which expose a message's data content to the BizTalk messaging layer. This in turn allows for a message to be routed to subscribers who are specifically interested in data condition (for example `Order Number == 12345`). Promoted properties are defined in a property schema, which is a special schema type within BizTalk Server. The property schema contains a flat list of elements (no records allowed) that represent the type of data we want the BizTalk messaging engine to know about. Once the property schema is created, we can associate specific fields in our message schema with the elements defined in the property schema. As we will see in practice later in this book, one key benefit of property schemas is that they can be used by more than one XSD schema. For instance, we could create a `NewEmployee` and `ModifiedEmployee` message that both map to a single `EmployeeID` property field. In this manner, we can associate messages of different types which have common data attributes.

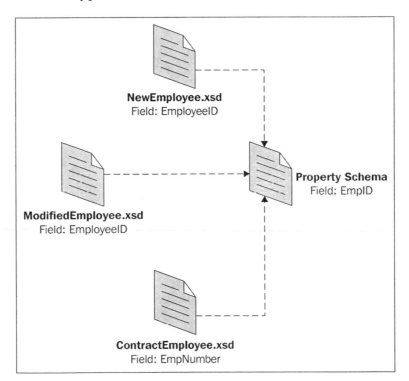

The BizTalk Schema Editor is a robust tool for building industry-standard XSD schemas. In a service-oriented architecture, the data contract is key, and understanding how to construct an XSD contract within BizTalk Server is an important skill.

What are BizTalk maps?

Rarely does data emitted from one system match the structure and content expected by another system. Hence, some sort of capability is needed to translate data so that it can be digested by a variety of consumers. **Extensible Stylesheet Language Transformations (XSLT)** is the industry standard for reshaping XML documents and the **BizTalk Mapper** is the tool used by BizTalk developers to graphically build XSLTs.

When creating a map, the BizTalk Mapper uses a straightforward design paradigm where the source schema is identified on the left side and the destination schema resides on the right side of the tool.

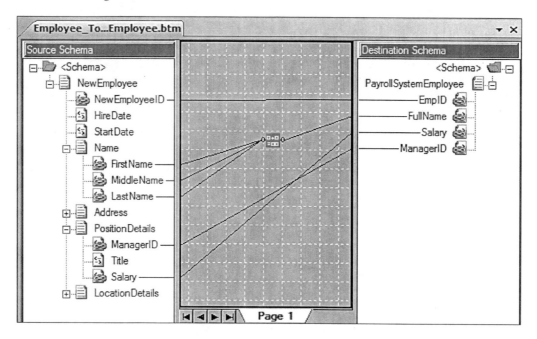

We are often lucky enough to be able to make direct connections between nodes. For instance, even though the node names are different, it is very easy to drag a link between a source node named **FName** and a destination node named **FirstName**. However, frequently you are required to generate new data in a destination schema that requires reformatting or reshaping the source data. This is where BizTalk Mapper **functoids** come to the rescue. What in the world is a functoid? Well, it is a small component which executes data manipulation functions and calculations on source nodes in order to meet the needs of the destination schema. There are over 75 functoids available in the BizTalk Mapper, which span a variety of categories such as string manipulation, mathematical calculations, logical conditions, and cumulative computation.

If you don't see exactly what you're looking for, you can use the *Scripting functoid* which enables you to write your own XSL script or .NET code to be executed within the map.

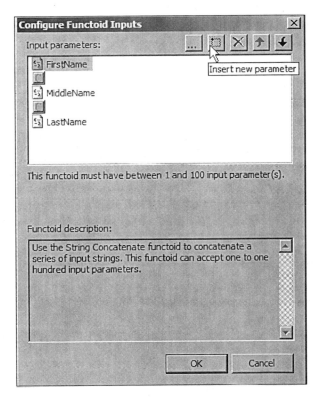

It's important to understand that the BizTalk Mapper is for data normalization logic only, NOT business logic. If you need to make business decisions, a map is not the right place to store that logic. For example, you would not want to embed complex discount generation logic within a BizTalk map. That sort of business logic belongs in a more easily maintained repository than in a map file. As a simple rule, the map should only be responsible for shaping the output message, not for altering the meaning of the data in its fields. Maps are great for transformation instructions, but a lousy place to store mission-critical business algorithms.

Configuring BizTalk messaging

Understanding how to design and arrange BizTalk messaging settings is an absolutely critical part of designing any BizTalk solution, let alone a service-oriented one.

Earlier in this crash-course on BizTalk Server, we discussed the BizTalk messaging architecture and its foundation in a publish and subscribe routing model. One of the most important parts of a messaging configuration is enabling the receipt of new messages. Without the ability to absorb messages, there's not much else to talk about. In BizTalk Server, messages are brought onboard through the combination of receive ports and receive locations.

Receive ports can be configured from within the BizTalk Server Administration Console. New receive ports support both "one-way" or "two-way" message exchange patterns. On the lefthand side of a receive port configuration, there are a series of vertically arranged tabs that display different sets of properties. Choosing the **Receive Locations** tab enables us to create the actual receive location which defines the URI that BizTalk will monitor for inbound messages. In the **Transport** section of a receive location's primary configuration pane, we can choose from the list of available BizTalk adapters. Once an adapter is chosen from the list, the **Configure** button next to the selected transport type becomes active. For a receive location exploiting the FILE adapter, "configuration" requires entering a valid file path into the **Receive folder** property.

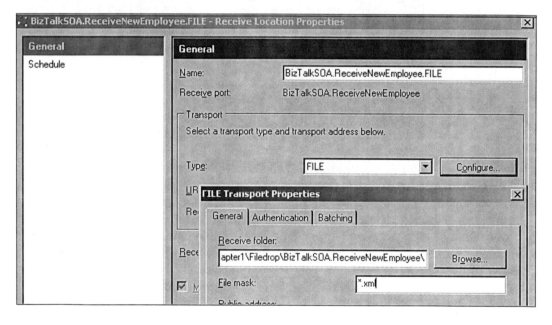

The next step in configuring BizTalk messaging is to create a subscriber for the data that is published by this receiving interface. BizTalk send ports are an example of a subscriber in a messaging solution. Much like receive locations, send ports allow you to choose a BizTalk adapter and configure the transmission URI for the message. However, simply configuring a URI does not complete a send port configuration, as we must pinpoint what type of message this subscriber is interested in. On the left side of a send port configuration window, there is a vertical set of tabs. The **Filters** tab is where we can set up specific interest criteria for this send port. For example, we could define a subscription that listens for all messages of a particular type that reach the MessageBox.

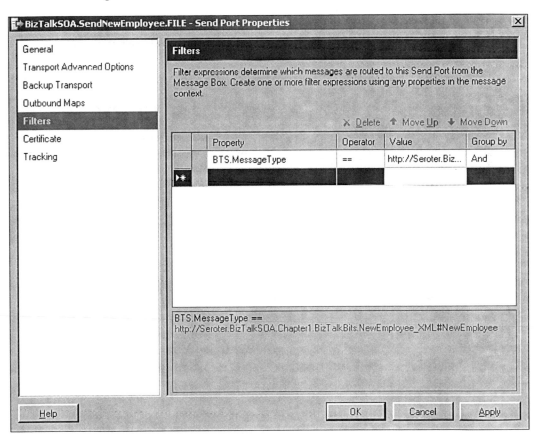

A send port can be in three distinct states. By default, a send port is `unenlisted`. This means that the port has not registered its particular subscription with BizTalk, and would not pull any messages from the MessageBox. A send port may also be `enlisted`, which is associated with ports that have registered subscriptions but are not processing messages. In this case, the messages targeted for this port stay in a queue until the port is placed in the final state, `Started`. A started port has its subscriptions active in the MessageBox and is heartily processing all the messages it cares about.

The BizTalk Server messaging engine is the heart and soul of a BizTalk solution. Here we saw how to create new input interfaces, and define subscribers for the published data.

Working with BizTalk orchestration

BizTalk Server includes a workflow platform, which allows us to graphically create executable, long-running, stateful processes. These workflows, called **orchestrations**, are designed in Visual Studio.NET and executed on the BizTalk Server. The Orchestration Designer in Visual Studio.NET includes a rich palette of shapes we can use to build robust workflows consisting of control flow, message manipulation, service consumption, and much more. The Orchestration Runtime is responsible for executing the orchestrations and managing their state data.

Orchestration is a purely optional part of a BizTalk solution. You can design a complete application that consists solely of message routing ports. In fact, many of the service-oriented patterns that we visit throughout this book will not require an orchestration. That said, there are a number of scenarios where injecting orchestrations into the solution makes sense. For instance, instead of subscribing directly to the "new employee" message, perhaps a payroll system will need additional data (such as bank information for a direct deposit) not currently available in the original employee message. We could decide to create a workflow, which first inserts the available information into the payroll system, and then sends a message to the new employee asking for additional data points. The workflow would then wait for and process the employee's response and conclude by updating the record in the payroll system with the new information. BizTalk orchestrations are a good fit for automating manual processes, or choreographing a series of disconnected services or processes to form a single workflow.

Orchestration "shapes" such as **Decide**, **Transform**, **Send**, **Receive**, and **Loop** are used to build our orchestration diagrams like the one below. This particular diagram below shows a message leaving the orchestration, and then another message returning later on in the flow. How does that message know which running orchestration instance to come back to? What if we have a thousand of these individual processes in flight at a single point in time? BizTalk Server has the concept of **correlation** which means that you can identify a unique set of attributes for a given message which will help it find its way to the appropriate running orchestration instance. A correlation attribute might be as simple as a unique invoice identifier, or a composite key made up of a person's name, order date, and zip code.

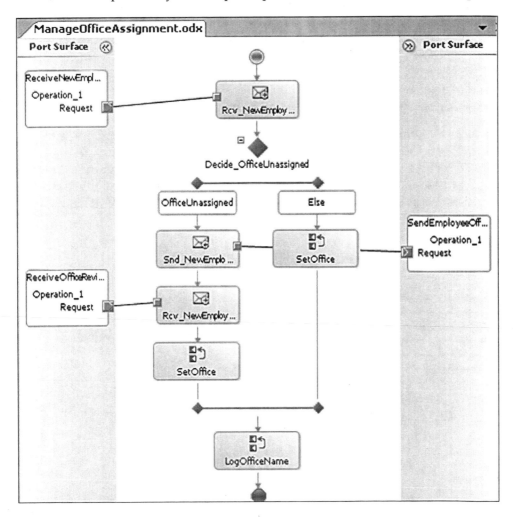

Orchestration is a powerful tool in your development arsenal and we will make frequent use of it throughout this book.

Summary

In this chapter, we looked at what BizTalk is, its core use cases, and how it works. In my experience, one of the biggest competitors to BizTalk Server is not another product, but custom-built solutions. Many organizations engage a "build versus buy" debate prior to committing to a commercial product. In this chapter, I highlighted just a few aspects of BizTalk that make it a compelling choice for usage. With BizTalk Server you get a well-designed scalable messaging engine with a durable persistence tier which guarantees that your mission-critical messages are not lost in transit. The engine also provides native support for message tracking, recoverability, and straightforward scalability. BizTalk provides you 20+ native application adapters that save weeks of custom development time and testing. We also got a glimpse of BizTalk's integrated workflow toolset that enables us to quickly build executable business processes that run in a load-balanced environment. These features alone often tip the scales in BizTalk Server's favor, not to mention the multitude of features that we have yet to discuss such as Enterprise Single Sign On the Business Rules Engine, Business Activity Monitoring, and more.

I hope that this chapter also planted some seeds in your mind with regards to thinking about BizTalk solutions in a service-oriented fashion. There are best practices for designing reusable, maintainable solutions that we will investigate throughout the rest of this book. In the next chapter, we'll explore one of the most critical technologies for building robust service interfaces in BizTalk Server: Windows Communication Foundation.

2

Windows Communication Foundation Primer

Good communication is as stimulating as black coffee, and just as hard to sleep after.

-Anne Morrow Lindbergh

Windows Communication Foundation (WCF) is a critical part of the Microsoft services strategy and a key part of the BizTalk Server 2009 platform. WCF is a rich and expansive topic, so this chapter will only focus on the key aspects of WCF, which prepares us for its usage in the later chapters.

In this chapter you will learn:

- What WCF is and why it matters
- How to construct and configure new WCF services
- Service hosting options
- How to call a WCF service from a client application

What is WCF?

In a nutshell, WCF is a framework for building and hosting services. Hosted by the Microsoft platform, WCF services make use of standard technologies to offer a wide range of cross-platform security, transaction, and communication capabilities.

Before WCF came along, .NET developers, who built distributed applications had to choose between communication schemes such as ASP.NET web services, .NET remoting, and MSMQ. This choice carried with it implications for how the component was designed, developed, deployed, and consumed. If you went with ASP.NET web services, you were committing to XML message formats and were handcuffed by limitations of the HTTP transport protocol. If you chose .NET remoting, you were able to process messages in an efficient fashion, but immediately limited yourself to .NET-only service clients. MSMQ is wonderful for disconnected applications, but in choosing it, you've eliminated any chance at having a synchronous, request-response conversation with a software client.

The goal of WCF is to unify these many technologies and provide a single transport-neutral development paradigm with common aspects for security, transactions, and exception handling. The service is implemented independent of the communication protocol strategy. This is a fairly revolutionary concept that introduces immense flexibility to service designers. Instead of building services with tightly coupled and rigid endpoints that do not welcome change, we can design flexible services that are capable of supporting a wide range of current and future consumers.

The service endpoint is king, and endpoints in WCF are defined using the easy-to-remember *ABC* acronym. The letter *A* stands for *addressing*, which refers to the actual URL of the service. The letter *B* stands for *binding*, which describes how we communicate with the service. Finally, the letter *C* stands for *contract*, which defines the operations and data elements that this service exposes. Let's look at each of these in detail.

Defining the contract

Unlike ASP.NET web services, WCF truly promotes a "contract first" design style where developers need to thoughtfully consider how the outside world will interact with their service. There is a clean separation between the interface definition and the actual implementation of the service. When building ASP.NET services, the developer typically takes a code-first approach, where .NET classes are decorated with attributes and exposed as services. In the WCF model, we focus first on the data being shared and what our interface to the outside world should look like (i.e. the contract). Only after this critical step is complete does the WCF developer begin to design the actual service implementation logic.

There are actually three different contracts you may define for a WCF service. These are:

- Service contract
- Data contract
- Fault contract

There's actually a fourth contract type corresponding the message itself, but I won't be covering that here. We'll investigate the service and data contract types right now, but save the fault contract for a later section in this chapter.

Service contracts

The **service contract** explains what your service can do. It's built using a .NET interface class and decorated with WCF attributes that identify it as a service contract. A basic service contract looks like this:

```
[ServiceContract()]
public interface IVendorContract
{
    [OperationContract()]
    void InsertVendor(string vendorId, string vendorName);

    [OperationContract()]
    bool DeleteVendor(string vendorId);
}
```

Notice that the interface has a ServiceContract attribute and each operation that we wish to expose publicly on our contract has an OperationContract attribute. Each of these metadata attributes has a series of optional parameters that let us explicitly define public characteristics of the service. For instance, we can add the Name and Namespace properties to the ServiceContract to better characterize this service in our environment. We can also add a series of properties to the OperationContract to control what the operation is named and the SOAPAction value is set to. Why give an alternate name to a service operation? Consider scenarios where you have an overloaded operation in your WCF service contract, and need each WSDL operation to have a unique public name. C# (and .NET) support overloading, but the WSDL standard no longer does.

```
[ServiceContract(Name="VendorService", Namespace="http://Seroter.
BizTalkSOA/Contracts")]
public interface IVendorContract
{
  [OperationContract(Name="InsertVendor")]
    void InsertVendor(string vendorId, string vendorName);
```

```
[OperationContract(Name="InsertVendorWithContact")]
void InsertVendor(string vendorId, string vendorName,
                                 string vendorContactName);

[OperationContract(Name="DeleteVendor")]
bool DeleteVendor(string vendorId);
}
```

Data contracts

As you can probably imagine, services often need to accept and return
comprehensive data entities in addition to simple type parameters. I might want
to model a data entity such as a customer instead of having a service operation
accept 15 individual string parameters. Complex data parameters are categorized
as **data contracts** in WCF. A data contract is a .NET class object decorated with the
DataContract attribute and whose public properties are flagged with DataMember
attributes. Public service operation definitions can only include complex types
identified as data contracts.

```
[DataContract()]
public class VendorType
{
    private string vendorId;
    private string vendorName;
    private string vendorContactName;

    [DataMember()]
    public string VendorId
    {
        get { return vendorId; }
        set { vendorId = value; }
    }

    [DataMember()]
    public string VendorName
    {
        get { return vendorName; }
        set { vendorName = value; }
    }

    [DataMember()]
    public string VendorContactName
    {
        get { return vendorContactName; }
        set { vendorContactName = value; }
    }
}
```

Much like the service contract, the attributes of the data contract allow for more fine-grained control of the entity definition. For instance, we may provide a Name and Namespace to the DataContract, while also adding some useful node ordering and existence attributes to the member elements.

```
[DataContract(Name="Vendor" Namespace = "http://Seroter.BizTalkSOA/
Types")]
    public class VendorType
    {
        private string vendorId;
        private string vendorName;
        private string vendorContactName;

    [DataMember(IsRequired=true, Order=0)]
        public string VendorId
        {
            get { return vendorId; }
            set { vendorId = value; }
        }

        [DataMember(IsRequired=true, Order=1)]
        public string VendorName
        {
            get { return vendorName; }
            set { vendorName = value; }
        }

        [DataMember(IsRequired=false, Order=2)]
        public string VendorContactName
        {
            get { return vendorContactName; }
            set { vendorContactName = value; }
        }
    }
```

If you omit the Order property from the DataMember attribute, then the nodes are ordered alphabetically, which may not be how you wish to organize your public schema.

Implementing contracts in services

Once we have decided upon an interface definition for a service, we are able to move forward with the service which implements this interface. For those of you who have previously built .NET interface classes, and then realized those interfaces in subsequent concrete classes, the WCF model is quite natural. In fact, it's the same. We build a concrete service class, and choose to implement the WCF service contract defined earlier. For this example, we take the previously-built interface (which has since had its Insert operations replaced by a single operation that takes a data contract parameter) and implement the service logic.

Consider creating distinct Visual Studio.NET projects to house the service contract and the service implementation. This allows you to share the contract project with service consumers without sharing details of the service that realizes the contract.

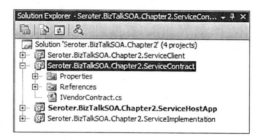

```csharp
public class VendorService : IVendorContract
{
    public void InsertVendor(VendorType newVendor)
    {
        System.Console.WriteLine("Vendor {0} inserted by service ...",
newVendor.VendorId);

    }

    public bool DeleteVendor(string vendorId)
    {
        System.Console.WriteLine("Vendor {0} deleted ...", vendorId);
        return true;
    }
}
```

A WCF service may have metadata attributes applied to it in order to influence or dictate behavior. For instance, WCF has very robust support for creating and consuming transactional services. While specific attributes are applied directly to the service contract to affect how the service respects transactions, the attributes on the concrete service itself establish the way the service processes those transactions. In order to identify whether a service will accept transactions or not, an attribute is added to the service contract.

```
[ServiceContract(Name="VendorService", Namespace="http://Seroter.
BizTalkSOA/Contracts")]
    public interface IVendorContract
    {
        [OperationContract(Name="DeleteVendor")]
    [TransactionFlow(TransactionFlowOption.Allowed)]
        bool DeleteVendor(string vendorId);
    }
```

However, this doesn't dictate the implementation details. That is left for attributes on the service itself. The `ServiceBehavior` attribute has numerous available properties used to shape the activities of the service. Likewise, an `OperationBehavior` applied to the implemented contract operations enables us to further refine the actions of the operation. In the following code snippet, I've instructed the service to put a tight rein on the transaction locks via the `Serializable` isolation level. Next, I commanded the `DeleteVendor` operation to either enlist in the flowed transaction or create a new one (`TransactionScopeRequired`), and to automatically commit the transaction upon operation conclusion (`TransactionAutoComplete`).

```
[ServiceBehavior(TransactionIsolationLevel=
                    System.Transactions.IsolationLevel.Serializable)]
    public class VendorService : IVendorContract
    {
    [OperationBehavior(TransactionAutoComplete=true,
                                TransactionScopeRequired=true)]
        public bool DeleteVendor(string vendorId)
        {
            System.Console.WriteLine("Vendor {0} deleted ...", vendorId);
            return true;
        }
    }
```

Be aware of the nuances of where WCF attributes may be applied (e.g. service contract, concrete service, service operation) and the rich capabilities that these metadata tags can offer you.

Critical point

While this example showed how to attach transactions to services, but you need to be extremely cautious and judicious with the usage of transactions across service boundaries. While WCF makes this seem transparent, try to make your services as encapsulated as possible so that they have few explicit or implied dependencies on other services.

Throwing custom service faults

Whenever possible, you should avoid returning the full exception stack back to the service caller. You may inadvertently reveal security or implementation details that allow a malicious user to engage in mischief. Within WCF, **a fault contract** is a custom data contract that allows you to shape the exception being returned to the service consumer. Let's say we defined a controlled fault contract that looks like this:

```
[DataContract(Name = "InsertFault")]
public class InsertFaultType
{
  private string friendlyMessage;

  [DataMember()]
  public string FriendlyMessage
  {
    get { return friendlyMessage; }
    set { friendlyMessage = value; }
  }
}
```

So far, that looks like any old data contract. And in reality, that's all it is. However, we associate this fault contract with a particular operation by adding the `FaultContract` attribute to the operation in the service contract.

```
  [OperationContract(Name="InsertVendor")]
[FaultContract(typeof(InsertFaultType))]
  void InsertVendor(VendorType newVendor);
```

While implementing the service, we explicitly produce and throw these custom exception types back to the service consumer. This is done by catching the .NET exception, and creating a new fault object from the custom fault we created earlier. Then, we throw a new `FaultException` typed to our custom fault definition.

```
public void InsertVendor(VendorType newVendor)
{
    try
```

```
    {
        //do complex database update ...
    }
    catch (System.Data.SqlClient.SqlException sqlEx)
    {
        //log actual fault to admin log

        //throwing SQL exception back to caller is bad.
        //Create new exception out of custom fault contract
        InsertFaultType insertFault = new InsertFaultType();
        insertFault.FriendlyMessage = "Insert operation failed";

        //throw custom fault
        throw new FaultException<InsertFaultType>(
            insertFault,
            "illegal insert");

    }
}
```

By defining and throwing custom service faults, you achieve better control over how your service communicates to the outside world and better insulate yourself from critical implementation leakage.

Choosing an endpoint address

It's great that we've talked about the important *C* (the contract) in the *ABC*s of WCF endpoints, but the story is far from complete. So far, we have a service definition completely devoid of transport information. That is, where does someone go to consume this service? The goal of the endpoint address is to:

- Tell us the communication scheme
- Tell us the location of the service

WCF provides a number of out-of-the-box communication schemes for accessing WCF services. These include options such as:

- HTTP
- TCP
- MSMQ

When looking at a service URI such as `https://rseroter:8081/VendorService/SecureVendorService.svc`, what am I able to infer from this WCF address? First, I can see that I'm using an HTTP/S scheme in order to secure my HTTP transmission channel via SSL certificates. Next, I can tell that the domain hosting this service is called `rseroter` and uses port 8081 for the HTTP/S traffic. Finally, I can gather the path of the service that I wish to call.

We'll see shortly how to actually set up a WCF service to listen on the address of your choice. For now, simply note that the address of a service is a key part of the whole service endpoint.

The role of service bindings

The WCF service binding (or the *B* in the WCF endpoint *ABCs*) is the channel stack that ties up how a service actually transmits data across the wire. The stack is made up of individual elements that make up the message communication. This includes elements that control security options, session capacity, and transaction capabilities. They are also used to determine how a message is actually encoded during transmission, whether that is in text/XML, binary format, or the new MTOM (Message Transmission Optimization Mechanism) format.

WCF provides a series of bindings for the available WCF transports which offer the most compatible and logical component order for a given transport. Let's review the key bindings that are also available with BizTalk Server 2009 as adapters:

- **BasicHttpBinding**: This binding works great for ASMX SOAP clients that only support the SOAP 1.1 Basic Profile. By default, there is no security aspect enabled, no session or transaction capabilities, and its default data encoding is plain text. This is your "safe bet" binding that is the most interoperable for clients that don't support the latest WS* web services standards.

- **WSHttpBinding**: Like the `BasicHttpBinding`, this binding is for HTTP and HTTP/S traffic. This is a rich HTTP-based binding with full support for transactions, sessions, and a default message-based security scheme. With the `WSHttpBinding`, you have the choice of not only encoding the payload in plain text, but also the more compressed MTOM format.

- **NetTCPBinding**: If you need fast, secure connectivity between WCF endpoints, then the `NetTCPBinding` is an excellent choice. Data is transferred over TCP in binary format while still getting full support for sessions, transactions, and the full range of security options.

- **NetNamedPipeBinding**: If your client is communicating with a WCF service and both resides on the same physical server, then this is the binding for you. The `NetNamedPipeBinding` uses IPC (named pipes) to transport data in a binary encoding with a secure transmission channel.

- **NetMsmqBinding**: This binding uses queuing technology that is ideal for disconnected applications. Data is transferred in a binary encoding with rich security options available, but no support for sessions. That makes sense because in a queue scenario, the publisher and subscriber are not aware of each other.

If the situation arises where none of the above set of bindings meet your needs, you can always craft a custom binding, which mixes and matches available binding elements to your liking. What if your service consumer can only send binary messages over HTTP? The out-of-the-box HTTP bindings don't support such an encoding, but we could configure a custom binding that matches this business requirement. Or what if you need a transmission protocol not offered in the standard WCF toolset? We'll see in Chapter 9 that the WCF SQL Server Adapter delivers a custom binding, which includes SQL Server communication as a valid service transport. Such control over the WCF channel stack is a key aspect of the framework's flexibility.

Note that there are additional bindings provided by WCF in the .NET Framework 3.5, which are not explicitly set up as BizTalk adapters. These include `WSDualHttpBinding` (for duplex communication between endpoints), `WS2007FederationHttpBinding` (which supports federated security scenarios), and `NetPeerTcpBinding` (for peer-to-peer networking).

Hosting services

Now that we've identified the core components of a WCF endpoint, the giant remaining question is: how do I make this service available to consumers? You are able to host your service in a variety of places, including:

- Self-hosting: You can create a managed .NET application such as a Windows Form or Console application that acts as the host for your service. A self-hosted service can use any of the available WCF bindings, but offers the least infrastructure for service hosting. This avenue is typical of demonstration or proof-of-concept scenarios and not really considered enterprise-grade.

- Windows Service: You could choose to build a Windows Service that hosts your service in a more managed fashion. Also considered a form of self-hosting, it too can support the full range of WCF bindings. This is a bit better than manually building a service host because through the Windows Services environment, you get more manageability and support for failure recovery, automatic startup, and association with a specific Windows identity.

- IIS: For Windows Server 2003 environments, you can serve up WCF services that have HTTP and HTTP/S endpoints. Here you get the full power of an enterprise web server and the availability, process separation, and host lifecycle management that comes along with it.

- The premier WCF hosting environment is IIS 7.0 alongside Windows Process Activation Service (WAS), available in Windows Server 2008 and Windows Vista. With IIS 7.0, you can host services that rely not only on HTTP communication, but also on three other WCF protocols (TCP, MSMQ, Pipes). So you get an integrated IIS experience regardless of the transport protocol. This is a fantastic way to get web server benefits (process recycling, health monitoring, and so on) for non-HTTP based services.

- In a short while, Microsoft will release a new set of IIS server extensions code named `Dublin`, which will make "IIS + WAS" an even more ideal host for WCF services in the future. Check out the last chapter of this book for a brief synopsis.

For our examples here, I'll use a self-hosted service. While it is very simple to use IIS 7.0 to host our services, the self-hosted paradigm forces us to create (and learn) the host activation plumbing that IIS nicely hides from you. In our case, the host is a Console Application project in Visual Studio.NET. Let's look at the complete host, and then dissect it a bit.

```
using System.ServiceModel;
using System.ServiceModel.Channels;
class Program
{
    static void Main(string[] args)
    {
        string address = "http://localhost:8081/VServiceBase";
        Binding httpBinding = new BasicHttpBinding();
        ServiceHost vendorHost = new ServiceHost(
            typeof(VendorService),
            new Uri(address));

        vendorHost.AddServiceEndpoint(
```

```
        typeof(IVendorContract),
        httpBinding, "");
    vendorHost.Open();
    Console.WriteLine("Vendor host opened ...");

    Console.ReadLine();

    vendorHost.Close();
    }
  }
```

So what do we have here? First, I created a string to hold my base address. A base address acts as a root for the service from which a series of endpoints with relative addresses may hang.

Next, I created an object for the `BasicHttpBinding`. We could have used any WCF binding here, but given that I chose an HTTP base address, I chose one of the available WCF bindings that support HTTP.

Now comes the important part. The `ServiceHost` object essentially instantiates the service, configures the endpoint, applies security, and starts to listen on the requested URI. The constructor I used for the `ServiceHost` first accepts the service implementation class object. The second parameter is an array of base addresses for the service. Note that we could have multiple base addresses, but only one per URI scheme. That is, I could have both an HTTP base address and TCP base address for my service and then have endpoints defined that use either of the available base addresses.

On the next line of the Console application, I call the `AddServiceEndpoint` operation on my `ServiceHost` instance. This operation accepts the contract used by the service, the binding of the endpoint, and optionally, the relative address. Notice that our endpoint has the full *ABC*s of WCF applied. Finally, I opened the host which led to the service endpoint being available for consumption.

Now, you may look at this and wonder why you'd want to hardcode this type of connection information into your host. How do you deal with service promotion through multiple environments where the address constantly changes, or achieve all this flexible goodness that WCF evangelists always talk about? This is where we gently shift into the concept of storing service configurations in an external XML file. If there is one thing you will learn from your forays into WCF, it's that configuration is key and configuration files get pretty darn big.

If we add an application configuration to the Console Application in Visual Studio. NET, then all the address, binding, and endpoint decisions are moved from code to configuration. Our self-hosted service above has much simpler code when a configuration file is used.

```
class Program
  {
    static void Main(string[] args)
    {
        ServiceHost vendorHost =
            new ServiceHost(typeof(VendorService));

        vendorHost.Open();
        Console.WriteLine("Vendor host opened ...");
        Console.ReadLine();
        vendorHost.Close();
    }
  }
```

Much shorter, eh? The application configuration (`app.config`) file associated with this self-hosted service looks like this:

```
<configuration>
  <system.serviceModel>
    <services>
      <service name="Seroter.BizTalkSOA.Chapter2.
ServiceImplementation.VendorService">
      <endpoint
        address=""
        binding="basicHttpBinding"
         contract="Seroter.BizTalkSOA.Chapter2.ServiceContract.
IVendorContract" />
        <host>
          <baseAddresscs>
            <add
              baseAddress="http://localhost:8081/VServiceBase" />
          </baseAddresses>
        </host>
      </service>
    </services>
  </system.serviceModel>
</configuration>
```

Notice how the values (for example base address, binding, contract, and service implementation) previously spelled out in code are now all present in a configuration file. As you can imagine, it's quite simple to add new endpoints, change base addresses, and switch binding parameters in an XML configuration file.

As far as I can determine, the only reason you would choose to embed WCF endpoint details in the service host code would be when either (a) the address and channel stack are NEVER expected to change, or (b) the address and channel stack are set dynamically based on runtime conditions. Other than this, storing these transport values in an external configuration file provides the greatest level of flexibility and extensibility for WCF host solutions.

Is this all there is to a hosted WCF service? Hardly so. Once the endpoint has been defined, we then decide which binding settings to modify. For instance, I could explicitly set up a `basicHttpBinding` configuration and define service timeout values, message size limits, and a specific security scheme. There are wide array of service variations that may be designed by manipulating these binding configurations.

While binding configurations play a key role in refining the way the service operates over the wire, WCF **behaviors** are used to provide custom extensions to the WCF runtime. There are four places where behaviors may be applied in a WCF solution:

- Contract
- Operation
- Endpoint
- Service

For example, we can apply a `serviceMetadata` behavior to the service in order to allow clients to investigate the service WSDL. Also, at the service level, we are capable of controlling the number of concurrent calls via the `serviceThrottling` behavior. Most importantly, it's fairly straightforward to build new behaviors that can be customized and reused by multiple services. For instance, we could build a custom interceptor, which logs all inbound messages to a database. We'll see examples of custom behaviors in future chapters.

Consuming WCF services

Now comes the most important part: using the service! How you go about consuming a WCF service depends greatly on the type of client application used.

Non-WCF clients

If you plan on calling a WCF service from a non-WCF client, then have no fear, you're still in great shape. One of the design goals of WCF (and any quality SOA solution) is interoperability, which means that a WCF services should be consumable on a wide variety of platforms and technology stacks.

Now, it is still the responsibility of the service designer to construct a service that's usable by non-WCF applications. For instance, a broadly used service would offer a basicHttpBinding to ensure that applications based on the .NET Framework 2.0, or JRE 1.4 would have no problem consuming it. An interoperable service would also use security schemes, which rely upon commonly available certificates for transport security.

Let's assume that a WCF service with a basic HTTP endpoint has been exposed. Let's also assume that this service has a metadata "behavior" attached to it, so that we can interrogate its WSDL contract. If you have a .NET Framework 2.0 application that typically consumes classic ASMX services (ASP.NET web services), they can consume a WCF in the exact same fashion. That is, add a new **Web Reference** to the WCF service metadata definition.

If you have Visual Studio.NET 2008 installed, the **Add Web Reference** option isn't immediately available on the project. You first right-click the **Project** and choose the **Add Service Reference** menu item. At the bottom of the resulting window, you'll find a button labeled **Advanced** which you should click.

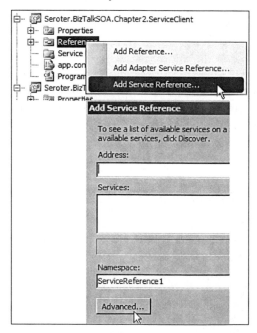

The next window that opens is a settings window, which has a button at the bottom for those who wish to add a traditional "web reference" that leverages older .NET technology.

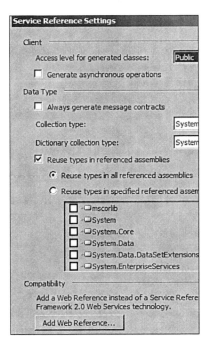

Choosing the **Add Web Reference** button finally opens up the traditional service browser, where we plug in the URL of our service and see the corresponding metadata.

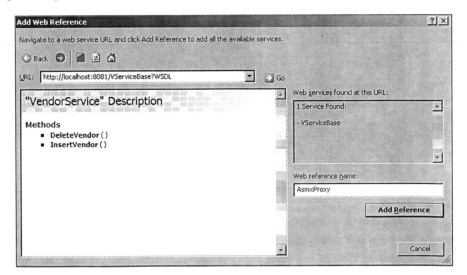

In the subsequent code which calls this service, the developer would use the assigned web reference just as if they were calling any standard SOAP web service.

```
Console.WriteLine("Vendor client launched ...");
try
{
  AsmxProxy.VendorService svc = new AsmxProxy.VendorService();
  AsmxProxy.Vendor newVendor = new AsmxProxy.Vendor();
  newVendor.VendorId = "1234";
  newVendor.VendorName = "Watson Consulting";
  newVendor.VendorContactName = "Watson Seroter";

  svc.InsertVendor(newVendor);
Console.WriteLine("Vendor " + newVendor.VendorId + " inserted ...");
 Console.ReadLine();
}
catch (System.Web.Services.Protocols.SoapException ex)
{
//grab "insert fault" part of message
   Console.WriteLine(ex.Detail.InnerText);
  Console.ReadLine();
}
```

The result? The HTTP host was opened successfully by WCF, and after the client executed the insert operation, the service wrote its confirmation message to the host console.

However, if our service fails and throws our custom fault message, our client code catches it as a SOAP exception, and still has access to the custom fault details. Below notice that the exception's detail object contains the XML message of the InsertFault type.

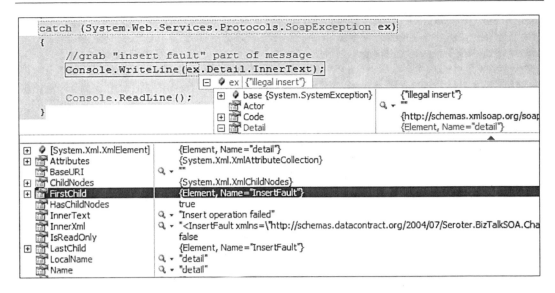

```
catch (System.Web.Services.Protocols.SoapException ex)
{
    //grab "insert fault" part of message
    Console.WriteLine(ex.Detail.InnerText);

    Console.ReadLine();
}
```

⊟ ⚡ ex	{"illegal insert"}	
⊞ ⚡ base {System.SystemException}	{"illegal insert"}	
▦ Actor	""	
⊞ ▦ Code	{http://schemas.xmlsoap.org/soap	
⊟ ▦ Detail	{Element, Name="detail"}	

⊞ ⚡ [System.Xml.XmlElement]	{Element, Name="detail"}	
⊞ ▦ Attributes	{System.Xml.XmlAttributeCollection}	
▦ BaseURI	""	
⊞ ▦ ChildNodes	{System.Xml.XmlChildNodes}	
⊞ ▦ **FirstChild**	**{Element, Name="InsertFault"}**	
▦ HasChildNodes	true	
▦ InnerText	"Insert operation failed"	
▦ InnerXml	"<InsertFault xmlns=\"http://schemas.datacontract.org/2004/07/Seroter.BizTalkSOA.Cha	
▦ IsReadOnly	false	
⊞ ▦ LastChild	{Element, Name="InsertFault"}	
▦ LocalName	"detail"	
▦ Name	"detail"	

WCF clients

If you have the benefit of using a WCF application to call a WCF service, then the full might of Microsoft's communication stack is laid before you. You are no longer constrained by HTTP-only communication and you can exploit a wide range of encoding, security, and transaction capabilities in your service consuming application.

Critical point

While WCF-to-WCF communication scenarios offer a rich set of communication options, technically any WS*-compliant application should be able to take advantage of a majority of WCF's service characteristics. For example, an Oracle application which understands WS-Security can effectively participate in secure conversations with a WCF service.

The easiest way to consume WCF services from a WCF application is to generate a proxy class that shields us from the plumbing necessary to call the service. A WCF proxy can be generated in one of two ways. First, we use the **ServiceModel Metadata Utility Tool** (svcutil.exe) command line tool if we want full control of the way the proxy class is generated. This tool takes the service metadata and generates a .NET source code file that may be used to call the WCF service.

The power in this little utility lies in the ability to apply a cornucopia of command line parameters, which define attributes of the .NET source code file such as its programming language, namespace, output location, and a whole lot more. For instance, executing the following command on our service results in a full WCF proxy class and merges the new WCF configurations with the existing configuration file for the client application.

```
Svcutil.exe http://localhost:8081/VServiceBase?WSDL /
    out:WCFProxy.cs /language:c# /config:app.config /mergeConfig
```

Because I built the WCF service proxy manually, my client application must have both the System.ServiceModel and System.Runtime.Serialization assemblies added as project references.

Consuming the WCF proxy class looks quite similar to consuming the ASMX proxy class. In fact, the only real difference that you'll notice here is more explicit interaction with the client proxy class. Notice that we work with the proxy class within a "try" block and catch any exceptions (including our custom one) in well defined "catch" blocks. While it is tempting to apply the C# "using" statement to WCF proxies, that practice can actually lead to swallowed exceptions and should be avoided. See http://msdn.microsoft.com/en-us/library/aa355056.aspx for more details. The other slight difference is that the WCF proxy class has an overloaded constructor. In this case, I'm passing in the name of the service endpoint name, which resides in the application configuration file.

```
WcfProxy.VendorServiceClient svc = new WcfProxy.VendorServiceClient
    ("BasicHttpBinding_VendorService");
try
  {
WcfProxy.Vendor newVendor = new WcfProxy.Vendor();
  newVendor.VendorId = "9876";
  newVendor.VendorName = "Noah Partners";
  newVendor.VendorContactName = "Noah Seroter";
  svc.InsertVendor(newVendor);
Console.WriteLine("Vendor " + newVendor.VendorId + " inserted ...");
  svc.Close();
  }
  catch (System.ServiceModel.FaultException<WcfProxy.InsertFault> ex)
    {
Console.WriteLine(ex.Detail.FriendlyMessage);
Console.ReadLine();
    }
catch (System.ServiceModel.CommunicationException) { svc.Abort(); }
catch (System.TimeoutException) { svc.Abort(); }
catch (System.Exception) { svc.Abort(); throw; }
```

If you're looking for an easier way to generate a WCF proxy class, look no further! Visual Studio.NET also offers an **Add Service Reference** option, which enables us to generate our proxy class from within our development environment.

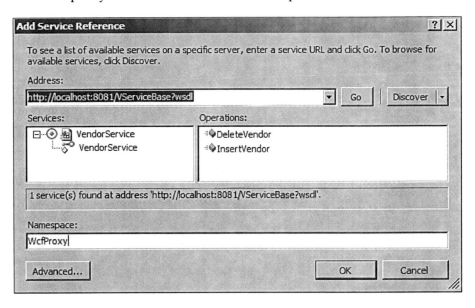

By either using the **ServiceModel Metadata Utility Tool** explicitly to generate proxy classes, or instead using Visual Studio.NET (which uses svcutil.exe underneath the covers), you have some efficient options for generating WCF-compliant code for use by service clients.

Summary

Windows Communication Foundation is a broad, powerful framework for designing, building, hosting, and consuming services. WCF unifies the many distributed application technologies in the Microsoft platform under a single programming model. The service developer is now freed from programming to the constraints of a given transport, and can instead focus on building robust services that take advantage of the latest industry standards for security, transactions, stateful sessions, and more.

The importance of WCF to BizTalk Server 2009 cannot be understated. In the next chapter, we will look at how to both expose and consume powerful WCF services from the BizTalk Server engine.

3
Using WCF Services in BizTalk Server 2009

The path to greatness is along with others
-Baltasar Gracion

Now that I've whetted your appetite with a quick look at BizTalk and WCF development, we're ready to start the main course. Let's dig into how BizTalk Server takes advantage of the power of WCF to consume and expose services. We will start this chapter with a look at how BizTalk and WCF complement each other and then explicitly show how to both consume and expose WCF services from BizTalk Server. Then, we'll see how to interact with both one-way and two-way messaging patterns and conclude by seeing how to consume services with and without orchestration in the middle. Throughout this chapter, I will demonstrate integration with numerous WCF bindings including **WSHttp**, **NetTcp**, and **NetPipe**.

In this chapter, you will learn:

- The different roles of BizTalk Server and WCF in a solution
- Where WCF fits into the BizTalk architecture
- How to generate WCF services out of BizTalk artifacts
- How to consume WCF services from BizTalk artifacts

Relationship between BizTalk and WCF

So are WCF and BizTalk Server competing technologies, or complementary ones? Let's review the role of each.

BizTalk Server 2009	Enterprise offering for messaging solutions that require consistent lifecycle for design, build, and deployment
	Process orchestration made available through a stateful, durable workflow engine
	Adapters to numerous protocols, technologies, and line of business systems
	Route data through high-performing, scalable, and persistent publish-subscribe message broker
	Runtime services with built-in scalability and load balancing
	Supplementary modules such as Business Activity Monitoring, Single Sign On, and Business Rules Engine
Windows Communication Foundation	Unify existing .NET communication technologies under a single umbrella
	Offer rich cross-platform support for WS* extensions targeting security, transactions, and stateful sessions
	Variety of flexible service host containers available
	Significant amount of service configuration exists outside of compiled code

Given this information, we see that the intersection of these two technologies occurs at the point where the BizTalk messaging and orchestration engine need to communicate effectively with the outside world. WCF extends BizTalk Server's base capability to provide and consume rich service interfaces through new powerful security and customization options. BizTalk Server provides WCF solutions with an enterprise-class messaging engine, which brings along service orchestration and access to numerous adapters that WCF does not have out-of-the-box bindings for.

BizTalk WCF adapter

BizTalk Server 2006 R2 introduced us to the BizTalk WCF adapters. In reality, BizTalk Server has seven WCF adapters that directly correlate to a subset of bindings available in WCF. These adapters are:

- **WCF-BasicHttp**: Just like the built-in WCF binding, this adapter is your safest best for simple service clients that conform to SOAP Basic Profile 1.1
- **WCF-WSHttp**: When you need an HTTP endpoint juiced up with the robustness of WS* standards for greater security, transactions, and encoding, this is the ideal adapter

- **WCF-NetTcp**: If WCF technologies are on both ends of the channel, then this adapter provides the most efficient means for transporting information while still providing all the hearty WS* capabilities

- **WCF-NetMsmq**: In scenarios where disconnected operations are vital, this adapter provides integration with queuing through MSMQ

- **WCF-NetNamedPipe**: When you have the source or target WCF application on the same physical server as BizTalk itself, then the most adept adapter is this one

- **WCF-Custom**: When you need rich customization of the WCF endpoint, then you use this adapter to manipulate the binding details and add behaviors

- **WCF-CustomIsolated**: For WCF endpoints hosted by the local web server and requiring binding or behavior customizations, then choose this adapter

Note that there are additional WCF bindings available in the .NET Framework 3.5 but not directly supported within BizTalk adapters. These include **WS2007Http**, **WsFederationHttp**, **NetPeerTcp**, **WebHttp**, and **MsmqIntegration**.

So how do these adapters actually fit into the BizTalk architecture? As they are adapters, they reside at the edges of BizTalk Server. A message sent to a WCF-BasicHttp receive location might following the path below.

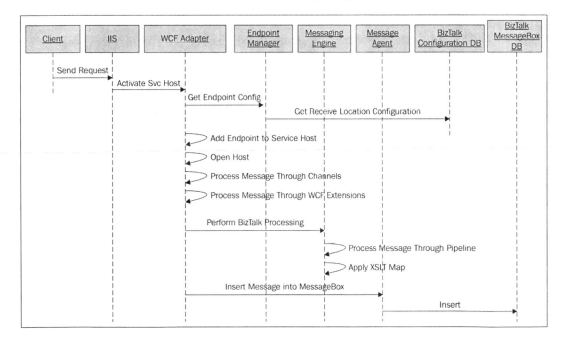

The inbound message arrives from the client to the IIS server and IIS determines the service endpoint to instantiate. The WCF service host is activated, the BizTalk Endpoint Manager is called in order to retrieve the settings of the receive location that matches the service endpoint. The message is processed through any relevant WCF channels and extensions before the message is passed off to the BizTalk Messaging Engine (residing in an isolated host). The Messaging Engine cycles through any receive pipeline components and maps before sending the message to the MessageBox via the BizTalk Message Agent.

 While WCF allows for behaviors on services, endpoints, contracts, and operation, BizTalk Server 2009 only applies WCF behaviors on services and endpoint.

In the previous chapter, we saw how WCF services require a service host in order to operate. In the BizTalk Server world, a **host** is a processing container which encompasses a wide range of runtime activities. BizTalk has the concept of an "in-process" host and an "isolated" host. An in-process host simply refers to the Windows Service that is owned and operated by BizTalk Server. An in-process host manages most BizTalk adapters, run the Orchestration Engine, and contains the Messaging Engine. A BizTalk isolated host is used when BizTalk Server does not own the lifecycle of the container process. For all practical purposes, this refers to processes hosted within the Microsoft Internet Information Services (IIS). The BizTalk web-based receive adapters (such as SOAP and HTTP) have to run in the same domain as IIS so therefore they run in the special BizTalk isolated host.

This all matters because the BizTalk WCF adapters have some flexibility when it comes to BizTalk hosting. All of the WCF bindings (including the HTTP-based ones) can be technically hosted by an in-process BizTalk host. By default, however, only the **WCF-NetTcp**, **WCF-NetMsmq**, **WCF-NetNamedPipe**, and **WCF-Custom** adapters run in the in-process host. If you wish to maintain an HTTP-based receive endpoint within an in-process host, you may use the WCF-Custom adapter and choose one of the HTTP-based bindings. For all these in-process adapters, the BizTalk Server receive location actually acts as the WCF service host. When you start the receive location, you are opening the WCF host. Likewise, when you disable the receive location, the WCF host is closed.

The BizTalk isolated host is used for the **WCF-BasicHttp**, **WCF-WSHttp**, and **WCF-CustomIsolated** adapters. While the BizTalk receive location still plays a role in the availability of the service, the adapter lifetime is actually managed by the IIS services. Starting and stopping the receive location linked to an isolated host impacts the ability to call the related service, but, does not physically impact the service host.

Is there any reason that you would host HTTP endpoints within a BizTalk in-process host instead of inside IIS 7.0? On the plus side, you get greater control over the service lifecycle and can define any URL you like. On the downside, you make it more difficult to participate in web server load-balancing and give up the rich set of service management features that IIS 7.0 offers.

Let's now take a look at how we actually use these WCF adapters to generate both services and metadata, as well as hosts for WCF endpoints.

Exposing WCF services from orchestrations

Our first task is to take a BizTalk orchestration workflow and expose one of its ports as a WCF-enabled web service. Fortunately for us, this is a fairly straightforward undertaking that requires no actual coding.

Setting up the project

The use case we will use throughout this chapter involves the ordering of pharmaceutical products. Our initial assignment is to define the shape of the data representing a "new order". I've built a schema named `NewOrder_XML.xsd` with a root node name of `NewOrder` and a structure which holds the characteristics of the order, the particular items that made up the order, and the corresponding sales territory information. The namespace of my schema, `http://Seroter.BizTalkSOA.Chapter3.OrderManagement.BizTalk/Contract`, will surface again once the service WSDL is generated.

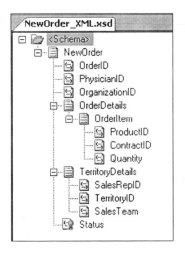

Now that we have a contract definition representing a new order, we assemble an orchestration workflow that consumes this data entity. Recall from Chapter 1 that a BizTalk orchestration depends on **messages** which equate to the data being sent and received by the orchestration. These messages are immutable so their data cannot be manipulated by the orchestration except during message creation. For our first simple orchestration, we have a message representing the inbound request, and a separate message for the acknowledgement returned to the caller. In this case, both messages are of the same schema type.

Once our messages have been defined, we sketch out the orchestration's sequential flow. In this case, let's do a very simple orchestration that receives the new order and then constructs and return response message with an altered `Status` value.

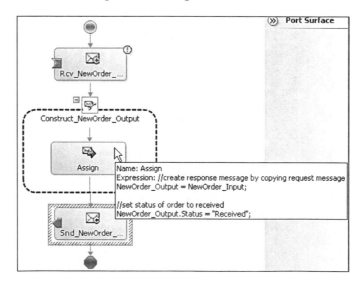

Finally, I set up a public, request-response logical port, which acts as the interface and entry point to the orchestration. This port has a single operation named SubmitNewOrder.

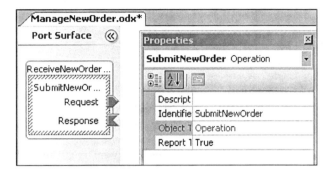

The final orchestration looks like this:

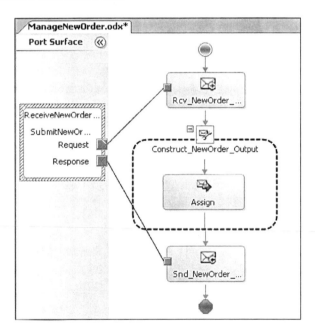

Notice that absolutely nothing we've done within this orchestration hints at its role as the realization of a WCF service. Ideally, an orchestration's ports are not tightly coupled to a runtime transport scheme, which in return means greater flexibility and reuse. The orchestration port only dictates a message type and message exchange pattern while remaining transport neutral. Before continuing on, I went ahead and built and deployed this project to ensure that my BizTalk application was created and refreshed.

Generating the WCF endpoint

Unlike most BizTalk receive adapters, which poll or listens to existing URIs (such as file locations, databases, queues), the WCF adapters require us to create new endpoints that BizTalk uses to get data absorbed into the system. Fortunately, Microsoft makes generating such endpoints fairly easy by introducing the **BizTalk WCF Service Publishing Wizard**.

Pitfall

Unlike the classic ASMX-based **BizTalk Web Services Publishing Wizard**, the BizTalk project in Visual Studio.NET does NOT have to be deployed in the Global Assembly Cache in order for the **BizTalk WCF Service Publishing Wizard** to locate it. However, if the BizTalk project assembly had been deployed at any time previously, then, the freshly updated assembly must be deployed to the GAC so that the Visual Studio wizard pulls the latest version of the assembly.

While one can launch the **BizTalk WCF Service Publishing Wizard** from the **Microsoft BizTalk Server 2009** folder on the **Start** menu, it's much simpler to trigger this wizard from within Visual Studio.NET itself. We initiate this wizard by going to the Visual Studio.NET **Tools** menu and choosing **BizTalk WCF Service Publishing Wizard**. What we see next is a new window that will walk us through all the steps necessary to generate the service and endpoint we desire.

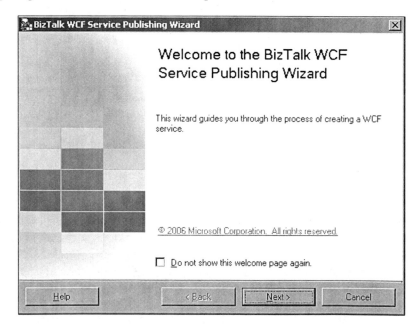

The first thing that this wizard needs to know is what type of WCF service we'd like to produce. Our choices are:

Endpoint type	Usage scenario
Service Endpoint	If you choose this type of endpoint, then this wizard will be responsible for generating a consumable WCF service that is hosted outside of BizTalk Server itself. Only WCF adapters that reside in the BizTalk Isolated Host (WCF-WSHttp, WCF-BasicHttp, and WCF-CustomIsolated) can be chosen here. Notice that you are able to allow metadata browsing of this service (through a WCF behavior) by selecting the **Enable metadata endpoint** checkbox. If you'd like the wizard to automatically create the BizTalk receive port/location which is linked to this freshly generated WCF service, then you may also select the corresponding checkbox that performs this action.
Metadata only endpoint (MEX)	Use this option if you have an existing, in-process BizTalk WCF endpoint whose metadata description you wish to expose on an IIS web server. Because BizTalk receive locations are never "typed" to a particular message schema, the in-process endpoints can't share any metadata that explains their expected data contract. Using a MEX endpoint, we can generate an IIS service that does nothing but expose the contract of the in-process endpoint. We'll see more of this option in the next section.

I went ahead and chose **Service endpoint** with a **WCF-WSHttp** transport while also enabling the metadata endpoint and auto-generation of a receive location in the BizTalk application named **BizTalkSOA**.

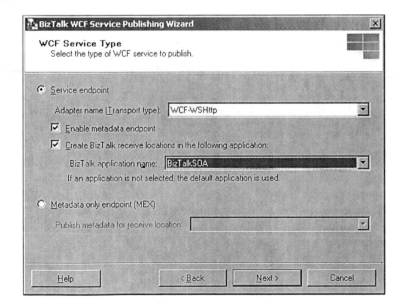

After selecting the desired service type, our next task is to identify which artifacts the wizard should use to generate the WCF service. Our current scenario will use the **Publish BizTalk orchestrations as WCF service** option, which means that key service attributes like data contract, communication pattern, and operation name are all retrieved from an existing orchestration's logical port. On the next page of the wizard, we are asked to designate which .NET assembly contains the orchestration that we'd like to use to generate the service. If we launched this wizard from within Visual Studio.NET when the BizTalk project is open, then the assembly's file path will be automatically populated by the wizard.

If the orchestration was successfully loaded by the wizard, then we should see the (public) orchestration ports available for selection. After accepting the current selected items, we enter a namespace for the service. In this case, I supplied the namespace http://Seroter.BizTalkSOA.Chapter3/Service.

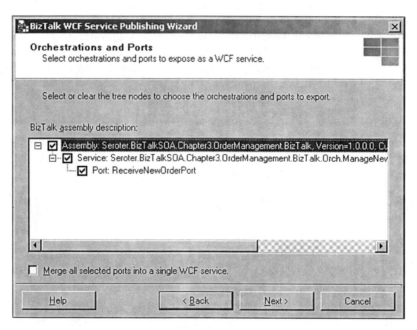

Finally, we need to specify the web server and address where our shiny new service will be deployed. Once we've picked a valid URL, we see a read-only view of the pending WCF service configuration. If everything looks good, then finish the wizard and wait for confirmation that all the necessary actions succeeded.

Configuring the Generated Components

We told the **BizTalk WCF Service Publishing Wizard** to build a receive location for us, so we should investigate exactly what we got as a result of that choice. In opening the **BizTalk Administration Console** and probing the **BizTalkSOA** application, we should see a new receive location with a staggeringly long name. It's hard to miss. Like all auto-generated messaging ports, this receive location is in a **Disabled** state. The next step is to enable this receive location, and in the **Orchestrations** section of the application, both bind and start the deployed orchestration.

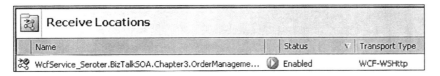

Double-clicking this new receive location reveals that it has been set up using the **WCF-WSHttp** adapter and the BizTalk isolated host. However, the real meat of this endpoint lies in the adapter configuration. We inspect this by clicking the **Configure** button next to the chosen adapter. The standard (non-custom) WCF adapters all have a similar look and feel to their configuration pages with the same set of tabs along the top. Here, we see the first critical piece of the endpoint: the address.

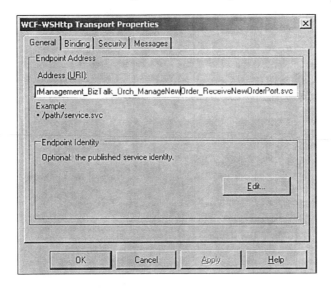

The second tab in this receive location configuration, named **Binding**, shows a subset of available **WCF-WSHttp** binding switches that we may alter for the adapter. Take note of the fact that while the default number of concurrent calls for a WCF service is 16, for performance reasons, the BizTalk WCF endpoint sets this value to 200. If we desire deeper control over this binding configuration, or wish to affix service behavior extensions, then the **WCF-CustomIsolated** adapter should be used instead.

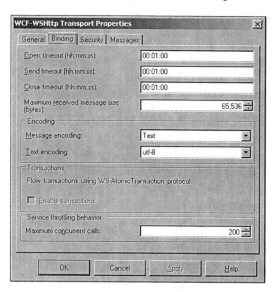

The third tab is named **Security** and provides us with a fairly straightforward way to apply standard WCF security schemes to our endpoint. We'll stick with the default **Message** security mode shown here.

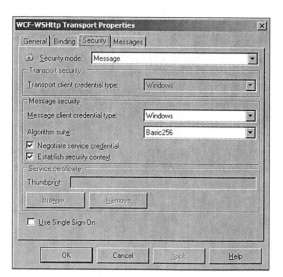

Finally, the last tab, named **Messages**, is where we tell BizTalk where to extract the message body from the WCF payload. We could send the entire SOAP payload to the BizTalk MessageBox (SOAP envelope included), or even rip out a specific node in the SOAP body. In our case, we just need the message body.

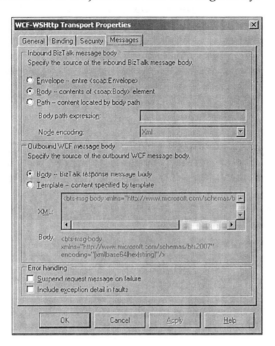

You may have noticed that nowhere in this receive location do we designate the *C* in the *ABCs* of WCF. Where is the *contract*? All BizTalk receive locations are type-less, and the WCF receive locations are no different. A BizTalk WCF endpoint exposes a generic contract that will accept any valid SOAP message. This is why the generation of a metadata endpoint is critical since otherwise we'd have no clear way to tell consumers how to structure the payload their service requests.

If you recall, our preceding run through the **BizTalk WCF Service Publishing Wizard** produced this receive location and an actual WCF service hosted in IIS 7.0. If we had tried to visit the service in our web browser immediately after the wizard had completed, we would have seen an error telling us that the receive location was offline. Note that the receive location for the associated WCF service must be enabled in order to browse the service. Once the receive location gets enabled, we should see a standard WCF service metadata page instead of an exception.

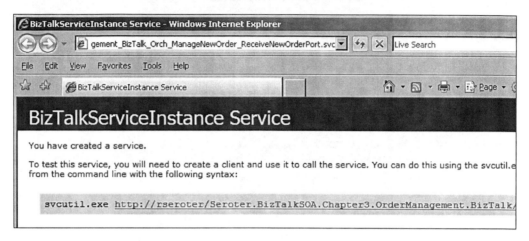

Let's take advantage of this metadata endpoint by referencing and consuming our new WCF service. In a new Visual Studio.NET console application we choose to **Add Service Reference** and point to the generated WCF service WSDL. Only a small bit of code is needed to consume this simple service. However, note the unwieldy type names that the orchestration-generated WCF service imparts upon us.

```
static void Main(string[] args)
{
    OrchSvc.Seroter_BizTalkSOA_Chapter3_OrderManagement_BizTalk_Orch_
ManageNewOrder_ReceiveNewOrderPortClient client =
        new OrchSvc.Seroter_BizTalkSOA_Chapter3_OrderManagement_BizTalk_
Orch_ManageNewOrder_ReceiveNewOrderPortClient("WSHttpBinding_
ITwoWayAsync");

            try
            {
                OrchSvc.NewOrder order = new OrchSvc.NewOrder();
                order.OrderID = "123";
                order.OrganizationID = "987";
                order.PhysicianID = "555";
                order.Status = "submitted";
                Console.WriteLine("Calling WCF service ...");
                client.SubmitNewOrder(ref order);
```

```
            Console.WriteLine("Result status is: " +
                order.Status);
            client.Close();
            Console.ReadLine();
        }
        catch (System.ServiceModel.CommunicationException) {
                client.Abort(); }
        catch (System.TimeoutException) { client.Abort(); }
        catch (System.Exception) { client.Abort(); throw; }
    }
}
```

At this point, we've designed an orchestration, exposed its port interface as a WCF service, and consumed that service from a WCF client.

Anatomy of a generated WCF WSDL

Attributes set while building a BizTalk project seep into the WSDL of a generated WCF service. Here is a quick look at which design-time properties map to runtime WSDL attributes.

BizTalk project attribute	WCF WSDL attribute

Value set for the **Service Namespace** in the **WCF Service Publishing Wizard**.	`<wsdl:definitions`
	`name="BizTalkServiceInstance"`
	`targetNamespace="http://Seroter.`
	`BizTalkSOA.Chapter3/Service"`
	
	`xmlns:tns="http://Seroter.`
	`BizTalkSOA.Chapter3/Service">`

Value set for the **Service Namespace** in the **WCF Service Publishing Wizard**.	`<xsd:schema`
	`targetNamespace="http://Seroter.`
	`BizTalkSOA.Chapter3/Service/`
	`Imports">`

Value set for **Target Namespace** in the BizTalk Schema.	`<xsd:import schemaLocation="..."`
	`namespace="http://Seroter.`
	`BizTalkSOA.Chapter3.`
	`OrderManagement.BizTalk/Contract"`
	`/>`

Value of the orchestration's **Namespace** attribute combined with the **Typename** of the orchestration, the name of the logical port being exposed and the name of the port **Operation**.	`<wsdl:message name="Seroter_`
	`BizTalkSOA_Chapter3_`
	`OrderManagement_BizTalk_Orch_`
	`ManageNewOrder_ReceiveNewOrderPort_`
	`SubmitNewOrder_InputMessage">`

BizTalk project attribute	WCF WSDL attribute

Value of the orchestration's **Namespace** attribute combined with the **Typename** of the orchestration and the name of the logical port being exposed.	`<wsdl:portType name="Seroter_`
	`BizTalkSOA_Chapter3_`
	`OrderManagement_BizTalk_`
	`Orch_ManageNewOrder_`
	`ReceiveNewOrderPort">`

Value of the orchestration's **Namespace** attribute combined with the **Typename** of the orchestration and the name of the logical port being exposed.	`<wsdl:binding name="WSHttpBinding_`
	`ITwoWayAsync" type="tns:`
	`Seroter_BizTalkSOA_Chapter3_`
	`OrderManagement_BizTalk_`
	`Orch_ManageNewOrder_`
	`ReceiveNewOrderPort">`

Value of the exposed orchestration port's **Operation** name.	`<wsdl:operation` `name="SubmitNewOrder">`

Exposing WCF services from schemas

In the last section, we looked at accepting a new product order in an orchestration and returning a response to the submitter. What if we only want a one-way channel and want multiple consumers to subscribe to this new order? This screams for a more event-driven scenario where the publisher asynchronously sends data that is handled and acted upon by unknown downstream systems (for example fulfilment systems, billing systems). In this case, we aren't interested in creating an orchestration that dictates our service contract, but rather, want to build a service on-ramp that simply gets data onto the message bus.

For this scenario, we will:

- Configure a TCP endpoint in BizTalk Server
- Generate a WCF metadata service hosted in IIS that clients use to discover the service and its true service URI
- Build the metadata endpoint using only schemas and no orchestrations

We will reuse the previously-built `NewOrder_XML.xsd` schema as the input message to the new service. This means that this new scenario requires no new development on our part. The scenario begins with the creation of a new receive port and location in the **BizTalkSOA** application found in the **BizTalk Administration Console**. The receive port has the following attributes:

Attribute	Value
Port type	One-way
Name	Seroter.BizTalkSOA.Chapter3.ReceiveNewOrder

Next, we'll take this receive port and add a new receive location to it with the following attributes:

Attribute	Value
Name	Seroter.BizTalkSOA.Chapter3.ReceiveNewOrder.WcfTcp
Transport Type	WCF-NetTcp
Receive Pipeline	XMLReceive
Transport Endpoint Address	net.tcp://localhost:9900/
	Seroter.BizTalkSOA.Chapter3.ReceiveNewOrder

Once the receive location is created, it should be started to ensure that it was configured correctly. An example of an incorrect configuration would be the designation of a URI port that was already in use by other processes. If this situation occurs, a message is added to the Application Event Log explaining the port collision.

Now as we talked before, BizTalk receive locations are never associated with a particular XSD schema. So, if we are assuming that our service client(s) does not have a copy of the service contract already, then we must provide a metadata endpoint that explains the type of message that our in-process receive location expects. In the previous section, we saw that the WCF endpoints generated from BizTalk orchestrations have verbose descriptions and burden you with lengthy attribute names. In many cases, you will want more fine-grained control over the service definition than what the **Publish BizTalk orchestrations as WCF service** selection in the **BizTalk WCF Service Publishing Wizard** can give you. In fact, unless you are desperate for the quickest possible way to generate WCF services and/or descriptions, there is no discernable reason to ever choose the **Publish BizTalk orchestrations as WCF service** option.

The alternative to using orchestrations to define the service contract and communication pattern is to build up the service definition graphically using a schema-only model. Selecting this alternative option allows us to manually name the service, choose a communication pattern, name the service operation, and choose the data contract(s).

To create such an endpoint, once again fire up the **BizTalk WCF Service Publishing Wizard** and choose the **Metadata only endpoint (MEX)** as the **WCF Service Type**. When we are asked which receive location we wish to produce metadata for, select the **Seroter.BizTalkSOA.Chapter3.ReceiveNewOrder.WcfTcp** location. After choosing to **Publish schemas as WCF service** on the next wizard page, we are given the opportunity to manually describe the new service.

Here, we apply friendlier names for service attributes, starting with the service description at the top. Note that this attribute cannot have dot operators in the name, so I called it **SeroterBizTalkSOAChapter3**. This value does NOT show up anywhere in the service itself, but is rather the name of the Visual Studio.NET solution file that the wizard generates for the web service. After renaming the service node **OrderService**, the existing two-way operation should be deleted. Next, a new operation is added by right-clicking the service, selecting **Add web method**, and choosing a **one-way** operation. After changing the operation name to **SubmitNewOrder**, we need to right-click the **Request** message and choose to **Select schema type**. This is where we indicate the input message type that our service expects. Browse to the appropriate BizTalk project assembly, and pick the only available schema type. Our service definition would now look like this:

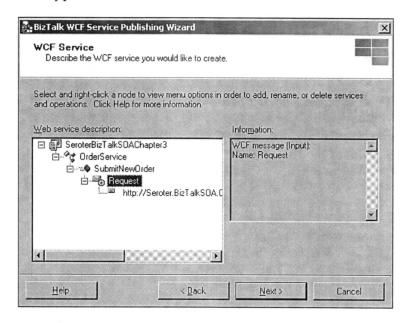

On the next page of the wizard, set the service namespace to `http://Seroter.BizTalkSOA.Chapter3/Service`. For the service location, I chose `http://localhost/Seroter.BizTalkSOA.Chapter3.OrderManagement.BizTalkMEX`. Once the wizard is completed, we have an IIS-deployed metadata endpoint that can be interrogated by WCF clients to reveal the contract and URL for our BizTalk-hosted service. Note that the status of the actual BizTalk endpoint (that is, receive location enabled or disabled) does not impact the availability of the MEX endpoint.

Is this the **only** way to expose metadata from in-process WCF receive locations? No, but it's the most straightforward way. In a later chapter, I'll show you a more roundabout way to do this that does not require an IIS-hosted metadata service.

Consuming WCF services from orchestrations

For BizTalk Server to play a full role within the service bus, it must be able to not only expose service endpoints, but also easily consume them. Let's take a look at how to create an orchestration, which accepts messages through the **WCF-NetTcp** receive location created earlier and also calls a WCF service that reveals a single endpoint based on Named Pipes.

We start by adding a new orchestration file named `LookupOrderContact.odx` to our existing BizTalk project in Visual Studio.NET. The orchestration starts up when a new order arrives. Therefore we should create a new orchestration message of type `Seroter.BizTalkSOA.Chapter3.OrderManagement.BizTalk.NewOrder_XML` named `NewOrder_Input`. After the order is received, we then call an existing WCF service, which provides us with more details about the customer placing the order. What do we need to know to call the WCF service from our orchestration? If you guessed the following, you'd be right:

* Schema contract(s) used
* Message exchange pattern (request/reply, request only)
* Service address and binding

Instead of having to manually produce these artifacts and configurations, we should use BizTalk-provided tools to do the work for us. If you wanted to reference a WCF service from a standard Visual Studio.NET project (for example class library, ASP.NET application), you could use the **Add Service Reference** option available by right-clicking the project. However, adding WCF references to BizTalk projects works a bit differently.

To add a WCF service reference, first right-click the BizTalk project and choose **Add** and then **Add Generated Items**. We are presented with a window that Visual Studio. NET uses to auto-construct BizTalk artifacts such as schemas based on adapter endpoints. We want to choose the **Consume WCF Service** option and click **Add**.

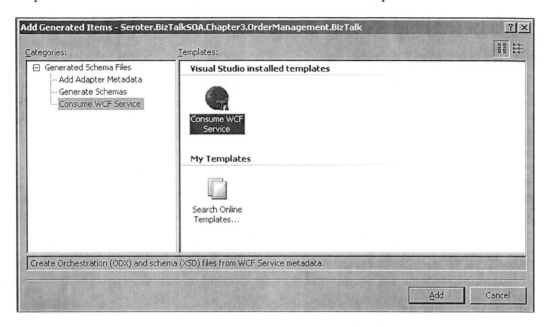

Now we get the pleasure of working with the **BizTalk WCF Service Consuming Wizard**. This is the twin brother of the **BizTalk WCF Service Publishing Wizard**, except that instead of generating new services, it produces the artifacts necessary to consume existing ones.

The first thing the wizard has to find out is where to get the metadata needed to craft the artifacts for BizTalk. If you only have a physical XSD and WSDL file (assuming someone went the true contract-first design route), then the second option in the wizard, **Metadata Files**, is best. However, if the target service is live and allows metadata queries, we can choose the first option. In our case, I have a running service with a **WCF-NetNamedPipe** endpoint and an explicit MEX endpoint. After choosing the metadata source as **Metadata Exchange Endpoint**, we then plug in the address of the metadata URL. In my case, this value is `net.pipe://localhost/Seroter.BizTalkSOA.Chapter3.OrderService/mex`. Notice that while only http(s) endpoints actually produce browsable metadata, any WCF endpoint can still expose metadata to query.

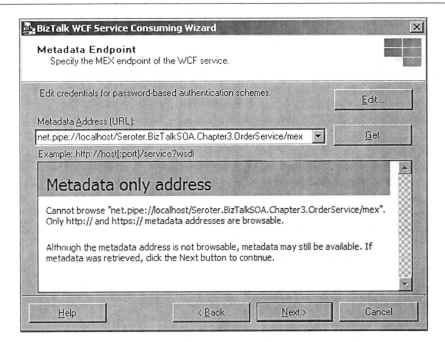

On the next wizard page (assuming that our service was accessible), we see a summary of what the wizard is about to import.

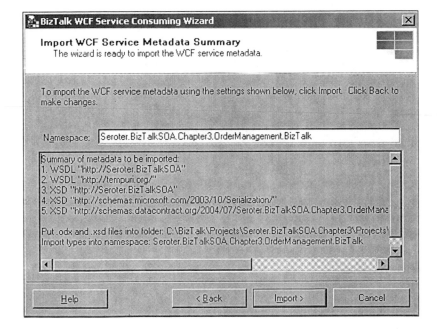

A number of files are generated including three different XSD schemas. These schemas describe the data types contained in the service contract. We also get two BizTalk binding files: one for the adapter type used in the metadata request (in our case, **WCF-NetNamedPipe**) and another we can optionally use to configure a **WCF-Custom** send port. In addition, the wizard emitted a new orchestration, which contains type definitions for multi-part messages representing the contract schemas, and, a port type that reflects the message exchange pattern of the target service.

Back in our primary orchestration, we now add the messages used for calling the service and handling the response. These messages (Contact_Request, Contact_Response) are created by using the multi-part message types defined in the wizard-generated orchestration.

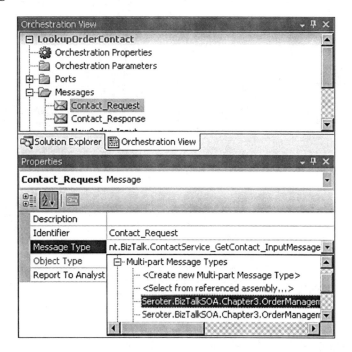

The service input message is represented as a complex (schema) type, so a BizTalk map is necessary to instantiate the new orchestration message. This means our orchestration requires a **Construct** shape in concert with a **Transform** shape that points to a new map. The map is quite simple as all we need to do is transfer the data in the target schema's PhysicianID XML node to the destination schema's contactId node.

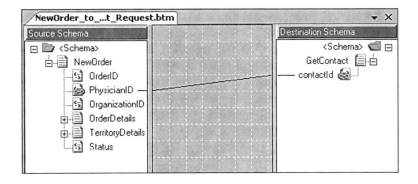

Once the map is finished, we add the **Send** and **Receive** shapes to the orchestration. The orchestration will send the request message and receive the response message. Once the shapes are dropped on the orchestration, and the corresponding **Message** properties are set on them, we create the logical port used by the orchestration to communicate with the service. After choosing to create and name a **New Configured Port**, we want to choose an *existing* port type for this port.

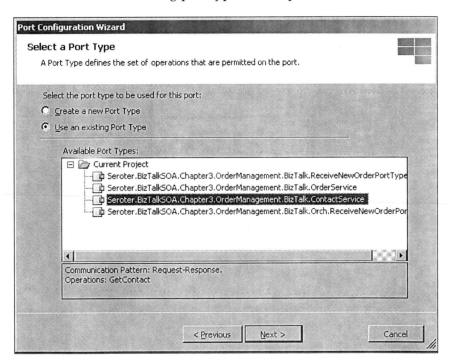

On the next wizard page, we confirm that the direction of the port is set to send a message and receive a response. We should now connect the service's send and receive shapes with the connectors on the logical port operation. Our final shape in the orchestration should be an **Expression** shape where a success confirmation is printed. If we want to extract data from the response message as proof that the response was successfully received, then we need to distinguish a field within the service response schema. In my case, I distinguished the Name element and printed that value out. To complete the orchestration, I added a new logical receive port for accepting the inbound order. The finished orchestration looks like this:

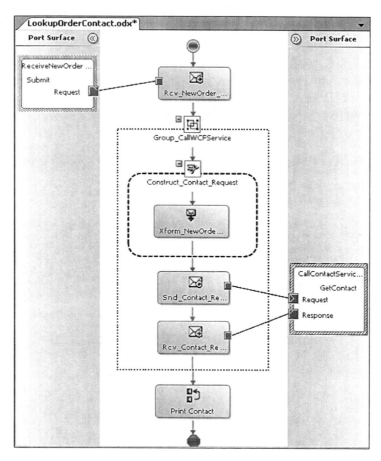

After deploying the orchestration, we have a few remaining tasks to perform from inside the **BizTalk Administration Console**. First, the generated BizTalk binding file should be imported so that our WCF send port is created automatically for us. Importing a binding is done by right-clicking the BizTalk application (in our case, named **BizTalkSOA**), choosing **Import** and then **Bindings**. Point this dialog box to the adapter-based binding (in our case, named `ContactService.BindingInfo.xml`) instead of the custom binding. After the import succeeds, we see a new (un-enlisted) send port that utilizes the **WCF-NetNamedPipes** adapter. That port should be turned on by right-clicking it and choosing **Start**.

Our final step is to bind and enlist the orchestration. We created a one-way **WCF-NetTcp** receive channel in the previous exercise and can reuse that receive port as our input to the orchestration. The orchestration binding is represented as follows:

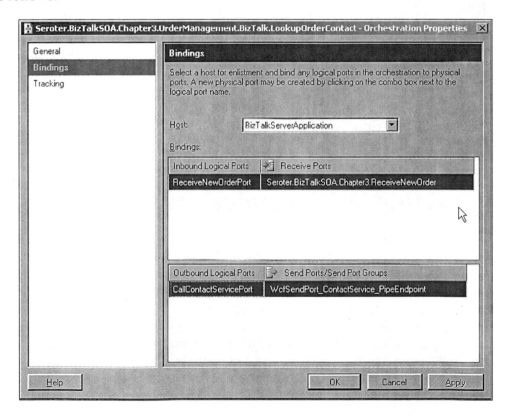

Once we start the orchestration, and ensure that the downstream service is up and running, we should trigger our client service. From the following screenshot, you can see that the client succeeded, the downstream service registered an invocation, and the orchestration successfully sent a trace message to the application Event Log.

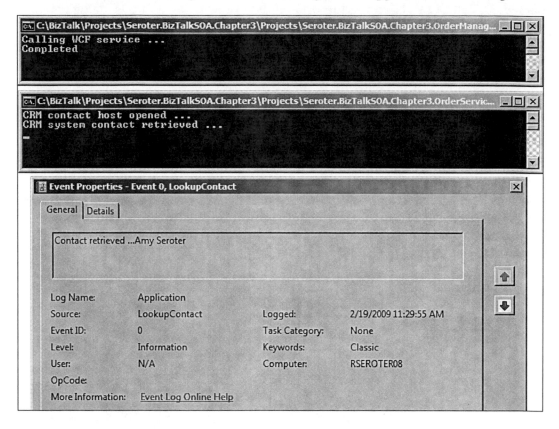

Consuming WCF services without orchestration

There are plenty of scenarios where orchestration is an unnecessary addition to service bus processing. Recall that an orchestration's prime benefit is the injection of a stateful, sequential series of steps to message processing. If the "processing" of a message can consist solely of the core BizTalk messaging components (receive ports, send ports, pipelines, maps, and subscriptions), then a messaging-only solution is the way to go. A general rule among BizTalk architects is that you avoid orchestration and concentrate on pure messaging when at all possible. This isn't because orchestration is intrinsically bad, but rather, because many situations actually don't require the overhead and complexity of a workflow.

That said, how nicely does the BizTalk bus play with WCF services when no orchestration is involved? Quite well, thank you. Let's look at how we may route inbound data to a WCF subscriber using only the message bus.

In our new scenario, we have a target service on our enterprise resource planning (ERP) system that accepts new order notices and uses WCF's **WsHttpBinding**. We'd like to call this service whenever a new product order enters the MessageBox. This subscriber does not need any direct knowledge of the upstream publisher or how the message arrived to the bus.

We start this example by referencing the target service from within Visual Studio. NET. This is done by once again right-clicking the BizTalk project and choosing to **Add** and then **Add Generated Items**. The **Consume WCF Service** is selected and when the **BizTalk WCF Service Consuming Wizard** launches, the **Metadata Exchange Endpoint** is picked as the source of the service metadata. Now we plug in the valid HTTP endpoint URI of our WCF service.

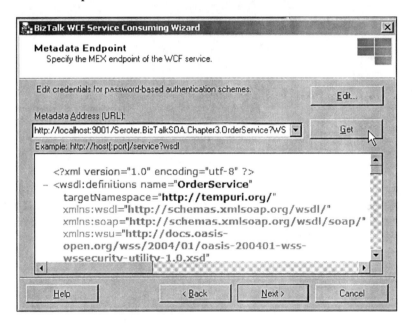

When the wizard completes, we have a set of metadata files (schemas, bindings, orchestration) that help describe the service and how to consume it. This example doesn't use orchestration, but we do still require one hand-built BizTalk artifact—a map. The WCF service expects the order data to be in a particular format, so we should design a map that gets applied by the outbound send port. The BizTalk map takes the repeating set of order items and puts them into their appropriate fields in the target schema.

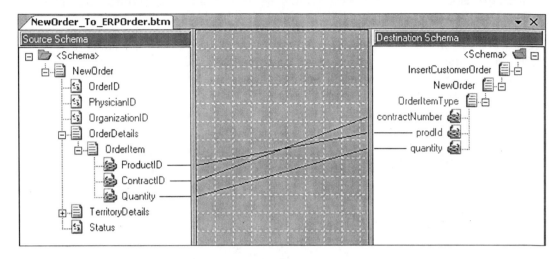

Now we build and deploy our updated project. Once that deployment has succeeded, we import the binding generated by the **BizTalk WCF Service Consuming Wizard**. For this scenario, let's import the **custom** binding (OrderService_Custom.BindingInfo.xml), so that we can see the different properties this adapter exposes. A send port is created for the **WCF-Custom** adapter, but notice that the binding specified by the adapter matches that of our service endpoint: **wsHttpBinding**.

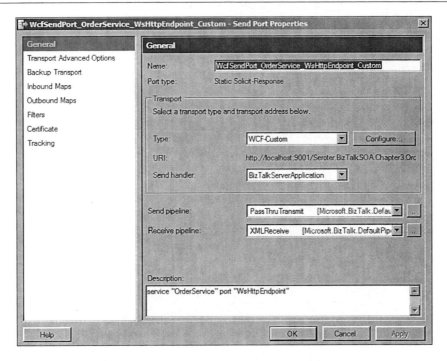

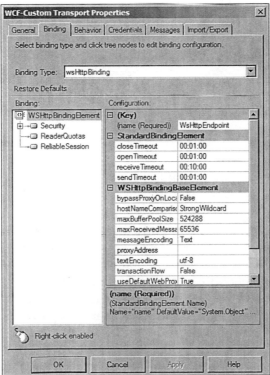

On the **General** tab of the adapter configuration, observe that there is a section called **SOAP action header**. This contains the SOAP action that will be attached to the outbound messages for this send port.

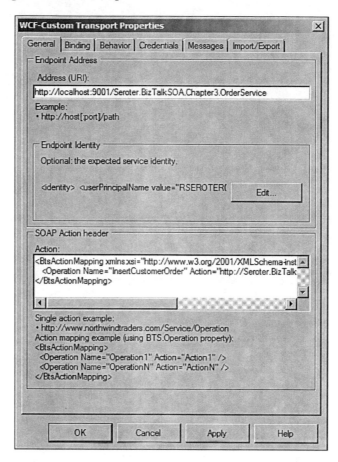

The `BtsActionMapping` wrapper in this textbox is used to support multiple **SOAPActions** values. However, this also means that something needs to set the **BTS.Operation** value, which the WCF adapter uses to choose the appropriate SOAP action from this collection. Typically this is set by the orchestration's logical send port operation name, but in the absence of an orchestration, we would have to set **BTS.Operation** value in a custom pipeline component. Before throwing up your hands and swearing loudly at this unnecessary complexity, breathe deeply and relax. Luckily, this textbox also supports an alternate format that is more supportive of simple content-based routing scenarios. A single SOAP action URI in this textbox is used when you want to apply the same **SOAPAction** header to all messages transmitted by the send port. For our scenario, let's switch this to the single **SOAPAction** header that corresponds to our target service operation.

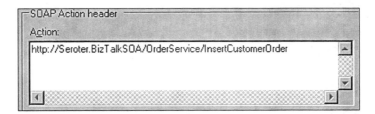

Next, we must apply our XSLT map to this send port. The map is a required component because our service is expecting a very specific data format that does not match the original structure of the data.

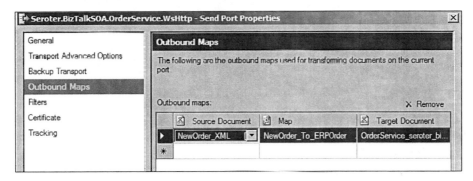

Our final step is to introduce a valid subscription for this send port. Without one, this port will never receive any messages published to the bus. Because we'd like to pull every order from the MessageBox, our subscription should be type-based, not context-based. A context-based subscription would say that we are subscribing to properties of the message (for example which port it arrived from) instead of anything relating to the message itself. We want to subscribe to all messages of a particular type. The subscription I applied can be seen in the following screenshot:

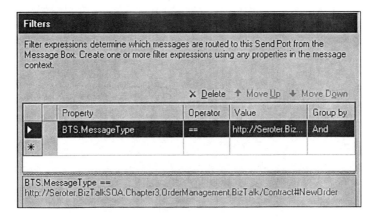

Now, technically we are finished. If we send a message into BizTalk, it should route to a listening send port, and produce the expected tracing statements. However, see the *pitfall* below to resolve an error with our current configuration.

Pitfall

The solution as it stands now will raise an exception. Why? The WCF service that BizTalk calls does not return a response message. However, the auto-generated BizTalk binding file was for a two-way send port. So, when the WCF service is called, the request is successful, but we end up with a **subscription not found** exception on the (empty) response message. We can fix this by creating a new one-way send port with identical configuration settings (adapter type, URI, binding, **SOAPAction**, and subscription) to the auto-generated port.

Summary

In this chapter, we began to see where BizTalk Server and Windows Communication Foundation intersect. WCF greatly enhances BizTalk Server by providing a flexible and extensible set of service endpoints that are capable of supporting a wide range of transmission, security, and encoding configurations. We now know how to generate services from BizTalk artifacts, whether those artifacts are schemas or orchestrations. We also looked at consuming existing services via orchestration or messaging-only patterns.

In the next chapter, we will investigate how to take the implementation knowledge we now have, and use it to actually architect service-oriented BizTalk solutions.

4
Planning Service-Oriented BizTalk Solutions

By failing to prepare, you are preparing to fail.
-Benjamin Franklin

Through the first three chapters of this book, we've looked at how to build BizTalk applications, WCF services, and BizTalk applications that use WCF services. However, simply knowing the nuts and bolts of working code doesn't mean that we're ready to architect maintainable, reusable, service-oriented applications. We need to become intimately familiar with standard patterns and always keep key principles in mind in order to truly build long-lasting SOA solutions.

In this chapter, you will learn:

- The definition of a service
- The core principles of a service-oriented architecture
- Which types of services can be exposed
- The standard message exchange patterns for services
- How the service-orientation principles apply to a BizTalk Server solution

The core principles of a service-oriented architecture

So what exactly is a service? A **service** is essentially a well-defined interface to an autonomous chunk of functionality, which usually corresponds to a specific business process. That might sounds a lot like a regular old object-oriented component to you. While both services and components have commonality in that they expose discrete interfaces of functionality, a service is more focused on the capabilities offered than the packaging. Services are meant to be higher-level, business-oriented offerings that provide technology abstraction and interoperability within a multipurpose "services" tier of your architecture.

What makes up a service? Typically you'll find:

- **Contract**: Explains what operations the service exposes, types of messages, and exchange patterns supported by this service, and any policies that explain how this service is used.
- **Messages**: The data payload exchanged between the service consumer and provider.
- **Implementation**: The portion of the service which actually processes the requests, executes the expected business functionality, and optionally returns a response.
- **Service provider**: The host of the service which publishes the interface and manages the lifetime of the service.
- **Service consumer**: Ideally, a service has someone using it. The service consumer is aware of the available service operations and knows how to discover the provider and determine what type of messages to transmit.
- **Facade**: Optionally, a targeted facade may be offered to particularly service consumers. This sort of interface may offer a more simplified perspective on the service, or provide a coarse-grained avenue for service invocation.

What is the point of building a service? I'd say it's to construct an asset capable of being reused which means that it's a discrete, discoverable, self-describing entity that can be accessed regardless of platform or technology.

Service-oriented architecture is defined as an *architectural discipline based on loosely-coupled, autonomous chunks of business functionality which can be used to construct composite applications*. Through the rest of this chapter we get a chance to flesh out many of the concepts that underlie that statement. Let's go ahead and take a look at a few of the principles and characteristics that I consider most important to a successful service-oriented BizTalk solution. As part of each one, I'll explain the thinking behind the principle and then call out how it can be applied to BizTalk Server solutions.

Loosely coupled

Many of the fundamental SOA principles actually stem from this particular one. In virtually all cases, some form of coupling between components is inevitable. The only way we can effectively build software is to have interrelations between the various components that make up the delivered product. However, when architecting solutions, we have distinct design decisions to make regarding the extent to which application components are coupled. Loose coupling is all about establishing relationships with minimal dependencies.

What would a tightly-coupled application look like? In such an application, we'd find components that maintained intimate knowledge of each others' working parts and engaged in frequent, chatty synchronous calls amongst themselves. Many components in the application would retain state and allow consumers to manipulate that state data. Transactions that take place in a tightly coupled application probably adhere to a **two-phase commit** strategy where all components must succeed together in order for each data interaction to be finalized. The complete solution has its ensemble of components compiled together and singularly deployed to one technology platform. In order to run properly, these tightly-coupled components rely on the full availability of each component to fulfill the requests made of them.

On the other hand, a loosely-coupled application employs a wildly different set of characteristics. Components in this sort of application share only a contract and keep their implementation details hidden. Rarely preserving state data, these components rely on less frequent communication where chunky input containing all the data the component needs to satisfy its requestors is shared. Any transactions in these types of applications often follow a **compensation** strategy where we don't assume that all components can or will commit their changes at the same time. This class of solution can be incrementally deployed to a mix of host technologies. Asynchronous communication between components, often through a broker, enables a less stringent operational dependency between the components that comprise the solution.

What makes a solution loosely coupled then? Notably, the primary information shared by a component is its interface. The consuming component possesses no knowledge of the internal implementation details. The contract relationship suffices as a means of explaining how the target component is used. Another trait of loosely coupled solutions is coarse-grained interfaces that encourage the transmission of full data entities as opposed to fine-grained interfaces, which accept small subsets of data. Because loosely-coupled components do not share state information, a thicker input message containing a complete impression of the entity is best. Loosely-coupled applications also welcome the addition of a broker which proxies the (often asynchronous) communication between components. This mediator permits a rich decoupling where runtime binding between components can be dynamic and components can forgo an operational dependency on each other.

Let's take a look at an example of loose coupling that sits utterly outside the realm of technology.

Completely non-technical loose coupling example

When I go to a restaurant and place an order with my waiter, he captures the request on his pad and sends that request to the kitchen. The order pad (the contract) contains all the data needed by the kitchen chef to create my meal. The restaurant owner can bring in a new waiter or rotate his chefs and the restaurant shouldn't skip a beat as both roles (services) serve distinct functions where the written order is the intersection point and highlight of their relationship.

Why does loose coupling matter? By designing a loosely-coupled solution, you provide a level of protection against the changes that the application will inevitably require over its life span. We have to reduce the impact of such changes while making it possible to deploy necessary updates in an efficient manner.

How does this apply to BizTalk Server solutions?

A good portion of the BizTalk Server architecture was built with loose coupling in mind. Think about the BizTalk MessageBox which acts as a broker facilitating communication between ports and orchestrations while limiting any tight coupling. Receive ports and send ports are very loosely coupled and in many cases, have absolutely no awareness of each other. The publish-and-subscribe bus thrives on the asynchronous transfer of self-describing messages between stateless endpoints. Let's look at a few recommendations of how to build loosely-coupled BizTalk applications.

Orchestrations are a prime place where you can either go with a tightly-coupled or loosely-coupled design route. For instance, when sketching out your orchestration process, it's sure tempting to use that **Transform** shape to convert from one message type to another. However, a version change to that map will require a modification of the calling orchestration. When mapping to or from data structures associated with external systems, it's wiser to push those maps to the edges (receive/send ports) and not embed a direct link to the map within the orchestration.

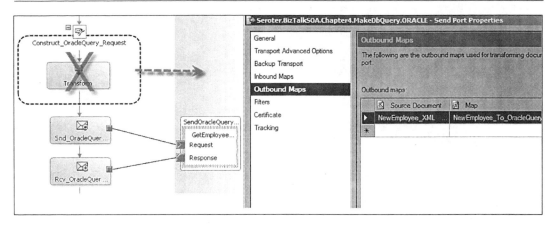

BizTalk easily generates schemas for line-of-business (LOB) systems and consumed services. To interact with these schemas in a very loosely coupled fashion, consider defining stable entity schemas (i.e. "canonical schemas") that are used within an orchestration, and only map to the format of the LOB system in the send port. For example, if you need to send a piece of data into an Oracle database table, you can certainly include a map within an orchestration which instantiates the Oracle message. However, this will create a tight coupling between the orchestration and the database structure. To better insulate against future changes to the database schema, consider using a generic intermediate data format in the orchestration and only transforming to the Oracle-specific format in the send port.

How about those logical ports that we add to orchestrations to facilitate the transfer of messages in and out of the workflow process? When configuring those ports, the **Port Configuration Wizard** asks you if you want to associate the port to a physical endpoint via the **Specify Now** option. Once again, pretty tempting. If you know that the message will arrive at an orchestration via a FILE adapter, why not just go ahead and configure that now and let Visual Studio.NET create the corresponding physical ports during deployment? While you can independently control the auto-generated physical ports later on, it's a bad idea to embed transport details inside the orchestration file.

On each subsequent deployment from Visual Studio.NET, the generated receive port will have any out-of-band changes overwritten by the deployment action.

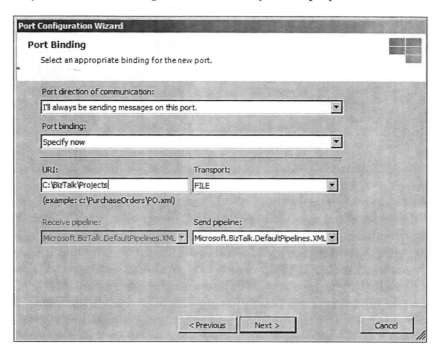

Chaining orchestration together is a tricky endeavor and one that can leave you in a messy state if you are too quick with a design decision. By "chaining orchestrations", I mean exploiting multiple orchestrations to implement a business process. There are a few options at your disposal listed here and ordered from most coupled to least coupled.

- **Call Orchestration** or **Start Orchestration** shape: An orchestration uses these shapes in order to kick off an additional workflow process. The **Call Orchestration** is used for synchronous connection with the new orchestration while the **Start Orchestration** is a fire-and-forget action. This is a useful tactic for sharing state data (for example variables, messages, ports) from the source orchestration to the target. However, both options require a tight coupling of the source orchestration to the target. Version changes to the target orchestration would likely require a redeployment of the source orchestration.

- Partner direct bound ports: These provide you the capability to communicate between orchestrations using ports. In the **forward partner direct binding** scenario, the sender has a strong coupling to the receiver, while the receiver knows nothing about the sender. This works well in situations where there are numerous senders and only one receiver. **Inverse partner direct binding** means that there is a tight coupling between the receiver and the sender. The sender doesn't know who will receive the command, so this scenario is intended for cases where there are many receivers for a single sender. In both cases, you have tight coupling on one end, with loose-coupling on the other.

- MessageBox **direct binding**: This is the most loosely-coupled way to share data between orchestrations. When you send a message out of an orchestration through a port marked for MessageBox direct binding, you are simply placing a message onto the bus for anyone to consume. The source orchestration has no idea where the data is going, and the recipients have no idea where it's been.

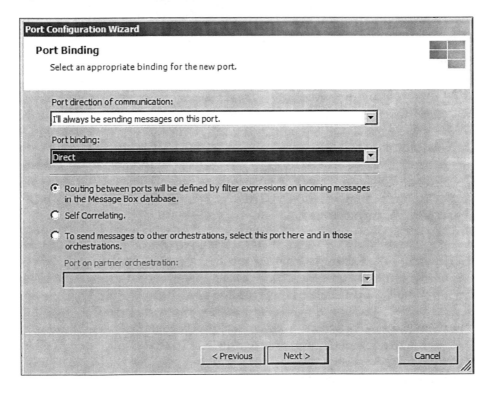

MessageBox direct binding provides a very loosely-coupled way to send messages between different orchestrations and endpoints. In Chapter 7, I'll show you how to use the BizTalk Business Rules Engine alongside orchestrations to seamlessly link, add, and replace orchestrations in a complex business process.

Critical point

While MessageBox direct binding is great, you do lose the ability to send the additional state data that a **Call Orchestration** shape will provide you. So, as with all architectural decisions, you need to decide if the sacrifice (loose coupling, higher latency) is worth the additional capabilities.

Decisions can be made during BizTalk messaging configuration that promote a loosely-coupled BizTalk landscape. For example, both receive ports and send ports allow for the application of maps to messages flying past. In each case, multiple maps can be added. This does NOT mean that all the maps will be applied to the message, but rather, it allows for sending multiple different message types in, and emitting a single type (or even multiple types) out the other side. By applying transformation at the earliest and latest moments of bus processing, you loosely couple external formats and systems from internal canonical formats. We should simply assume that all upstream and downstream systems will change over time, and configure our application accordingly.

Another means for loosely coupling BizTalk solutions involves the exploitation of the publish-subscribe architecture that makes up the BizTalk message bus. Instead of building solely point-to-point solutions and figuring that a SOAP interface makes you service oriented, you should also consider loosely coupling the relationship between the service input and where the data actually ends up. We can craft a series of routing decision that take into account message content or context and direct the message to one or more relevant processes/endpoints. While point-to-point solutions may be appropriate for many cases, don't neglect a more distributed pattern where the data publisher does not need to explicitly know exactly how their data will be processed and routed by the message bus.

When identifying subscriptions for our send ports, we should avoid tight coupling to metadata attributes that might limit the reuse of the port. For instance, you should try to create subscriptions on either the message type or message content instead of context attributes such as the inbound receive port name. Ports should be tightly coupled to the MessageBox and messages it stores, not to attributes of its publisher. That said, there are clearly cases where a subscriber is specifically looking for data that corresponds to a targeted piece of metadata such as the subject line of the email received by BizTalk. As always, design your solution in a way that solves your business problem in an efficient manner.

Abstraction

The SOA concept of abstraction is all about making your service a black box to consumers. All that the consumers see is an interface while possessing no visibility into the soft meaty center of the service. The underlying service could be very simple or mind-numbingly complex. It could have a very stable core, or be undergoing consistent upgrades. The service logic could integrate with a single backend system, or choreograph communication across ten applications. None of these things should matter to a service consumer who has an interface that provides an abstract perspective of the service itself.

This is where the art of service contract design plays an immense role. The contract needs to strike the right balance of information hiding, while still demanding information material to an effective service. Consider operation granularity. I have an application that requires a series of API calls in order to insert a new order for a product. First I need to check the available stock, then decrement the stock, and then add the new order to the system. If I were a brand new SOA developer, I might take that API, slap a SOAP interface on it, and declare our application to be service-oriented. Wrong answer! We don't always need to expose that level of granularity to the consumer. Let's bestow upon them a nice coarse-grained interface that hides the underlying system API messiness and simply accepts the product order through a `SubmitOrder` operation.

Completely non-technical abstraction example

When my order is taken at a restaurant, I don't have the opportunity (or desire!) to outline the sequence of steps I wish the chef to take in preparing my meal. Instead, I am asked a simple series of questions that are recorded and forwarded on to the kitchen. Inside the kitchen, a swift, complex set of actions are taken to get the food ready all at once. From my perspective while seated at the table, I simply made a single request and will get back what I expect. If the chef decides to try prepare a meal in a brand new way, that's of no consequence to me (unless it tastes bad). The underlying service may undergo mild or fundamental changes, but the ordering interface provided to me will remain fairly static.

Why does abstraction matter? A well-defined interface that successfully hides the service logic provides a way to change implementation details over time, while still respecting the original contract. Just because a service undergoes plumbing modifications doesn't mean that service consumers must take note of those changes or behave any differently. As long as the interface remains consistent, the service itself can accommodate either simple or radical changes. A nicely abstracted interface promotes loose coupling between the service sender and receiver while a contract that too deeply reveals implementation details can lead to tight coupling.

How does this apply to BizTalk Server solutions?

When thinking about abstraction and information hiding in BizTalk Server, I'd like to focus on how BizTalk functionality is exposed to the outside world. Here I'll highlight two ways to respect the abstraction principle in BizTalk Server.

First, let's talk about how orchestrations are consumed by outside parties. In truth, they are never directly exposed to a service consumer. It's impossible to instantiate a BizTalk orchestration without going through the adapter layer. So when we develop external service interfaces that front orchestrations, we should be diligent and not reveal aspects of our orchestration that the service consumer shouldn't know about. We can accomplish this in part by always starting our projects in a contract-driven manner by building the schema first, and then go about building an orchestration. If we design in reverse, it is likely that the orchestration's implementation logic seeps into the schema design. For instance, let's say that my orchestration sends employee data to a SQL Server database and also interacts with a web service exposed by a TIBCO messaging server. If I built my orchestration first, and then built up my schema along the way, I might be tempted to add fields to my employee schema where I can store a `TIBCO_Response` and capture and store a `SQL_Exception`.

Then if I used the **BizTalk WCF Service Publishing Wizard** to expose my orchestration as a service, I'd have an externally-facing schema polluted with information about my technical implementation. My service consumer should have no knowledge about what my orchestration does to complete its task.

Another critical way to show regard for the abstraction principle is by thoughtfully considering how to expose downstream system interfaces to upstream consumers. Let's say that you need to integrate with a Siebel application and insert new customer contacts. The WCF LOB Adapter for Siebel allows you to auto-generate the bits needed by a BizTalk orchestration to consume the target Siebel operations. When exposing that orchestration's port as a service interface, it would be a very bad decision to assign the Siebel-generated schema as our instantiating contract. There are two reasons I would avoid doing this at all costs:

- This tightly couples our service consumer to an implementation decision. Ignoring the fact that LOB system generated schemas are typically verbose and hard to digest, our service consumer should neither care nor know about how the orchestration processes the new customer. By sharing LOB system schemas as orchestration schemas, you've lost any opportunity to provide an abstract interface.

- A service typically offers a simplified interface to complex downstream activities. What if Siebel required three distinct operations to be called in order to insert a new customer? Should we expose three services from BizTalk Server and expect the service client to coordinate these calls? Absolutely not. As we discussed earlier, slapping SOAP interfaces onto existing APIs does not make an application service-oriented. Instead, we want to look for opportunities to offer services that aggregate downstream actions into a single coarse-grained exterior interface.

A good strategy for interfacing with LOB systems is to identify a single canonical schema that encapsulates all the data necessary to populate the downstream LOB systems regardless of how many individual LOB operations are needed. This strategy has two benefits. First, you obtain significant control over the structure of your service contract instead of being subjected to a data structure generated by an adapter. Secondly, we achieve a much more flexible interface that is no longer dependent on a particular implementation. What if the downstream LOB system changes its interface or the target LOB system changes completely? In theory, the service consumer can remain blissfully unaware of these circumstances as their interface is cleanly separated from the final data repository used by the service.

Interoperable

SOA-compatible services need to support cross-platform invocation and the service itself will often access a heterogeneous set of data and functions. Interoperability is all about making diverse systems work together and it **is** a critical component of a long-term SOA.

Similar to all of the core SOA principles, service interoperability needs to be designed early in the project lifecycle instead of being an afterthought addressed only moments before production deployment. Now interoperability doesn't mean that the service has to accommodate a mix of runtime host environments. A service that fails to run in both Microsoft IIS and BEA WebLogic hosting platforms doesn't mean that I've written a closed, poorly-designed service. When we talk about interoperability, we are concentrating on how a wide variety of disparate *clients* can access a single service. Is the fact that my service was written in .NET 3.5 and hosted by IIS 7.0 completely transparent to my Java, .NET, and Ruby users? If your service was written well, then the answer to that question should be "yes".

As for service implementation, you ideally want to empower your service to yank data from any available source. To do so, the service needs a means to access diverse sets of resources that may not natively expose simple interfaces. This is where a service/integration bus can truly shine. Some applications just won't naturally play nice with each other. But a service bus with built-in adapter technology can bridge those gaps and enable unfriendly systems to share and consume data from the outside. For example, the BizTalk Adapters for Host Systems produce no-code integration solutions for IBM mainframe technology. I can write a snazzy WCF service that chews on and returns data that dwells in VSAM host file and the service client remains blissfully unaware. The adapters in BizTalk Server enable us to build rich services that penetrate existing non-service-oriented applications and seamlessly weave their data into the service result.

So how do you achieve interoperability in your service environment? First and foremost, you want to adhere to the standard entities that typically describe services and their behavior. The "big four" technologies to keep in mind are WSDL (for service contract description), XSD (for message structure definition), SOAP (the protocol for sending service messages) and UDDI (for service registration and discovery). All of these technologies are considered "cross-platform" and are readily supported by both major and minor software vendors. Do you need to use each of these technologies in order to provide an interoperable service? Definitely not. Some find WSDLs to be obtuse and unnecessary and still others find XSD to be a lousy way to organize data. However, given BizTalk's embrace of these artifact types, I'll work within these confines.

 I'd be remiss if I didn't mention that service interoperability is also quite possible through services written in a RESTful manner. That is, services that don't use the more verbose SOAP interface and instead rally around HTTP URI significance, distinct "resources", transferring resource representations, and the well-defined HTTP verbs. RESTful services typically offer a looser concept of a "message contract" and don't provide a standard way to share the representations that the service expects or returns. Although WCF now has full support for RESTful services, the BizTalk WCF adapter does not readily expose or consume such endpoints. Note that I won't spend much time analyzing RESTful services in this book.

When building a service for interoperability, what do you need to consider? From my perspective, interoperability design comes in at four major points:

- **Endpoint choice**: If you truly intend for your service to be available to the widest range of consumers, then you need to pick an endpoint that is accessible to the masses. Simply put, pick a protocol like HTTP that everyone can support. Now, there's no shame in exposing WCF's **netTcpBinding** endpoint for targeted consumers, but be aware that you've instantly settled on a .NET-to-.NET only solution.

- **Data structure**: Properly selecting friendly XML data types and node behaviors is a vital part of building an interoperable service message. How are decimals handled? What's the precision of a floating point number for .NET versus. Java? For intricate calculations, those answers have a significant impact on the accuracy of data used by the service. Also don't forget about date/time handling either, as XSD has a very rigid `datetime` data type (CCYY-MM-DDThh:mm:ss), but either source or destination systems may enforce an alternate format.

- **Security scheme**: Cross-platform security can be a challenge, but without it, one cannot truly put forward an interoperable service. Even with the WS-Security standard itself, you are bound to come across existing service clients who support different versions or flavors of these standards, thus making pure interoperability impossible.

- **Transaction support**: The naturally stateless nature of most services makes the idea of a two-phase commit problematic to implement. When either exposing a service that must accept a transaction, or when the internal functions of a service require the assistance of a transaction, you want to lean heavily on standard mechanisms that can ensure the widest range of compatibility across platforms and technologies.

Completely non-technical interoperability example

For me, a true test of a quality ethnic restaurant is if the people working there are of the same ethnicity that the restaurant touts as its speciality. However, what if the chef doesn't speak the same language as the waiter? In this case, they rely on multiple means of interoperability. First, they can use a taxonomy consisting of letter codes or numbers to represent the meals requested by patrons. Secondly, they can employ a single translator who proxies communication between the personnel who don't natively speak the same language.

How does this apply to BizTalk Server solutions?

BizTalk Server is the most vendor-neutral product that Microsoft has ever manufactured. Its 25+ built-in adapters allow it to readily access an impressive set of industry-standard and vendor-specific technologies. The question is, how do we make BizTalk Server's external interface as interoperable as possible in order to support the widest range of client types? Let's evaluate BizTalk's interoperability support in the four areas outlined previously.

Deciding upon an on-ramp technology for the service bus is a critical task. Do we expose a FILE-based interface that supports legacy applications? How about a very simple HTTP interface that is sure to please basic web service clients? Each choice has tradeoffs. Fortunately for BizTalk architects, this needn't be such a gut-wrenching decision. BizTalk Server walls off the interface from the implementation logic in a very loosely-coupled fashion making it possible to support a mix of inbound channel technologies. Remember that the logical ports in an orchestration are not associated with a specific technology during design time. Also recall that even when an orchestration is bound to a physical messaging artifact at runtime, it is not bound to an individual **receive location**, but rather to the more encompassing **receive port**. A single receive port can contain countless receive locations which all accept data via different channels. As a result, we should carefully consider our service audience, and based on that assessment, configure the acceptable number of endpoints that accommodate our primary consumers. If we plan on building a very accessible service which also provides advanced capabilities for modern users, then a receive port filled with receive locations for both **WCF-BasicHttp** and **WCF-WSHttp** adapters makes sense. This way, our simple clients can still access the service using classic SOAP capabilities, while our forward-thinking clients can engage in a more feature-rich service conversation with us. If we later discover that we have service consumers who cannot speak HTTP at all, then BizTalk Server still affords us the opportunity to reveal more traditional endpoints such as FILE or FTP.

One place that interoperability between systems can subtly fail is when the data itself is transferred between endpoints. How one platform serializes a particular data type may be fundamentally different on an alternate platform. For instance, be sure that if you've defined a field as `nullable` that a standard mix of consumers can indeed accept a null value in that data type. Note that the `float` and `decimal` data type may have different levels of precision based on the platform so you could encounter unexpected rounding of numerical values. Also consider the handling of `datetime` values across environments. While the XSD `datetime` data type is quite rigid in format, you may choose to use an alternate date format embedded in a string data type instead. If you do so, you must ensure that your target service consumers know how to handle a `datetime` in that format. In general, a reliance on simpler data types is going to go a long way towards support for the widest variety of platforms. You can stay focused on this concept by building your XSD schema first (and complying with known types) prior to building a service that adheres to the types in the schema. Fortunately for us BizTalk developers, we're used to building the contract first.

Alongside the data structure itself, a service is more interoperable when the service contract is not needlessly complicated. A complicated WSDL definition would describe an XSD contract that possessed numerous nested, imported schemas with a distinct set of namespaces. You may find that some SOAP toolkits do not properly read WSDL files with these types of characteristics. While it can initially be seen as a huge timesaver that application platforms will auto-magically generate a WSDL from a service, you are often better off creating your own WSDL file that simplifies the portrayal of the service. Fortunately for us, both WCF and BizTalk Server support the usage of externally defined WSDL files as replacements for framework-generated ones.

Service security is a tricky concept due to the fact that support for cross-platform security technology has yet to extend into all major software platforms. WCF (and thus BizTalk Server) exploits the WS-Security set of standards, which offer platform-neutral security schemes, but, few vendors have offerings that fully support this standard. So, when architecting service security, you can either implement modern security schemes supported through WS-I standards, or, go the more traditional route of securing the transmission channel with Secure Sockets Layer (SSL) and/or securing the data throughout its journey by applying X.509 certificates and encrypting the payload.

The embrace of the service transaction standard is also slow in coming. WCF incorporates the **WS-AtomicTransaction** and **WS-ReliableMessaging** standards, but note that BizTalk Server only explicitly supports **WS-AtomicTransaction**. Be aware that you can make a BizTalk WCF adapter use **WS-ReliableMessaging** by manually constructing the binding in the WCF-Custom adapter. Also, BizTalk's support for service transactions only extends to the point of publication to the MessageBox, and the distribution of messages from the MessageBox.

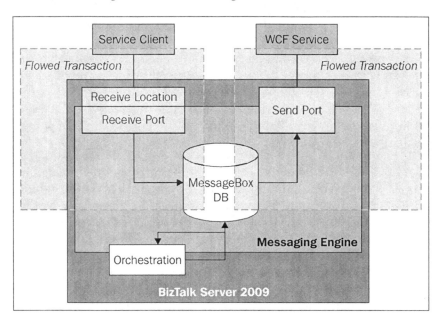

To design a BizTalk service to be interoperable, with both security and transaction concepts in mind, you may be forced to implement the security specifications available by the WS-I organization and educate service clients as to the types of frameworks and libraries they need to properly engage these advanced service capabilities.

Reusable

In my humble opinion, the principle of reusability is the most important aspect of a service-oriented architecture. I consider *reusability* to be a design time objective while *reuse* is an inadequate runtime success metric. In essence, reusability is all about effectively segmenting functionality into services which are capable of being used by others outside the scope of your immediate effort. Note the word *capable* in the previous sentence. Unless you can predict the future, it's hard to guarantee that a service module built today will satisfy all the future needs for similar capabilities. Even if no additional consumers decide that a service is of use to them, this doesn't mean that the service is a failure. By itself, the forethought and decisions made to make a service reusable makes the construction of the service a worthwhile effort.

Why does reusability matter? The answers may seem obvious, but I'll call out three explicit benefits:

- Future applications can harvest the functionality of the original service and accelerate their solution development while encouraging the adoption of composite applications. Some SOA advocates foresee a world where many applications consist of very little original functionality but rather, are simply aggregations of existing services exposed in the enterprise.

- A heavily reused service affords an organization the opportunity to make solitary changes that cascade to all consumers of that functionality. Let's say we have a service, which aggregates data from multiple underlying systems and returns a single, unified view of a *customer* entity. Assuming that most major applications in our enterprise use this service to get information about our customers, we can change the implementation (swap out data sources, add new sources, change logic) of this service and each consumer instantly gets the benefits.

- The architectural choices made in designing a reusable service will inevitably encourage the implementation of the other mentioned SOA principles such as loose-coupling, abstraction, and interoperability in addition to other core principles such as composability, encapsulation, and discoverability.

A reusable service can be of many diverse shapes and sizes. First of all, such a service could exhibit a coarse-grained interface that employs a static contract while supplying a distinct business function. For instance, a service with an operation named `PublishAdverseEvent` (which takes reports of patients experiencing negative effects from a medication) can be used by every system or business process that might produce this sort of data. This service takes a very specific payload, but it can be reused by the multiple systems that encounter this category of input data. Conversely, we might define a utilitarian service that archives information to a database through a loose contract that accepts any structured data as a parameter. This service also offers a reusable interface that can be applied to a varied set of use cases. Reusable services may have very generic logic or very specific logic, flexible contracts or rigid ones, and may be business-oriented or cross-cutting functional services. A key aspect of reuse is to define the service in such a way that it can be useful to those outside of your immediate project scope.

Completely non-technical reusability example

An intelligent restaurant owner doesn't hire a chef who is only capable of preparing grilled cheese sandwiches. Instead, they seek out chefs who are adept at not only repeatedly assembling the same meal, but also skilled at delivering a wide variety of different meals. The service offered by the chef, "preparing food", is a reusable service that accepts multiple inputs and produces an output based on the request made.

How does this apply to BizTalk Server solutions?

Virtually every component that comprises a BizTalk solution can be constructed in a reusable fashion. Take schemas for example. A single schema may be aggregated into other schemas, or simply applied to multiple different projects. For instance, a schema describing a standard `Address` node might be deemed an enterprise standard. Every subsequent schema that must contain an address can import that standard `Address` element. That's an example of an incomplete "part" that can only be useful as a component of another schema. You may also define an inclusive schema that depicts a standard enterprise entity such as a `Product`. Any ensuing project that requires processing on a `Product` would reference and reuse this pre-defined schema. Look for opportunities in your schemas to harvest enterprise entities and elements that may prove useful to those that follow you. When doing so, consider establishing and applying a project-neutral namespace that highlights those artifacts as multipurpose instead of project-specific.

Consider your experience when building BizTalk maps. In the development palette, you get access to 80+ **functoids** that provide a repeatable, consistent way to perform small fine-grained activities. When you encounter a situation where an out-of-the-box functoid won't suffice, BizTalk permits you to either build your own custom functoids, or, simply reference an external (reusable) component that holds the functionality you crave.

While the BizTalk **Scripting** functoid does allow you to embed isolated code directly into the map, the window for doing so is quite small and devoid of familiar code writing comforts such as Intellisense and debugging. This is a polite way of telling you that you should only embed simplistic code snippets in the map directly and leave complex or weighty logic to be written in externally maintained (and hopefully reusable) assemblies.

What about BizTalk pipelines and pipeline components? By nature, most pipeline components are built to serve a universal purpose well beyond the demands of a single consumer. Surely, you could choose to write an `archive` receive pipeline component that acted in a very specific way for a very specific message, but that would be bad form. Instead, a well-written archive component would accept any content and use configuration attributes to decide where to publish the archive log. When designing custom pipeline components, consider first writing all the code necessary to perform the desired function, and then scan your project for hard-coded references to aspects that are project-specific (such as Xpath statements, file path directives). Take those references and turn them into configuration properties that can be substituted by other applications at a later time.

WCF behaviors are now an asset to be reckoned with in a BizTalk environment. They serve a similar function to pipeline components in that they process the raw message as it travels in and out of the BizTalk bus. Reusable WCF behaviors can be written for message logging, caching, error handling, authorization, and more. What's more, WCF behaviors can be shared between BizTalk applications and standalone WCF services. This means that a well-written enterprise service behavior does not need to be duplicated just to be used in BizTalk Server.

> When should you use WCF behaviors versus BizTalk pipelines? They can both perform similar actions on the stream of data passing through BizTalk. However, BizTalk pipelines offer the advantage of knowing about the BizTalk **message type** and thus have clearly defined ways to deal with batching/de-batching and possess full control over creating or changing the full BizTalk message context including promoted properties. That said, the continued focus by Microsoft on WCF technology, and the ability to share WCF behaviors between BizTalk applications and standard WCF services means that where possible, you should strongly consider putting generic data processing logic into WCF behaviors instead of pipelines.

How about orchestration? On the surface, it might appear that orchestrations only serve distinct purposes and are lousy candidates for reuse. While it's true that many workflow processes are targeted to specific projects, there are clear ways to enjoy the benefits of reuse here. To begin with, consider the means by which a message enters the orchestration. It's very convenient to define a "specify later" orchestration port on the orchestration that is inevitably bound to a physical receive port. However, this type of port tightly couples itself to the receive port and thus reduces its potential for reuse. Wherever possible, look at the **Direct Binding** option and move your tight coupling to the MessageBox instead of a specific receive port. With direct binding, the orchestration simply subscribes directly on the MessageBox, so any publisher, whether a receive port or another orchestration, can flow messages into this orchestration.

We can also choose to perform orchestration decomposition and seek out reusable aspects of our orchestration that may serve other functions. For example, you may decide that every exception encountered across orchestrations should all be handled in the same fashion. Why build that same processing logic into each and every orchestration? Instead, you can define a single orchestration which accepts messages from any orchestration and logs the pertinent details to an exception log and optionally sends exception notifications to administrators. Our communal orchestration might accept *any* content and merely append the data blob to a common registry. Otherwise, the orchestration could accept a pre-defined OrchestrationException schema which all upstream orchestrations inflate prior to publishing their exception to the MessageBox. Seek out common processing logic and universal functionality that can be re-factored into a shared assembly and used across organizational projects.

Finally, let's talk about reuse in the BizTalk messaging layer. On the message receipt side, receive locations are quite multipurpose and compel no specific data format on the messages they absorb. If I define a FILE receive location, there is absolutely no reason that such a location couldn't be used to take in a broad mix of message types. However, let's be realistic and consider a case where a particular receive port is bound to a specific orchestration. This orchestration processes **adverse events** that have occurred with our medical products. The orchestration expects a very specific format which fortunately, the initial service consumer adheres to. Inevitably, the next consumer isn't so accommodating and can only publish a message shaped differently than what the orchestration expects. Do we need to start over with a new orchestration? Absolutely not. Instead, we can reuse the exact same receive port, and even offer to add a new receive location if the existing service endpoint is inaccessible to the new client. To support the incompatible data structure, a new map which converts the client format to the orchestration format can be added to the receive port. In this scenario, the orchestration was completely reusable, the receive port was reused, and optionally, the single receive location may have been reused.

On the message transmission side, BizTalk send ports also offer opportunities for reuse. First off, send port maps allow for a mismatched collection of messages to funnel through a single endpoint to a destination system. Let's say I have a solitary send port that updates a company's social events calendar through a service interface. Even though party notices come from varied upstream systems, we can flow all of them through this sole send port by continually affixing new maps to the send port. We don't need a new send port for each slightly different message containing the same underlying data, but rather, can aggressively reuse existing ports by simply reshaping the message into an acceptable structure. Secondly,

BizTalk allows us to define **dynamic ports**, which rely on upstream processes to dictate the adapter and endpoint address for the port. A single dynamic port might be used by countless consumers who rely on runtime business logic to determine where to transmit the data at hand. Instead of creating dozens of static send ports, which are solely used to relay information (i.e, no mapping), we can repeatedly reuse a single dynamic send port.

Identifying Standard Message Exchange Patterns

When we talk about **Message Exchange Patterns**, or MEPs, we're considering the direction and timing of data between the client and service. How do I get into the bus and what are the implications of those choices? Let's discuss the four primary options.

Request/Response services

This is probably the pattern that's most familiar to you. We're all comfortable making a function call to a component and waiting for a response. When a service uses this pattern, it's frequently performing a **remote procedure call** where the caller accesses functionality on the distant service and is blocked until either a timeout occurs or until the receiver sends a response that is expected by the caller.

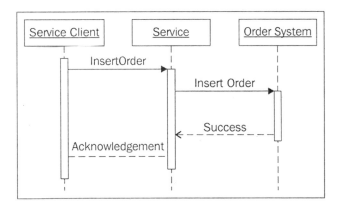

As we'll see below, while this pattern may set developers at ease, it may encourage bad behavior. Nevertheless, the cases where request/response services make the most sense are fine-grained functions and mashup services. If you need a list of active contracts that a hospital has with your company, then a request/response operation fits best. The client application should wait until that response is received before moving on to the next portion of the application. Or, let's say my web portal is calling an aggregate service, which takes contact data from five different systems and mashes them up into a single data entity that is then returned to the caller. This data is being requested for immediate presentation to an end user, and thus it's logical to solicit information from a service and wait to draw the screen until the completed result is loaded.

BizTalk Server 2009 has full support for both consuming and publishing services adhering to a request/response pattern. When exposing request/response operations through BizTalk orchestrations, the orchestration port's Communication Pattern is set to **Request-Response** and the **Port direction of communication** is equal to **I'll be receiving a request and sending a response**. Once this orchestration port is bound to a physical request/response receive port, BizTalk takes care of correlating the response message with the appropriate thread that made the request. This is significant because by default, BizTalk is a purely asynchronous messaging engine. Even when you configure BizTalk Server to behave in a request/response fashion, it's only putting a facade on the standard underlying plumbing. A synchronous BizTalk service interface actually sits on top of a sophisticated mechanism of correlating MessageBox communication to simulate a request/response pattern.

When consuming request/response services from BizTalk from an orchestration, the orchestration port's Communication Pattern is set to **Request-Response** and the **Port direction of communication** is equal to **I'll be sending a request and receiving a response**. The corresponding physical send port uses a solicit-response pattern and allows the user to set up both pipelines and maps for the inbound and outbound messages.

One concern with either publishing or consuming request/response services is the issue of blocking and timeouts. From a BizTalk perspective, this means that whenever you publish an orchestration as a request/response service, you should always verify that the logic residing between inbound and outbound transmissions will either complete or fail within a relatively brief amount of time. This dictates wrapping this logic inside an orchestration **Scope** shape with a preset timeout that is longer than the standard web service timeout interval.

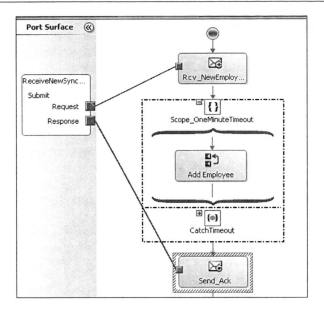

For consuming services, a request/response pattern forces the orchestration to block and wait for the response to be returned. If the service response isn't necessary for processing to continue, consider using a **Parallel** shape that isolates the service interaction pattern on a dedicated branch. This way, the execution of unrelated workflow steps can proceed even though the downstream service is yet to respond.

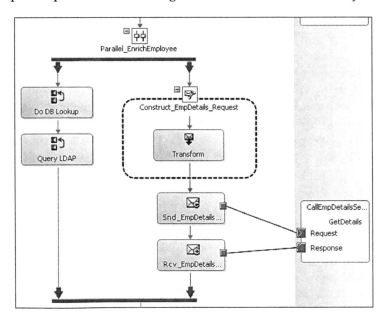

One-way services

This is your straightforward *fire and forget* pattern. The message is sent unidirectionally and asynchronously to a waiting receiver. If you grew up building components with fine-grained functional request/reply interfaces, this idea of throwing a message out of your application and not expecting anything back may seem a bit useless. However, this manner of service communication is a powerful way to build more event-driven applications and embrace non-blocking service invocation patterns. A one-way service interface may send a message to a single destination (a point-to-point solution), a defined list of recipients (multi-cast solution) or be a general broadcast (pub/sub solution). The key is, the caller remains unaware of the journey of the message once it is swallowed up by the service.

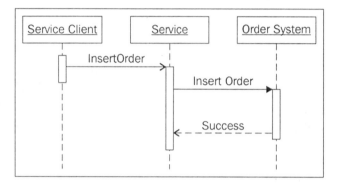

In scenarios where the sender and receiver may not both be online or active at the same time, a one-way service pattern offers a way to buffer this communication. For instance, I can build a service that offers an operation called `PublishCustomerChange` which takes a `Customer` entity possessing modified data attributes. The service itself may decide to queue up requests and only update the legacy Customer Management application during scheduled intervals throughout the day. However, the service may still receive requests all day, but because there is no expectation of a response to the submitter, the service can decide to prioritize the processing of the request until a more convenient time.

Pitfall

While the communication between endpoints may appear to be one-way, the default behavior of a WCF service returning *void* is to still provide a passive acknowledgement (or negative acknowledgement) that everything has run successfully. To prevent this completely and have a truly asynchronous service operation, set the `IsOneWay` property of an `OperationContract` attribute within the WCF service.

BizTalk Server 2009 is at its finest when working with one-way messaging patterns. Messages flow into the MessageBox and inherently cascade down to many places. When freed from the restraints of an expected service response, BizTalk Server can more powerfully chain together data and processes into far-reaching solutions. Consider a message sent to BizTalk via a one-way service interface. The loosely-coupled orchestrations and send ports can simply subscribe to this message's data, type, or attributes and act upon it. There is no concern for doing anything else but acting upon the data event. When a request/response receive port is designated as the service publisher, there can feasibly be only a single subscriber (and responder) to the request.

While all the BizTalk WCF adapters support one-way patterns, only the **WCF-NetMsmq** adapter requires it. MSMQ was designed for disconnected systems, and thus do not expect publishers to the queue to wait for any business data response.

Request/Callback services

There are cases where the caller of a service wants the benefits of non-blocking asynchronous service invocation, but also needs an actual data response from the service. In this case, a callback pattern can best fit your needs. In this situation, the caller acts as both a service consumer and a service provider. That is, the caller must be able to both send a message, and host an endpoint that the service can send a subsequent response to. You can consider this an asynchronous request/response pattern.

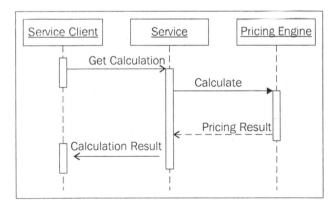

This can be a complicated pattern for service callers to accommodate. The caller has to design some intelligent strategies to correlate out-of-band responses with the original request made. During request/response invocations, the caller is blocked and doesn't proceed until the response has arrived. A sequence of processing is preserved. In a callback scenario, the client receives service responses well after the initial request. They have to make sure that:

- The response corresponds to a given request
- The response remains relevant to the application

Additionally, the client application should take into account the fact that a response may never actually arrive.

How does the service know where to send its response message back to? Typically the inbound request contains a pointer to the callback URI. The SOAP header is a good place to cram this sort of metadata instead of polluting the actual data message with context information.

WCF has some fairly rich support for callbacks through bindings such as the **NetTcpBinding** and **NetNamedPipeBinding**. While HTTP is inherently stateless and doesn't naturally support bidirectional communication, WCF provides a special HTTP binding named **WSDualHttpBinding**, which creates a matching pair of directional channels under the covers. A WCF developer can add callback *contracts* to a service contract and allow WCF clients to seamlessly call services and have an event raised when the service response is eventually received.

Sounds great, right? Unfortunately, the BizTalk WCF adapters do not openly support the **WSDualHttpBinding** or callback contracts in general. Instead, as we'll investigate in depth during Chapter 6, we need to get creative through the use of dynamic ports or polling strategies to implement a general purpose, cross platform callback patterns. That said, I will show you in Chapter 6 how you CAN effectively use the WSDualHttpBinding within a BizTalk receive location.

Publish/Subscribe services

This final MEP is actually an extension of the one-way MEP. Instead of a sender and receiver of a service, consider the parties to be a publisher and subscriber. In a publish/subscribe MEP, data objects are sent to an endpoint where a dynamic set of interested entities yank a copy of the data for their own purpose. There is a one-to-many relationship between the publisher and subscribers. The data is published to the service in an asynchronous fashion with no expectation of a direct response.

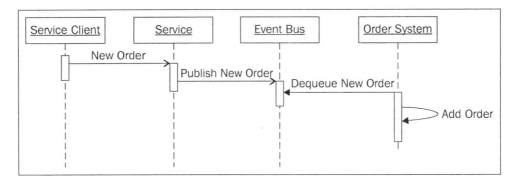

BizTalk excels at the publish/subscribe service pattern. BizTalk can optionally subscribe on three distinct pieces of information:

- **Message context**: Each message that arrives into BizTalk Server has a property bag called **context** attached to it. Regardless of whether the data is in a structured data format (such as XML) or a binary blob (such as a PDF file), any object reaching the BizTalk MessageBox has context attached. Message subscribers can decide to register interest in topics associated with the message metadata found in context. For instance, a subscriber might choose to listen for all messages that arrived at a specific file location. Hence, their send port subscription would equal `BTS.ReceivedFileName`.

- **Message Type**: A message with a structured data format can be typed by the BizTalk endpoint prior to publication to the bus. The **type** value is typically equal to the namespace of the XML message plus the name of the root node. BizTalk subscribers can choose to pull any message that matches the data type they are interested in.

- **Message Content**. Developers can single out fields in a message schema for **promotion** which means that they are available for routing decisions within the BizTalk bus. When a message arrives into BizTalk, and a matching schema is found, the data elements designated for promotion have their values yanked out of the payload and put into context. Downstream subscribers can now specify data-level subscription topics. Hence, instead of pulling all new employees from the bus (based on a message type subscription), we could extract only those where `EmployeeCountry == Germany` using a content based subscription.

Pitfall

While BizTalk Server offers a variety of subscription topic mechanisms (context, type, or content), you are limited by the subscription operators available. For instance, you cannot create a subscription where "Organization CONTAINS Hospital". That is, you do not have options for wildcard searches or dynamic subscriptions in a send port. To achieve such a capability, you'd have to rely on orchestrations or custom pipeline components.

This manner of service invocation shifts the idea of a service from being just a functional component in a fancy SOAP wrapper to being an on-ramp to a distributed computing bus, where the publisher relinquishes knowledge and control of the data's processing path.

Types of services

There are multiple ways to look at types of services, and I've chosen to consider the types of services based on the category of message they accept.

RPC services

A **Remote Procedure Call (RPC)** is a means of executing a function on a distant object. These remote invocations are meant to appear as if they were happening locally and typically following the request/response communication pattern. If you've written DCOM or CORBA components before, then this is a familiar concept. As SOAP gained traction, this was initially seen as just another way to execute remote functions but in a more interoperable way. However, this encourages a very point-to-point mentality.

RPC-style services follow the "Gang of Four" *Command pattern* where objects (in our case, messages) correspond to the action you wish to perform. In essence, you are sending a message that tells the remote service what to do. For example, the payload of an RPC-style service request meant to create a new customer entity would look like this:

```
<soap:Envelope xmlns:soap="http://schemas.xmlsoap.org/soap/envelope/">
  <soap:Body>
    <InsertNewCustomer xmlns="http://Seroter.BizTalkSOA.RPCExample">
      <ID>010022</ID>
      <Name>Amy Clark</Name>
      <FacilityID>LHS2001</FacilityID>
    </InsertNewCustomer>
  </soap:Body>
</soap:Envelope>
```

While this type of command message may be acceptable for service requests that return a specific response (`GetCustomerDetails` or `VerifyAddress`), it is not a good practice for messaging solutions. Why? Architecturally, this is fairly tight coupling where the client confidently knows exactly what the service is supposed to do with their request and by the nature of the request, is demanding such behavior (`DeleteCustomer`). That's fairly presumptive, no? If the client truly had the ability to do this action themselves, they wouldn't need the service at all! In truth, the caller is only capable of making polite requests to the service where it remains the prerogative of the service to handle that request as it sees fit. For example, a demand to `AddNewCustomer` may not be a simple, synchronous event. The service may require human validation of the customer entry, or even decide that it doesn't want to add this new customer for reasons such as content duplication, failure of business rules, or simply irrelevance to the system.

Where does RPC play in BizTalk Server solutions? The classic ASMX service generator had a choice of producing **bare** or **wrapped** services that dictated whether the service operation followed an RPC style or not. The default style, **wrapped**, would enclose the message payload with the name of the service operations.

The **BizTalk WCF Service Publishing Wizard** offers no choice of messaging style. In fact, any WCF service generated either from schemas or orchestrations will follow the document-style outlined below. The name of the service operation is not part of the SOAP payload. If you wish to promote an RPC style service and aren't satisfied with the metadata generated by the BizTalk, you have the option to author your own RPC-oriented WSDL and provide that as the primary facade definition. Either way, the adapter is quite forgiving with each format, as it can either strip out nodes from parent elements, or conversely, add a wrapper to an inbound data object.

Document services

A document-style service is one in which the payload represents an encapsulated data structure devoid of any sort of instruction of what to do with it. As you can imagine, this type of service operation is much more coarse-grained and accepts plumper messages that are more self-describing. The service has all it needs to perform its action and doesn't rely on a stateful series of actions that provide context to the operation. If we re-factored our above RPC-style payload to be more document-centric, it might look like this:

```
<soap:Envelope xmlns:soap="http://schemas.xmlsoap.org/soap/envelope/">
  <soap:Body>
    <NewCustomer xmlns="http://Seroter.BiztalkSOA.RPCExample">
      <ID>010022</ID>
      <Name>Amy Clark</Name>
      <FacilityID>LHS2001</FacilityID>
```

```
        </NewCustomer>
    </soap:Body>
  </soap:Envelope>
```

Notice that instead of having a functional directive as the focus of the message payload, we are highlighting the data entity that is travelling across the wire. Either the single recipient or the broad list of subscribers can decide how they handle a `NewCustomer` and what they do with the data to fit their needs.

While this type of service can be used for request/response operations, they typically make lots of sense for scenarios where one application simply needs to exchange data with another application. These services can follow a one-way MEP when data is only being shared in a point-to-point manner, or could also be a one-way MEP with a publish/subscribe flavor where any interested party could have at the data.

Does BizTalk Server support this document-centric service type? It certainly does. As mentioned above, all BizTalk-generated WCF service endpoints define a document-centric contract. We'll chat about this more in the next chapter as we analyze the best ways to construct a schema for service exposure. Specifically, we'll talk about how we should both identify and shape our schemas to avoid functional presumption and encourage reusable data entities.

Event services

Finally, let's consider the step-brother of the document-style service: the event service. For event services, when something of note occurs, the service is invoked and a message explaining the event is distributed. Unlike the document message, the event message typically contains a limited amount of information. You're basically telling the service that something important happened, but not sharing too much data or instructing it as to what to do next.

In these scenarios, it's quite possible that the service recipient will have to call back to the source system to actually get the relevant data set. Consider the `NewEmployee` event notification. When a new employee is added to the HR system, our service is called and the `NewEmployeeEvent` message is transmitted. Let's say that BizTalk fans this message out to all downstream systems that care about employee data. Our French office's security badge application has a service exposed which accepts the `NewEmployeeEvent` message and then peeks to see which country the new employee is associated with. If that country is France, then their service calls back to the source HR system to retrieve the full employee profile. What exactly is in this truncated event message if not the full document? Stay tuned for when we dissect the event message and consider how best to use it.

In the BizTalk sense, this sort of service is a very nice use of the event-driven message bus and is a great fit for one-way or pub/sub MEPs. Assuming that BizTalk accepts these event messages via its inbound service adapters, what are the possible outcomes? Three options are:

- Fan the message out to downstream services that have their own event-handling logic.
- Spawn a new orchestration workflow that performs event processing logic.
- Generate additional event messages within the bus based on content in the original message.

While event messages are typically asynchronous in nature, the life cycle of event processing can actually exploit all three service types identified in this chapter. In the sequence diagram below, I show how an initial event message (Order Event) may give way to a command request (GetOrderDetails) and a document-style response (OrderDetails).

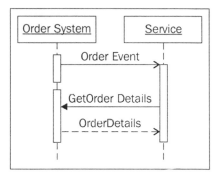

The thought of using BizTalk Server for this sort of event-style routing may be counter to classic impressions of BizTalk as a simple point-to-point broker. We've moved beyond that antiquated concept and should consider BizTalk a serious option when architecting robust service-oriented event processing systems.

Summary

We covered a lot of ground in this chapter in our quest to discover the key principles underpinning service-oriented design and evaluating how to champion these concepts within BizTalk Server 2009. Proper planning of a service oriented solution goes a long way towards ongoing agility and future return on investment that is critical to defining the success of a SOA.

BizTalk is an ideal tool for building loosely-coupled, interoperable solutions that maximize reusable components. The mix of platform-neutral technology adapters and a foundational message bus based on a publication/subscribe pattern results in BizTalk being uniquely positioned to do much more than facilitate point-to-point application interfaces. While BizTalk supports RPC messages over a request/response channel, we've also seen the benefits we can secure by rotating our thinking and embracing asynchronous messaging based on more loosely-coupled document or event messages.

In the following chapters, we will build on the concepts that we've touched upon here. In the next chapter, we'll look specifically at ways to implement many of the contract and endpoint concepts introduced so far.

5
Schema and Endpoint Patterns

Simply pushing harder within the old boundaries will not do.
-Karl Weick

How you go about designing your service interface will go a long way towards the long term success and stability of your overall service. As we saw in the last chapter, a well-built service should only reveal its location, available operations, and the messages it exchanges with clients. The service's internal plumbing should remain safely tucked away from those who intend to consume the interface. We will spend the majority of this chapter looking at how to practically implement a series of key schema and endpoint patterns.

In this chapter you will learn:

- Good practices for building schemas that coincide with the service type you've chosen
- When and how to build canonical schemas
- The benefits and limits of schema reuse
- How data types and node characteristics translate into client code
- The ways to use generic schemas in your solutions
- Strategies for building contract-first endpoints

Service-oriented schema patterns

Schemas are a critical component of the service contract. They not only announce the data model that a service recognizes, but more conceptually, they allow our service to adhere to the principles laid out in the previous chapter. Abstraction is a key aspect of an SOA, and a well-built schema provides a sufficient level of opaqueness to the underlying service processing. Interoperability, another vital piece of a far-reaching service, should be taken into consideration at the earliest phases of schema design. Finally, the concept of reusability is readily embraced in schema design, and we will see numerous examples in this chapter.

Let's now look at a series of ways as to we can take these service-oriented principles and apply them to schemas designed in BizTalk Server 2009. Throughout this chapter, I will use examples that revolve around receiving details about a subject's activities in an ongoing clinical drug trial. This includes actions such as enrolling into a trial, participating in a screening, and withdrawing from the trial.

Designing schemas based on service type

In the last chapter we defined three different service types:

- RPC Services: Messages correspond to actions we wish to perform.
- Document Services: The data entity is transmitted, absent instruction of what to do with it.
- Event Services: Messages represent explanations of events that have occurred.

The **BizTalk WCF Service Publishing Wizard**, unlike the classic **BizTalk Web Services Publishing Wizard**, does not offer the option of **Bare** (document-style services) or **Wrapped** (RPC-style services). All BizTalk-generated WCF endpoints exhibit a document-centric pattern. Therefore, if you wanted to accept an RPC-style WCF message into of BizTalk Server, you'd have to explicitly build your request schema in that RPC fashion.

So how would you build this sort of schema for a "new enrollment" in our drug trial? We start out with a command root node name, and include the parameters we need to insert this record into our clinical trial system.

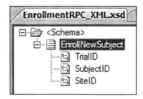

Notice by transmitting this sort of message, the caller gets the impression of invoking a function called `EnrollNewSubject` on my remote system.

What would a more document-centric design of this schema look like? In this case, we'd want to share the entire `enrollment` entity with the service. That is, provide a fully encapsulated form of the data object that relies on no existing context about this interaction.

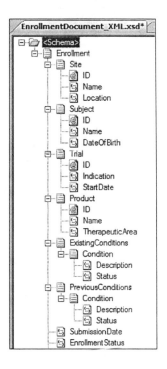

In this schema, the root is the type of document being exchanged and no indication is given as to what the service has to do with it. Meanwhile, it contains a full spectrum of information about this particular enrollment and should not require additional enrichment prior to acting upon it.

How do event-style message differ? In this case, the message is a reflection of something of interest that has occurred. In the previous chapter, I mentioned that in some cases event messages trigger callbacks to the source system for more information. However, do not consider that scenario an excuse to distribute tiny, nondescript event messages that contain nothing but foreign key pointers.

If you choose to only send data pointers in an event message, you are saying that either (a) the user doesn't need the actual data in order to make decisions, or (b) the downstream consumer is guaranteed to have access to the source system for data enrichment. I consider a correctly-sized event message to be one that contains enough information to be actionable.

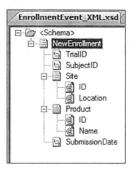

This schema is for the **New Enrollment** event published by the business partner that manages the clinical trial process. While it's certainly possible to include the "document" in an event message, in my case above, I've chosen to include only a few pieces of data that are most critical to event subscribers. Interest in enrollments will be limited to the location of the clinical site, which product is being administered, and which trial this is part of. If the receiver of the event requires any more enrollment information than this, then I'll ask them to seek it out in their own regional systems.

Critical point:

In reality, these schema structure distinctions are purely architectural ideals. We're really talking about how a message looks as it is exchanged between endpoints. The name of a root node, or how exactly the schema is structured doesn't directly relate to what the service is capable of doing. However, the forethought that goes into deciding on a more event-driven approach versus a RPC approach does impact how you build the service and infrastructure that uses the service message.

When building any schema in a distributed architecture, the tricky concept of **idempotence** must be addressed. Wikipedia defines *idempotence* as:

> *In computer science, the term idempotent is used to describe methods or subroutine calls that can safely be called multiple times, as invoking the procedure a single time or multiple times results in the system maintaining the same state.*

Source: http://en.wikipedia.org/wiki/Idempotence

Simply put, because it's never a good idea to rely on the infrastructure between distributed systems, the messages should support repeated delivery without consequence. For instance, a typical request/response query (such as getting the address of a customer) is idempotent. It doesn't matter if I initiate this request fifteen times in a row, the state of the customer's address remains static. However, if I execute a `withdrawal` command repeatedly, then I better expect my bank account to continually decrease.

So how do we account for this? The *Enterprise Integration Patterns* book from Hohpe and Woolf calls out two ways:

- Built in "de-duplication" process where duplicates are detected and ignored
- Define messages themselves to be idempotent

A non-idempotent RPC message may demand that my salary was increased by five thousand dollars. While I might appreciate that message "accidentally" traveling through our payroll system five or six times, my employer would not. An idempotent version of that message would instead declare what the current salary number should be (such as fifty thousand dollars) so that the repeated transmission would result in the same value being present in the target system. However, this isn't foolproof as it does not take into account the changes being made to that same entity by other systems.

RPC and document-style services can be quite prone to this problem. What if you have repeated changes to an "enrollment" document published and the message bus processes them out of order so that the latest one is overwritten by the earlier one? You can try and exploit timestamps and the like, but this remains a tricky issue.

One way to avoid this is to rely on event messages with required lookups by the subscriber. Deviating from our clinical trial scenario for a moment, let's consider the life cycle of employee changes in an HR system. A given employee record could get updated at a few distinct intervals in the day, and the opportunity exists for messages to slip out of sequence. However, if you have an event-style message that tells subscribers that the employee's data has changed (and nothing else), then the subscriber simply goes and pulls the latest employee profile from the source system themselves. It doesn't matter if I send that event message sixty times in a row; I'm not actually distributing any state data that is dependent on arrival order. The downside to this strategy is an increase in network traffic, and an assurance that all subscribers can indeed access the source system.

Canonical schemas

Once again, let's quote Wikipedia on *canonical models*:

> *In enterprise application integration, the "canonical data model" is a design pattern used to communicate between different data formats.*

Source: `http://en.wikipedia.org/wiki/Canonical`

Without designing a canonical, or intermediary, data format you can end up with a mess of point-to-point translations that leads to a brittle application.

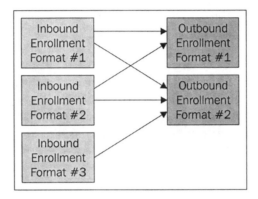

By injecting a common schema, you can reduce coupling between the source formats and destination formats. At any one time, a message only needs to be translated to or from the canonical format.

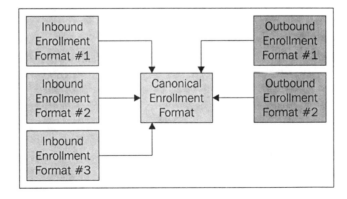

So where do we implement this in BizTalk solutions? I specifically recommend this approach when interacting with auto-generated schemas. The WCF LOB adapters available in BizTalk Server 2009 will automatically generate schemas that comply with the selected system interface. Naturally, this schema exhibits extremely tight coupling to the destination platform. If we use these schemas in our orchestrations, or worse, in exposed services, we've instantly made either incremental or far-reaching change a more complicated endeavor. We've also failed miserably at the SOA goal of abstraction.

That said, in some cases you clearly need to interact with LOB schemas from within an orchestration. Consider the scenario where some of the LOB schema fields are populated through enrichment via other messages. Clearly I need the more stateful orchestration environment to host more complex message creation.

Let's demonstrate an additional example. The LOB adapters expose fairly **CRUD (create-read-update-delete)** types of operations on databases such as SQL Server 2008. As we've discussed in the book so far, a service is a more business-oriented module that should extend higher than simply slapping a SOAP interface on low-level APIs. The "Enrollment" document-style schema I created earlier may actually be a canonical schema that sits in between a variety of input formats and destination systems. Let's say my database that stores enrollment information has the following structure:

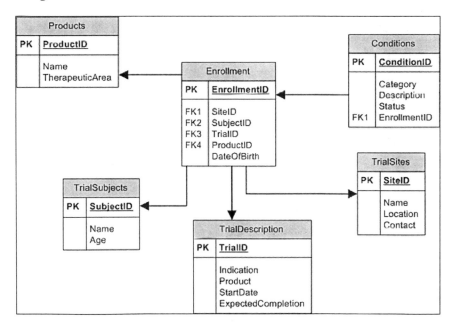

If I solicit schemas from the SQL Server WCF adapter for these tables, I'll end up with a series of message types. It would be a fairly poor decision to expose each schema as a distinct service operation. Instead, I have an intermediate enrollment schema that abstracts the more complex set of individual services needed to insert a new subject enrollment.

A well thought-out canonical schema doesn't simply have copies of the same nodes and structures from all the schemas that rely on it. While clearly the canonical format needs to capture the right data to serve its purpose, put consideration into how the logical composite entity should look and take a more business-centric view of the data. Specifically, remove redundant fields, reorganize elements into a natural hierarchy, reconsider data types, and evaluate occurrence and restriction boundaries.

Pitfall

Be careful about going overboard on canonical schemas and introducing accidental complexity. For messaging-only solutions, you may be fine with the schema formats demanded by the source and destination systems. When your scenario involves the injection of processing logic (for example rules or orchestration), then it becomes more attractive to decouple components through the use of canonical schemas.

Building and applying reusable schema components

Schemas in BizTalk Server 2009 can be built to support reusability in a variety of ways. Let's look at four of them.

If I want to put the content of one schema into the definition of another, I can either **import** or **include** it. When the target namespace between the schemas differs, then the **import** option must be used. For example, let's say that we design a schema which represents a subject (or patient) that is planning to enroll in a drug trial.

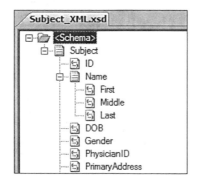

Next, we have a basic **Enrollment** schema that looks like this:

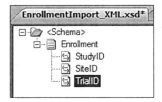

If we click the uppermost node named **<Schema>** in the `Enrollment` schema, we get
a set of global settings available in the Visual Studio.NET **Properties** window. Select
the ellipse next to the **Imports** property to launch the schema selection pane. Clicking
the **Add** button will allow us to pick which schema in our project (or referenced
projects) we wish to import. After selecting the **Subject** schema, and before clicking
Ok on the pop up, we can see the namespace prefix and action that we're about
to perform.

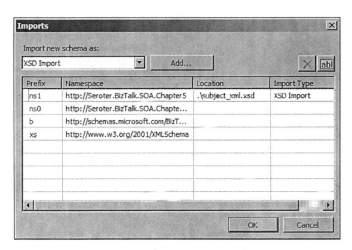

Once the import is complete, our schema tree view should look no different.
However, if we glance at the XSD schema view pane, we can see a new
`<xsd:import>` command injected at the top of the schema.

```
<?xml version="1.0" encoding="utf-16" ?>
- <xs:schema xmlns:ns0="http://Seroter.BizTalk.SOA.Chapter5/Import"
    xmlns:b="http://schemas.microsoft.com/BizTalk/2003"
    xmlns:ns1="http://Seroter.BizTalk.SOA.Chapter5"
    targetNamespace="http://Seroter.BizTalk.SOA.Chapter5/Import"
    xmlns:xs="http://www.w3.org/2001/XMLSchema">
    <xs:import schemaLocation=".\subject_xml.xsd"
      namespace="http://Seroter.BizTalk.SOA.Chapter5" />
```

How do we exploit this imported schema? Let's create a new record in the `Enrollment` schema. The **Properties** window for that node includes an attribute called **Data Structure Type**. Notice that we now have a **ns1:Subject** available as a data type.

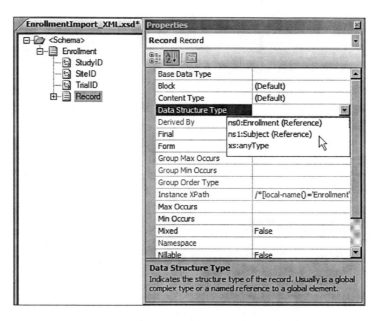

Choosing the `Subject` data type causes the previously created `Record` to be replaced with the full `Subject` schema structure from our other schema.

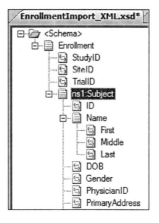

Note that any changes made to the imported schema are automatically reflected in the master schema.

If the schema you wish to reuse is in the same namespace as the master schema, then you have to perform a schema `include`. Including one schema in another is fairly similar to the import procedure. Before this exercise, I updated the schemas so that the **Enrollment** and **Subject** schemas reside in the same namespace. We once again highlight the **<Schema>** node in the **Enrollment** schema and choose **Imports** from the **Properties** window. Be sure to change the value in the drop-down list from the default value, **XSD Imports**, to **XSD Includes**. Notice that after picking the `Subject` schema again the **Namespace** and **Schema** values match the default namespace of the master schema.

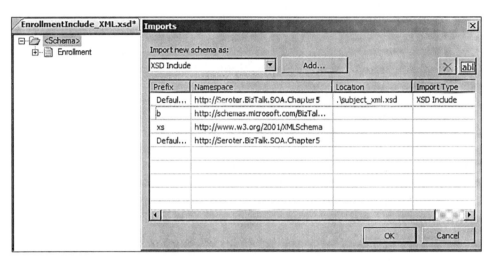

The source of the **Enrollment** XSD file now includes an XML `<xsd:include>` statement pointing to the included schema. That's not the only difference from the Import operation. Notice that the schema tree now has a ghosted `Subject` node at the top of it. We can now create a new record under the **Enrollment** node and point the **Data Structure Type** to **Subject**.

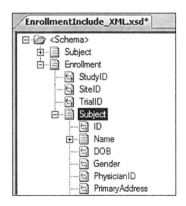

When working with included schemas, you may experience some unexpected behavior when generating XML instances for the schema. As the schema above stands, if I choose to **Generate Instance**, the Subject node will be the one generated as the root node, not the expected Enrollment element. The way to get around this is to click the uppermost **<Schema>** node, choose the **Root Reference** property, and explicitly define **Enrollment** as the root of the schema.

In the off chance that you wish to use another schema, and make a variation to it, then this is where the redefine option comes in. In this scenario, you reference a schema (in the same namespace) and you have the option of making modifications to it. You need to be cautious with redefinitions as you break your connection to the original schema.

The final type of schema reuse comes into play when designing global types that can be employed by other schemas. So far we've seen reuse of entire schemas, but what if we have a set of standard types that by themselves are not standalone messages, but instead are snippets of data structures? For instance, let's take an address as an example. A typical address structure exists in all sorts of schema types and is probably duplicated over and over again. We could define a global address type and use that in all our relevant schemas.

We can do this by first creating a new schema and defining a record that outlines the **Address** structure.

Next, we click the record name, select the **Data Structure Type** property, and manually type in a value such as **AddressType**. The Schema Editor now reflects the construction of a new global type.

```xml
<?xml version="1.0" encoding="utf-16" ?>
- <xs:schema xmlns:b="http://schemas.microsoft.com/BizTalk/2003"
    xmlns="http://Seroter.BizTalk.SOA.Chapter5/GlobalTypes"
    targetNamespace="http://Seroter.BizTalk.SOA.Chapter5/GlobalTypes"
    xmlns:xs="http://www.w3.org/2001/XMLSchema">
  - <xs:complexType name="AddressType">
    - <xs:sequence>
        <xs:element name="Type" type="xs:ID" />
        <xs:element name="Street" type="xs:string" />
        <xs:element name="City" type="xs:string" />
        <xs:element name="State" type="xs:string" />
        <xs:element name="PostalCode" type="xs:string" />
        <xs:element name="Country" type="xs:string" />
      </xs:sequence>
    </xs:complexType>
    <xs:element name="Address" type="AddressType" />
</xs:schema>
```

The next thing to do is actually delete the Address node. Why is that? Because we don't actually need or want the element of the AddressType in this schema. All we actually want is the type declaration, which survives after the record is deleted. Our schema now shows no nodes in the tree, but we can see within the XSD that a global type exists.

```
AddressType_XML.xsd

<Schema>

<?xml version="1.0" encoding="utf-16" ?>
- <xs:schema xmlns:b="http://schemas.microsoft.com/BizTalk/2003"
    xmlns="http://Seroter.BizTalk.SOA.Chapter5/GlobalTypes"
    targetNamespace="http://Seroter.BizTalk.SOA.Chapter5/GlobalTypes"
    xmlns:xs="http://www.w3.org/2001/XMLSchema">
  - <xs:complexType name="AddressType">
    - <xs:sequence>
        <xs:element name="Type" type="xs:ID" />
        <xs:element name="Street" type="xs:string" />
        <xs:element name="City" type="xs:string" />
        <xs:element name="State" type="xs:string" />
        <xs:element name="PostalCode" type="xs:string" />
        <xs:element name="Country" type="xs:string" />
      </xs:sequence>
    </xs:complexType>
</xs:schema>
```

If we import this schema in our **Subject** schema (which we have to do because they are in different namespaces), and create a new record called **Addresses**, we can now choose **AddressType** as the **Data Structure Type** for this record.

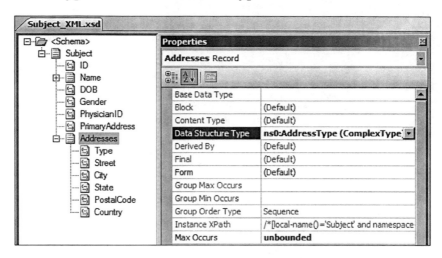

As you would hope, the relationship between the **Subject** and **Address** is retained even when the **Subject** is imported into the **Enrollment** schema. We've daisy chained three schemas in a very reusable way.

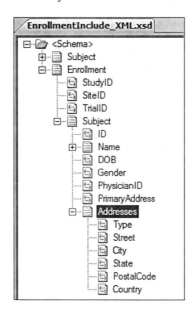

Finally, what's the impact of using `imports/includes/redefines` in your BizTalk-generated WCF endpoints? All three are supported by the **BizTalk WCF Service Publishing Wizard**. However, service consumers may experience issues when a schema possesses a `redefine` command, so use that with caution. Even with multiple nesting of included schemas, the WCF svcutil.exe had no problem interpreting the contract. However, this is an area where interoperability can be a problem. As a best practice, try to limit excessive schema reuse if you cannot be sure of the types of clients consuming your service.

Node data type conversion for service clients

You may have noticed that the **Schema Editor** provided by BizTalk Server 2009 delivers a comprehensive list of data types for schema nodes. In this table, I call out each schema type, what it is, and what .NET type it converts to when consumed by the WCF `svcutil.exe` proxy generation tool.

BizTalk XSD Type	Description	.NET Type
anyURI	Can be any absolute or relative Uniform Resource Identifier Reference	System.String
base64Binary	Holds Base64-encoded arbitrary binary data (e.g. PDF, JPEG)	System.Byte[]
boolean	Supports the mathematical concept of binary value logic (0/1 or true/false)	System.Boolean
byte	Holds an 8-bit value	System.SByte
date	Object with year, month, and day properties	System.DateTime
dateTime	Object with year, month, day, hour, minute, second, and timezone properties	System.DateTime
decimal	Contains a subset of real numbers with support for at a minimum of 18 decimal digits	System.Decimal
double	A double precision 64-bit floating point type	System.Double
duration	Represents a duration of time consisting of year, month, day, hour, minute and second	System.String
ENTITIES	Separated list of ENTITY references	System.String
ENTITY	Unparsed entity that may include non-XML content	System.String
float	A single precision 32-bit floating point type	System.Single

BizTalk XSD Type	Description	.NET Type
gDay	Equal to a day recurring each month	System.String
gMonth	Equal to a month recurring each year	System.String
gMonthDay	A calendar date (month + day) recurring each year	System.String
gYear	A period of a single year	System.String
gYearMonth	A particular calendar month in a specific year	System.String
hexBinary	Represents arbitrary hex-encoded binary data	System.Byte[]
ID	Definition of document-global unique identifiers	System.String
IDREF	A reference to a unique identifier (ID)	System.String
IDREFS	Separated list of IDREF references	System.String
int	A 32-bit signed integer	System.Int32
integer	A signed integer of arbitrary length	System.String
language	Set of language codes called out in RFC 3066 (e.g. en-US)	System.String
long	64-bit signed integer	System.Int64
Name	XML string with no whitespace	System.String
NCName	Name that conforms to namespace standard (e.g. no colons)	System.String
negativeInteger	Encompasses all strictly negative integers	System.String
NMTOKEN	Set of XML "name tokens" excluding spaces or commas	System.String
NMTOKENS	Separated list of NMTOKENS	System.String
nonNegativeInteger	Encompasses all positive integers (including zero)	System.String
nonPositiveInteger	Encompasses all negative integers (including 0)	System.String
normalizedString	Contains whitespace-replaced strings (meaning all carriage returns, tabs, etc have been replaced)	System.String
positiveInteger	Encompasses all strictly positive integers	System.String
QName	Qualified name as a combination of namespace name and part name	XmlQualifiedName
short	Set of 16-bit integers	System.Int16

BizTalk XSD Type	Description	.NET Type
string	String of any set of XML allowable characters, including whitespace	System.String
time	Instant of time recurring each day	System.DateTime
token	Set of strings with whitespace replacement of leading/trailing spaces, carriage return, line feed, tab, and any instance of two or more spaces.	System.String
unsignedByte	8-bit unsigned value	System.Byte
unsignedInt	32-bit unsigned integer	System.UInt32
unsignedLong	64-bit unsigned integer	System.UInt64
unsignedShort	16-bit unsigned integer	System.UInt16

It's interesting to see how some types are handled. For maximum interoperability, stick with very common types like `string` and `int`. As you move into floating point numbers, consider using the decimal type instead of the `float` type so that you can get the maximum precision on your numbers and not fall prey to rounding errors.

One interesting data type to note, that I don't come across very often, is the `ID/IDREF`. `ID/IDREF` is a concept left over from DTD where you can define relationships between XML nodes. The ID value acts as a primary key (and must be unique in the message) while the `IDREF` field points to the ID field.

In a schema, I have sections of dependent elements that are not structured in a way to enforce the relationship. For instance, recall that one version of my **Enrollment** schema has a repeating list of addresses in order to account for `home`, `work`, and `alternate` addresses. I may have a new element in this schema named `PrimaryAddress` that references which of the included addresses we should treat as the default one. Using basic XML data types, there is no way to enforce that the `PrimaryAddress` node can only contain a value that corresponds to the repeating list of addresses. However, if I update my schema to apply ID/IDREF data types to the corresponding address nodes and then validate the below XML snippet in the BizTalk Schema Editor, I get the exception **Reference to undeclared ID is 'Alternate'**.

```
<ns0:Subject xmlns:ns0="http://Seroter.BizTalk.SOA.Chapter5/Import">
  <ID>ID_0</ID>
  <Name>
    <First>First_0</First>
    <Middle>Middle_0</Middle>
    <Last>Last_0</Last>
  </Name>
  <DOB>DOB_0</DOB>
  <Gender>Gender_0</Gender>
  <PhysicianID>PhysicianID_0</PhysicianID>
```

```
  <PrimaryAddress>Alternate</PrimaryAddress>
  <Addresses>
    <Type>Home</Type>
    <Street>Street_0</Street>
    <City>City_0</City>
    <State>State_0</State>
    <PostalCode>PostalCode_0</PostalCode>
    <Country>Country_0</Country>
  </Addresses>
  <Addresses>
    <Type>Work</Type>
    <Street>Street_0</Street>
    <City>City_0</City>
    <State>State_0</State>
    <PostalCode>PostalCode_0</PostalCode>
    <Country>Country_0</Country>
  </Addresses>
</ns0:Subject>
```

Hence, while it remains difficult-to-impossible to build strong relationship semantics into a schema, consider ID/IDREF if you need to enforce basic referential integrity in your service schema.

Node feature mapping for service clients

When applying robust boundary and logic conditions to your service schema, it is critical to understand how those rules are translated from the WSDL to your client code.

Note that the **BizTalk WCF Service Publishing Wizard** is infinitely better than the classic **BizTalk Web Services Publishing Wizard** when it comes to respecting the initial schema. Whereas the WCF wizard keeps all schema properties intact after metadata publication, the ASMX wizard removes occurrence limits, default values, and complex type groupings.

Element grouping

Let's first look at complex type grouping. When you erect a standard XSD schema, by default, the schema expects all the XML nodes to be in the sequential order set forth by the schema. However, you have options to be more flexible than that. The question is though, how well do WCF clients support a schema structure possessing such flexibility? We can evaluate this by first setting up a **Screen Result** schema, which outlines the results of a physician screening of a drug trial subject. The original structure looks like this:

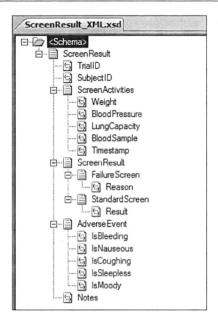

The **ScreenActivites** record contains elements explaining a sequence of steps that must be reported in a specific order. I can ensure this is the case by clicking the **ScreenActivities** record, and setting the **Context Type** property equal to **Complex Content**. As soon as that value is set, a **Sequence** group is added to the **ScreenActivites** node.

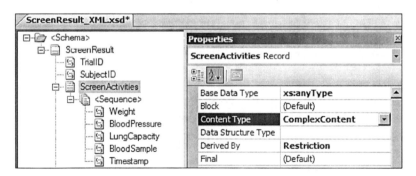

The second record of note, **ScreenResult**, will contain either a "success" or "failure" node based on the physician's evaluation of the screening visit. We want our schema to expect only one of these two possible values. Once again, we can set the **Context Type** to **Complex Content** on this record, but this time, after the **Sequence** group shows up we should select it and flip the **Order Type** to **Choice**. This means that the schema expects one of the two records to be there.

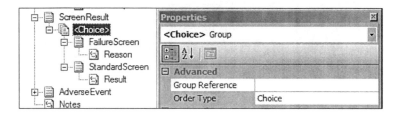

Finally, we have the **AdverseEvent** record, which holds a list of Boolean values about possible side effects we are keeping an eye out for. In this case, we can use an alternate way to dictate the record behavior. After selecting the record, and setting the **Group Order Type** to **All**, I've told the schema that all these nodes need to be here, but, they can exist in any order. One of the only real differences here is that there is no visual indication of the record's grouping behavior. I'll point out another difference in just a moment.

At this point, we want to expose this schema as a WCF service so that we can investigate how these grouping principles are (or aren't) applied in the WCF client that consumes it. I created a very simple, one-way WCF service (and metadata endpoint) using the **Expose schemas as web service** option of the **BizTalk WCF Service Publishing Wizard**. After starting the generated receive location (so that the service is enabled and browsable) I pointed my client application at the WSDL of the service.

Investigating the generated .NET types reveals something curious. The object representing the ScreenActivities node is defined like this:

```
public partial class ScreenResultScreenActivities {
        private string[] textField;
        /// <remarks/>
        [System.Xml.Serialization.XmlTextAttribute()]
        public string[] Text {
            get {
                return this.textField;
            }
        }
}
```

It does not contain all the sub types (`Weight`, `BloodPressure`) that were child nodes in the schema. This is because the **ScreenActivities** node had its **Sequence** characteristic set by changing its **Content Type** property. When we did this, the **Base Data Type** was automatically set to **xs:anyType**. Hence, the subsequent .NET class does not know about the actual contents of the **ScreenActivities** node. We can correct this by going back to our schema and removing the **xs:anyType** as the **Base Data Type**, and regenerating our WCF service endpoint.

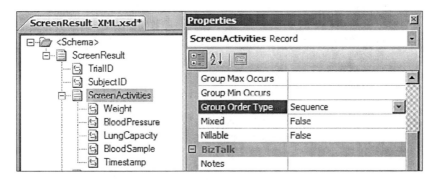

 When setting the complex type grouping behavior, just set the **Group Order Type** property instead of changing the **Content Type** property. This will prevent serialization problems down the line.

How does the generated .NET type class respect the schema grouping that we defined? Notice in the code snippet below that for the sequence node `ScreenActivities`, the corresponding class properties have order attributes in their serialization instruction.

```
[XmlElementAttribute(Form=XmlSchemaForm.Unqualified, Order=0)]
  public string Weight {
    get {
    return this.weightField;
  }
}
[XmlElementAttribute(Form=XmlSchemaForm.Unqualified, Order=1)]
  public string BloodPressure {
    get {
    return this.bloodPressureField;
  }
}
```

What about the **ScreenResult** element that is has a `choice` grouping? In this case the **ScreenResult** .NET object has an Item property that will hold either the `FailureScreen` or **StandardScreen** objects.

```
[XmlElementAttribute("FailureScreen", typeof(FailureScreen)]
[XmlElementAttribute("StandardScreen", typeof(StandardScreen)]
  public object Item {
    get {
    return this.itemField;
    }
    set {
    this.itemField = value;
    }
  }
}
```

Finally, how is the concept of `all` XSD grouping handled by .NET client code? As you might expect, the code looks much like the `sequence` code, minus the mandatory node ordering attribute.

```
[XmlElementAttribute(Form= XmlSchemaForm.Unqualified)]
public bool IsBleeding {
  get {
        return this.isBleedingField;
      }
  set {
        this.isBleedingField = value;
      }
}

[XmlElementAttribute(Form= XmlSchemaForm.Unqualified)]
public bool IsNauseous {
    get {
        return this.isNauseousField;
      }
    set {
        this.isNauseousField = value;
      }
}
```

Overall then, XSD grouping clearly holds up pretty well when interpreted by WCF service clients.

Element properties

Next, we need to confirm how element properties are mapped from XSD definitions to .NET client code. Specifically, let's look at how occurrence limits nullability and default values are handled. I've gone ahead and modified our existing **ScreenResult** schema so that these new element properties are present. To do this I set:

- The **ScreenActivities** node to have a minimum occurrence of 1, and a maximum occurrence of 5.

- The **Timestamp** node, which is a **xsd:dateTime**, has its **Nillable** property set to **True**

- The **BloodSample** default amount is set to **Two Vials**

The resulting XSD resembles this:

```
– <xs:element minOccurs="1" maxOccurs="5" name="ScreenActivities">
  – <xs:complexType>
    – <xs:sequence>
        <xs:element name="Weight" type="xs:string" />
        <xs:element name="BloodPressure" type="xs:string" />
        <xs:element name="LungCapacity" type="xs:string" />
        <xs:element default="2 Vials" name="BloodSample" type="xs:string" />
        <xs:element name="Timestamp" nillable="true" type="xs:dateTime" />
      </xs:sequence>
    </xs:complexType>
  </xs:element>
```

After rebuilding the WCF endpoint via the **BizTalk WCF Service Publishing Wizard** and then updating our client's service reference, we can see how these modified attributes are reflected. The `ScreenActivities` type does NOT capture the occurrence limits from the XSD, but does show a default value for `BloodSample`, and a `nullable` type for the `Timestamp` property.

```
public partial class ScreenResultScreenActivities {

        private string weightField;

        private string bloodPressureField;

        private string lungCapacityField;

        private string bloodSampleField;

        private System.Nullable<System.DateTime> timestampField;

        public ScreenResultScreenActivities() {
            this.bloodSampleField = "2 Vials";
}
```

Keep in mind that any well thought out limits on XML node occurrences won't cascade down into the .NET clients that call your service.

Element restrictions

The last set of schema attributes to evaluate is restrictions placed on XML nodes. I've updated our existing **ScreenResult** schema by changing:

- The failure screen reason will only accept an enumeration

- The **Notes** field has a maximum field length of 150 characters

- Added a regular expression pattern to the **SubjectID** field that looks for two letters and 5 numbers

All of these element restrictions are set by clicking on a schema node and changing the **Derived By** value to **Restriction**. This opens up an array of new attributes that can be applied to the selected node.

```
- <xs:element name="ScreenResult">
  - <xs:complexType>
    - <xs:sequence>
        <xs:element name="TrialID" type="xs:string" />
      - <xs:element name="SubjectID">
        - <xs:simpleType>
          - <xs:restriction base="xs:string">
              <xs:pattern value="[A-Z]{2}[0-9]{5}" />
            </xs:restriction>
          </xs:simpleType>
        </xs:element>
    + <xs:element minOccurs="1" maxOccurs="5" name="ScreenActivities">
      - <xs:element name="ScreenResult">
        - <xs:complexType>
          - <xs:choice minOccurs="1">
            - <xs:element name="FailureScreen">
              - <xs:complexType>
                - <xs:sequence>
                  - <xs:element name="Reason">
                    - <xs:simpleType>
                      - <xs:restriction base="xs:string">
                          <xs:enumeration value="Adverse event detected" />
                          <xs:enumeration value="Incomplete data" />
                          <xs:enumeration value="Data not recorded properly" />
                        </xs:restriction>
```

Once more, we can rebuild our BizTalk project, redeploy it, and rerun the **BizTalk WCF Service Publishing Wizard**. As we would hope, the enumeration that existed in the schema node is cleanly translated to a .NET enumeration type in the service client. However, neither the field length restriction nor the regular expression pattern flowed down to the generated .NET classes.

So what can we glean from this investigation into node validation? While .NET translates an impressive amount of XSD validation logic into its service client objects, there are clearly gaps in the concepts that get mapped across. This means that you should be cautious into building too much data validation into your schemas if you expect your clients to adhere to it. Also, going overboard and meticulously configuring each schema node only makes later modification that much more difficult. For instance, setting default values and adding enumerations are nice, but what happens when a default value changes, or new enumeration choices are needed? It may be better to actually avoid these types of tempting restrictions in the spirit of abstraction and loosely coupling service expectations from client requirements.

Exploiting generic schemas

While I've been preaching so far about all the benefits and capabilities of structured schemas, there are real cases where you need to be exceedingly flexible in the way you take data in. You may want to open up an inbound on-ramp that takes any sort of message in, and let the message bus figure out how to type it and route it. Or a particular message type may have a portion that expects variable content and you wish to accommodate any XML structure.

First, let's look at how to make a part of a specific schema expect generic content, and see what the resulting WCF service endpoint would look like. We can add generic placeholders to an XML schema through the use of the XSD "any" node type. There are two key attributes of the any node which dictate how the XML parser treats the content embedded here. The **Namespace** property can contain any of these values:

Value	Description
##any	The default value; this means that the XML content can be part of any document namespace.
##targetNamespace	XML content must be associated with target namespace of the document.
##local	Data not associated with any namespace are allowed
##other	XML content associated with other namespace besides the target
List of values	Data can be associated with any of the comma separated namespace values

You have a variety of choices for how to qualify the XML content with a namespace. However, the second attribute of the `any` node is just as vital as the namespace instruction. The **Process Contents** property specifies how an XML parser should evaluate the XML content in the `any` node.

Value	Description
Strict	The default value, this means that the parser will look at the namespace of the XML content and must find a corresponding schema for validation
Lax	The parser tries to find the schema and validate the XML content, but if it fails, it won't raise an exception
Skip	The parser ignores the XML content and does not try to validate it

So if you have a namespace value of **##any** and set the **Process Contents** to **Skip**, you can send along virtually any XML structure you'd like. Of course, you may still want to provide a bit of verification by limiting the allowable namespaces or still requiring the BizTalk parser to find a schema that matches the generic payload.

I went ahead and changed our **Enrollment** schema by adding a new **SiteSpecificData** record which has an **any** element underneath it. If my solution simply took this content and crammed it into a database field for archival purposes, I could be confidently lazy and accept any namespace and skip schema validation on that generic node.

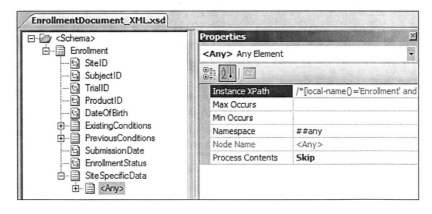

We can then publish this schema as a WCF endpoint and see how service consumers would interact with this open payload. The code in the auto-generated client object shows that the generic node expects nothing but an `XmlElement` object.

```
public partial class Enrollment{
        private string studyIDField;
        private string siteIDField;
```

```
        private string trialIDField;

        private Subject subjectField;

        private System.Xml.XmlElement siteSpecificDataField;
}
```

This is a fairly useful technique when you want to develop schemas that are expected to handle a variety of yet-unknown clients in the future.

The situation may also arise when you wish to make the entire payload of the service generic. That is, the service is capable of accepting any content, and the message bus is responsible for figuring out what to do with it. This is one situation where you cannot use the **Publish schemas as WCF service** option in the **BizTalk WCF Service Publishing Wizard**. You may recall my earlier statement that there is virtually no need to ever expose orchestration as services instead of exposing schemas. Well, here is that one fringe exception to that statement.

The **publish schemas** option of the **BizTalk WCF Service Publishing Wizard** always expects us to choose a schema from an existing assembly. We cannot choose simple types, or generic types. Hence, we need to cheat and build a temporary orchestration that can force the wizard to build a service just how we want it. We start out by creating a new orchestration and adding a message of type **System.Xml. XmlDocument**. Next we put a single **Receive** shape connected to a one-way logic receive port. The "finished" orchestration looks like this:

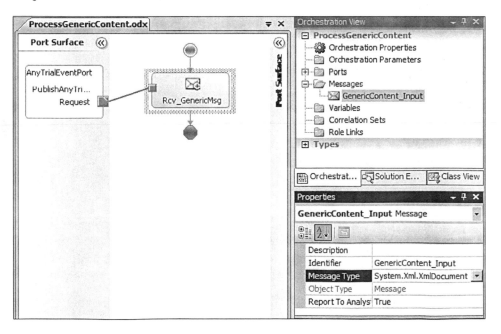

After deploying the updated solution, we should walk through the **BizTalk WCF Service Publishing Wizard** and choose to publish an orchestration port as a service.

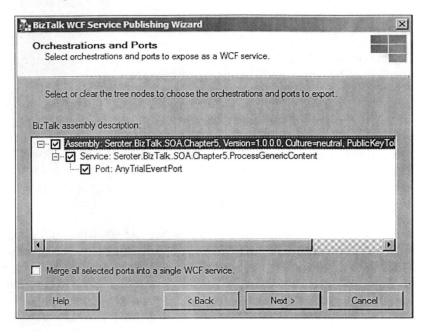

The WCF service reference in the client application defines a request message that accepts a generic object as its input.

```
public partial class PublishAnyTrialEventRequest {
    [MessageBodyMemberAttribute(Namespace="", Order=0)]
    public object part;
    public PublishAnyTrialEventRequest() {
    }
    public PublishAnyTrialEventRequest(object part) {
        this.part = part;
    }
}
```

Clearly you have to use this pattern with caution, as you must be confident that these messages are expected by the message bus and that you know how to handle each and every one that arrives. Also, your service consumer has absolutely no direction as to the shape of the data that the service expects and must use some other means to inflate the request message.

Service-oriented endpoint patterns

What can we do to make our endpoints as service-oriented as possible? We can retain our focus on reusability, abstraction, interoperability, and loose coupling in order to accomplish this. One way to do this is embrace data mapping and not be hamstrung by the idea that the bus should only accept a single canonical schema. If we don't force service callers to all implement a specific data format, we can instead grow our set of callers organically and bring on new clients with ease.

Building reusable receive ports

One key way to make our services as interoperable as possible is to offer a range of inbound transmission channels. While it would be ideal if all our service clients were running the latest versions of the .NET framework, in reality, we are frequently interacting with either dated or cross-platform service consumers. Also, while we may have all service consumers on the same platform, they may all define a particular data entity in slightly different ways. Let's look at how we'd accommodate each of these scenarios.

In this first scenario, consider an environment where our service callers each represent different vendors, and thus each have different service capabilities. One vendor has existing VPN access and is quite modern in their development framework and wants to use the TCP protocol. Another vendor is forced to go through a public Internet connection and its service client only supports SOAP Basic Profile 1.1. As we've already discussed so far, neither of these considerations need to factor into the development of our BizTalk components. Let's assume we have a new schema that holds registration details for physicians wishing to administer a clinical trial for a new medicine. The corresponding orchestration takes in this physician registration message and processes it accordingly. Nothing in this orchestration has to influence which type of inbound receive channel we wish to use.

When this orchestration is deployed, we get to bond the logical receive port to the physical one. In this case, we have a single receive port, but have the option of multiple receive locations. Each receive location corresponds to a different input mechanism whether it be a classic FILE adapter, or WCF channels such as HTTP, or MSMQ. Given how easy it is to add new receiving endpoints, it is good form to offer multiple input channels that accommodate the widest range of consumers.

Now what if the physician registration message that my orchestration accepts was different than the format that each vendor had been transmitting for years prior? If I want the lowest service consumer impact, I'd want to let them send whatever format they use, and simply normalize it to the canonical format required by my orchestration. I have two real choices here:

- Create facade endpoints for each (new) service client so that each client has a strongly typed service to call. All of these facade endpoints can still be part of the same physical receive port and maps are applied to get the data into a common format.

- Create a single, generic endpoint that on boards all registration messages and applies an assortment of maps to reshape the data into our common format.

Choosing the former option requires more maintenance for all parties, but follows better form. The latter option is quite flexible, but raises the risk of improperly formatted data reaching the bus.

So, when it comes to reusing receive ports, consider not only applying multiple receive locations but also adding multiple maps to accommodate a single receive location. A physical receive port offers a valuable level of abstraction to the message bus and any linked orchestrations so that we can control significant behavior at the outermost perimeter of the messaging infrastructure. We can use the same receive port over and over for a related process by simply standing up new input channels and applying new maps to the canonical format.

Constructing a contract-first endpoint

Earlier we discussed the fact that BizTalk Server receive locations are inherently "type-less". That is, they dictate no specific contract. While the **BizTalk WCF Service Publishing Wizard** does a fairly efficient job building metadata endpoints, there are simply cases where you want more control over the contract being exposed to service clients. Fortunately for us, the BizTalk WCF adapters do a nice job of allowing externally defined WSDL definitions to front the BizTalk endpoints.

Earlier in the book, I alluded to the fact that you can technically host an HTTP-based WCF endpoint within the BizTalk in-process host. That is, you don't have to use IIS. For the example we walk through here, I'll use that particular hosting pattern. To legitimately do contract-first service development, you build a schema and WSDL file first, and massage the resulting application to accommodate that contract definition. We can start out with a simple `SiteRegistration` schema which provides all the details we need to associate a site with a particular clinical trial.

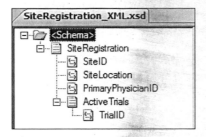

The next step is to create a basic WSDL, which uses this schema and defines the message exchange pattern and operations that our contract supports. My straightforward WSDL looks like this:

```xml
<?xml version="1.0" encoding="utf-8"?>
<wsdl:definitions name="HelloService"
  targetNamespace="http://Seroter.BizTalk.SOA.Chapter5.ContractFirst"
 xmlns:wsdl="http://schemas.xmlsoap.org/wsdl/"
 xmlns:soap="http://schemas.xmlsoap.org/wsdl/soap/"
 xmlns:tns="http://Seroter.BizTalk.SOA.Chapter5.ContractFirst"
 xmlns:xsd="http://www.w3.org/2001/XMLSchema">
 <!-- declare types-->
 <wsdl:types>
 <xsd:schema elementFormDefault="qualified" xmlns="http://Seroter.
BizTalk.SOA.Chapter5.ContractFirst" targetNamespace="http://Seroter.
BizTalk.SOA.Chapter5.ContractFirst">
    <xsd:element name="SiteRegistration">
      <xsd:complexType>
        <xsd:sequence>
          <xsd:element name="SiteID" type="xsd:string" />
          <xsd:element name="SiteLocation" type="xsd:string" />
          <xsd:element name="PrimaryPhysicianID" type="xsd:string" />
          <xsd:element name="ActiveTrials">
            <xsd:complexType>
              <xsd:sequence>
                <xsd:element minOccurs="0" maxOccurs="unbounded"
name="TrialID" type="xsd:string" />
              </xsd:sequence>
            </xsd:complexType>
          </xsd:element>
        </xsd:sequence>
      </xsd:complexType>
    </xsd:element>
  </xsd:schema>
  </wsdl:types>
<!-- declare messages-->
```

```
<wsdl:message name="SiteRegistrationRequest">
  <wsdl:part name="part" element="tns:SiteRegistration" />
</wsdl:message>
<!-- decare port types-->
<wsdl:portType name="CustomSiteRegistration_PortType">
  <wsdl:operation name="PublishSiteRegistration">
    <wsdl:input message="tns:SiteRegistrationRequest" />
  </wsdl:operation>
</wsdl:portType>
<!-- declare binding-->
<wsdl:binding name="tns:CustomSiteRegistration_Binding" type="tns:
CustomSiteRegistration_PortType">
  <soap:binding transport="http://schemas.xmlsoap.org/soap/http"/>
  <wsdl:operation name="PublishSiteRegistration">
    <soap:operation soapAction="PublishSiteRegistration"
style="document"/>
    <wsdl:input>
      <soap:body use ="literal"/>
    </wsdl:input>
  </wsdl:operation>
</wsdl:binding>
<!-- declare service-->
<wsdl:service name="CustomSiteRegistrationService">
  <wsdl:port binding="CustomSiteRegistration_Binding" name="CustomSi
teRegistration">
    <soap:address location="http://localhost:4044/
SiteRegistrationService"/>
  </wsdl:port>
</wsdl:service>
</wsdl:definitions>
```

While the **BizTalk WCF Service Publishing Wizard** produces a fairly clean WSDL file, we are clearly establishing more structural control by building these contracts by hand.

The next step is to switch to the **BizTalk Administration Console** and create a new one-way receive port/receive location combo. I've chosen the **WCF-Custom** adapter for the receive location which means that the in-process, **BizTalkServerApplication** host is used.

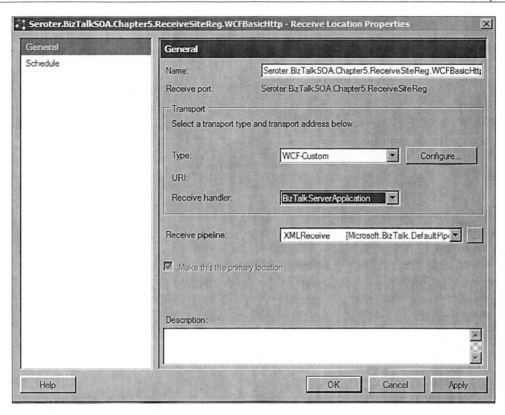

Now we need to configure this custom endpoint. Skip ahead to the **Binding** tab within the **WCF-Custom Transport Properties** window. I've decided that this custom WCF adapter will exploit the **basicHTTP** binding.

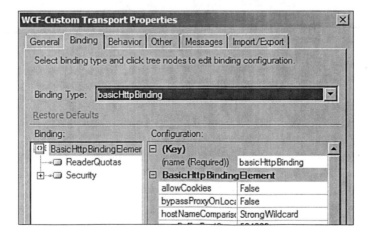

Now, we can switch back to the **General** tab and assign an HTTP address for this endpoint. I've chosen an arbitrary port number and URI (`http://localhost:4044/SiteRegistrationService/service.svc`) to represent this endpoint.

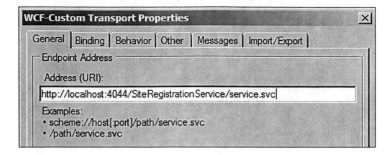

Finally, let's add a new behavior to this endpoint so that service clients can interrogate the WSDL. On the **Behavior** tab, we right-click the **Service Behavior** node and choose to **Add Extension**. In the **Select Behavior Extension** window, we should choose the **serviceMetadata** entry. Then, we must be sure to flip the **serviceMetadata** property named **httpGetEnabled** to **True**. If you recall from our WCF discussion earlier, we use this behavior to explicitly turn metadata retrieval on and off.

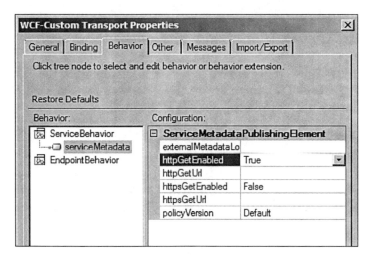

If we enable this receive location, and browse to the chosen URL, we'll be presented with the standard WCF service description page.

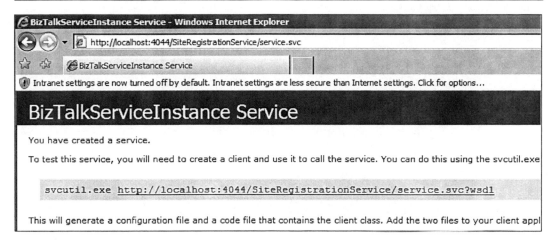

However, if we look at the available WSDL, we'll notice a generic `BizTalkSubmit` operation and no explicit schema. This makes sense because our receive location has absolutely no idea what type of data we plan on passing to it. Let's help it out, shall we? Go back to the receive location we created, open the adapter configuration window, switch to the **Behavior** tab and choose the **serviceMetadata** behavior listed there. This behavior has a property named **externalMetadataLocation** where we can specify which outside WSDL file should be a substitute for whatever the receive location would have generated on its own. I populated this property with the URL of my hand-built WSDL.

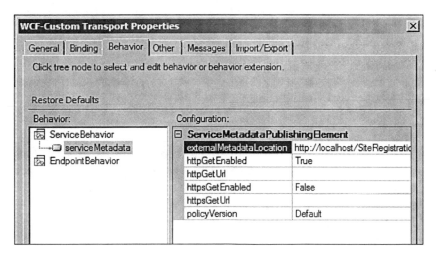

Pitfall

The WSDL file must be accessed through an HTTP or HTTPS channel by the adapter. If you try and point to a WSDL using a file system URI, the receive location will fail to start and throws an error. You can resolve this by placing the WSDL in an IIS web directory and referencing it there.

Now if I browse this service again, I see that the custom WSDL file is served up instead of the auto-generated one.

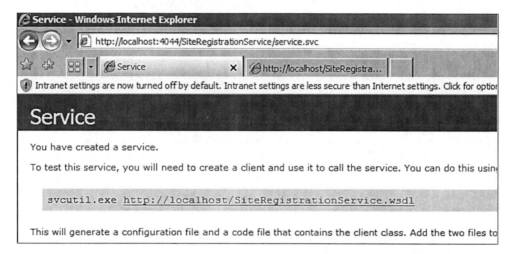

Notice that I could also use this pattern to accept "generic" content into my receive location and avoid the throwaway orchestration demonstrated in the previous section. Our custom-built WSDL could designate an arbitrary payload for our service operation.

This pattern demonstrates a clean way to attach "type" details to a WCF receive location in a very loosely-coupled way. Note however, that there is no practical reason to avoid hosting our services in IIS 7.0 and choosing the in-process hosting instead. The best part is, an endpoint hosted in IIS can still take advantage of the **externalMetadataLocation** property set in the corresponding receive location. Hence, this little trick isn't just for in-process hosting but rather, available to any WCF adapter in any hosting environment.

Consider using the "custom" WCF adapters in all situations. In doing so, you get easy access to binding configurations and behaviors that are inaccessible from the transport-specific WCF adapters. Also, if you need to upgrade the capabilities of the port in the future, there is no need to create new ports and rebind existing processes.

Summary

Throughout this chapter, we looked at how to apply the basic SOA principles when designing our service schemas and inbound endpoint. Applying a level of forethought to our schema design prior to coding allows us to consider how our messaging solution should behave, and how best to accommodate the current and future clients of our service.

In the next chapter, we build upon these concepts and tackle the brave world of asynchronous message patterns.

6

Asynchronous Communication Patterns

The beauty of independence, departure, actions that rely on themselves.
-Walt Whitman

Arguably the signature aspect of a service-oriented architecture based on messaging is the prevalence and embrace of the asynchronous message exchange pattern. In the last chapter, we looked at how to construct practical schemas and design smart endpoints. Now we build upon those concepts and see how combining well-built messages and endpoints with an event-driven, asynchronous infrastructure can help us realize our aim of a loosely coupled architecture.

In this chapter, you will learn:

- The inherent value of asynchronous communication
- The patterns for implementing asynchronous processing in WCF solutions
- How to take advantage of asynchronous communication in BizTalk solutions
- Mechanisms for returning results from asynchronous operations
- The role of queue-based services

Why asynchronous communication matters

In earlier chapters, we've discussed the benefits of chaining services together in an asynchronous fashion. I'm sure that for many developers, deciding upon asynchronous communication requires an enormous leap of faith. It feels much safer to simply make a linear series of synchronous calls where our client application only advances once we are assured that our message reached its destination. However, if you remain hesitant to embrace asynchronous patterns, consider the wide range of benefits you will be missing out on. These benefits are:

- **No client blocking**: By definition, a synchronous operation requires the caller to block and wait for the operation to return its expected response. The code can perform no other tasks. In an asynchronous model, the client engages in "fire-and-forget" behavior and relies on other mechanisms to determine any desired results from the service invocation.

- **Support for long-running processes**: This relates to the previous benefit, but it's worth calling it out independently. When the client is freed from concerns of timeouts and blocking, they can safely trigger operations that take minutes or days to complete. A service invoked asynchronously can perform a variety of additional tasks when freed from the constraints of required responses.

- **Encourages event-driven, not procedural applications**: It's nearly impossible to build anything but linear applications when relying upon synchronous communication patterns. Call one service, wait for result, then call another. In an asynchronous world, both caller and services spawn events and rely less on strict procedural sequences and instead become more free-flowing in their processing.

- **Fewer operation dependencies**: This is a big one for me. If your solution utilizes a message bus, then applying asynchronous patterns means that you can engage in a very loosely-coupled relationship with the downstream recipients of your data. Experiencing a high burst of inbound data? No problem as a BizTalk Server will throw disproportionally more processing power at receiving messages than processing them. If no immediate response is expected, then BizTalk can gracefully scale down from a flood of requests. What if the downstream system is offline? Once again, this is of no real concern to the publisher because once they connect to the bus, they are no longer on the hook for handling infrastructure errors down the line.

Now, asynchronous programming isn't always easy, which is why it may not yet be part of your standard arsenal of patterns. What are some challenges of asynchronous communication?

- **Building messages with required context**: When calling a series of synchronous operations on a stateful service, you have the luxury of the service retaining context of previous interactions. You can transmit small, discrete messages that only pertain to the current operation while knowing that the service can augment any gaps using knowledge retained from preceding calls. However, in a loosely-coupled, stateless, asynchronous environment, the messages need to encapsulate all the data needed by the service to handle independent service invocation.

- **Obtaining results to asynchronous calls**: Just because you execute a fire-and-forget function, it doesn't mean that you have no interest in the result of the service invocation. Even if the caller is able to obtain a result from the asynchronous service, they still need to determine the relevance of this message. What if the result came back after such a long period of time that a subsequent service call has superseded it? Properly correlating relevant response events and data from the service back to the initiator can be a tricky concept fraught with opportunities to take a wrong turn.

- **Reliable delivery of data**: One of the most justified concerns regarding asynchronous programming is centered on reliability. When a developer calls a synchronous operation, they are able to proactively detect any infrastructure or service exceptions that may occur. The caller does not proceed until the service has completed its operation set. If you aspire to fully embrace asynchronous messaging patterns, then you will need to know that when you require reliability, it's there, and that any exceptions will be properly captured and handled by the service provider.

Throughout the remainder of this chapter, we will look at how to explicitly address these concerns and demonstrate ways to incorporate asynchronous patterns into your applications.

Using asynchronous services in WCF

WCF has support for both client-side and server-side asynchronous programming scenarios. By "client-side" programming, I mean that a service built with a request/response operation can appear asynchronous to the client. For example, let's look at a simple sequence diagram that shows what I mean.

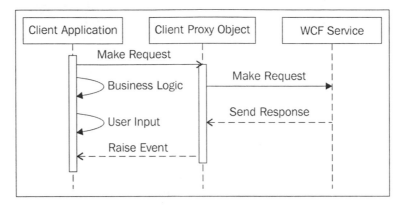

The WCF client proxy class is responsible for simulating the asynchronous communication, while the actual service still exposes only a synchronous operation. Let's look at an example of how we would physically create a client-side asynchronous experience in a WCF solution.

Creating the synchronous service

We start out by creating a new, empty Visual Studio.NET 2008 solution. Then we add a project of type **WCF Service Library** to the solution. This project type automatically adds an interface class, service class, and application configuration file. I've changed the interface class content so that it reflects the **adverse event** object that we'll be working with throughout this chapter. An adverse event is a patient experience with a drug that has caused them problems. My service interface (and corresponding data classes) now looks like this:

```
[ServiceContract(Namespace="http://Seroter.BizTalkSOA.Chapter6")]
public interface IAdverseEventSync
{
    [OperationContract]
    AdverseEventAction SubmitAdverseEvent(AdverseEvent NewAE);
}

[DataContract(Namespace="http://Seroter.BizTalkSOA.Chapter6")]
public class AdverseEvent
{
```

```csharp
    [DataMember]
    public string Product { get; set; }
    [DataMember]
    public int PatientID { get; set; }
    [DataMember]
    public int PhysicianID { get; set; }
    [DataMember]
    public AECategoryType Category { get; set; }
    [DataMember]
    public DateTime DateStarted { get; set; }
    [DataMember]
    public ReportedByType ReportedBy { get; set; }
    [DataMember]
    public string Description { get; set; }
}
[DataContract(Namespace="http://Seroter.BizTalkSOA.Chapter6")]
public class AdverseEventAction
{
    [DataMember]
    public string SubmissionID { get; set; }
    [DataMember]
    public string Product { get; set; }
    [DataMember]
    public int PatientID { get; set; }
    [DataMember]
    public bool doCeaseMedication { get; set; }
    [DataMember]
    public bool doReduceDosage { get; set; }
    [DataMember]
    public bool doAdmitHospital { get; set; }
    [DataMember]
    public bool doScheduleFollowup { get; set; }
    [DataMember]
    public string AdditionalNotes { get; set; }
}
[DataContract]
public enum AECategoryType
{
    [EnumMember]
    InjectionSoreness = 0,
    [EnumMember]
    Swelling = 1,
    [EnumMember]
```

```
    Headache = 2,
    [EnumMember]
    Bleeding = 3,
    [EnumMember]
    Sickness = 4,
    [EnumMember]
    Rash = 5,
    [EnumMember]
    Other = 6
}

[DataContract]
public enum ReportedByType
{
    [EnumMember]
    Patient = 0,
    [EnumMember]
    Physician = 1,
    [EnumMember]
    SalesRep = 2,
    [EnumMember]
    Other = 3
}
```

Notice that we have a single, synchronous service operation defined. This operation accepts an adverse event, and returns the resulting action that the submitter should take.

We now need an actual service implementation of this interface. In a separate class file, I have my very simple service that looks like this:

```
 public AdverseEventAction SubmitAdverseEvent(AdverseEvent NewAE)
 {
        AdverseEventAction AEAction = new AdverseEventAction();
        AEAction.SubmissionID = Guid.NewGuid().ToString();
        AEAction.PatientID = NewAE.PatientID;
        AEAction.Product = NewAE.Product;

        //initialize values
        AEAction.doAdmitHospital = false;
        AEAction.doCeaseMedication = false;
        AEAction.doReduceDosage = false;
        AEAction.doScheduleFollowup = false;
        AEAction.AdditionalNotes = "";

        TimeSpan aeDuration= DateTime.Now.Subtract(NewAE.DateStarted);
```

```
        if (NewAE.Category == AECategoryType.InjectionSoreness &&
aeDuration.Days > 3)
        {
            AEAction.doReduceDosage = true;
        }

        return AEAction;
    }
```

For this basic scenario, we're checking to see if someone is still experiencing soreness more than three days after a drug injection. Our next step is to actually host this WCF service, so that it is visible to the outside world. Up until now, we've focused primarily on self-hosting, but I'm going to switch gears and take advantage of IIS 7.0 and Windows Process Activation Services (WAS) for hosting our WCF services.

Let's add a **WCF Service** Web Site project to our existing Visual Studio.NET solution.

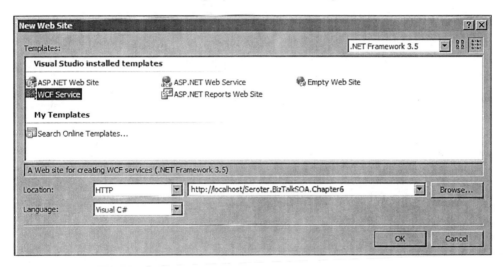

Once again, we are provided some sample classes and implementation objects by this Visual Studio.NET project type. We can freely delete the **Service1.cs** class files as we won't be putting actual service implementation logic into this host container. Next, we have to add a reference to our existing WCF service library project. After that, we change the directive at the top of the **Service.svc** file so that it points to the service type residing in our referenced library. That single line at the top should read:

```
<%@ ServiceHost Language="C#" Debug="true" Service="Seroter.
BizTalkSOA.Chapter6.ServiceLibrary.
AdverseEventSyncService" %>
```

Almost there. All that remains to do is use the **WCF Service Configuration Editor** to update the **web.config** file to accurately reflect our referenced service configuration. We only need to modify the service name and the endpoint contract.

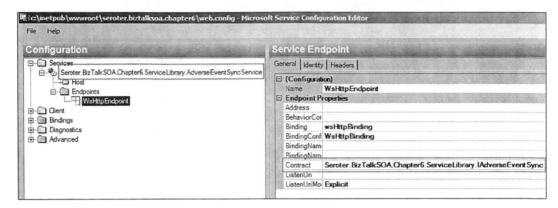

You may notice that we do not need to add either a base address or service address in order for this service configuration to be complete. When a service is hosted within IIS 7.0, the base address is equal to the address of the .svc file.

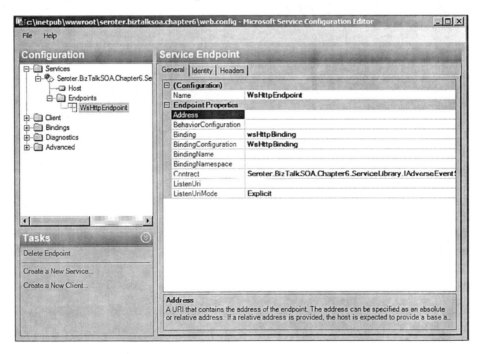

We can confirm a successful configuration by opening IIS 7.0, locating our new service, and browsing the `.svc` file. You should see the standard WCF service introduction page.

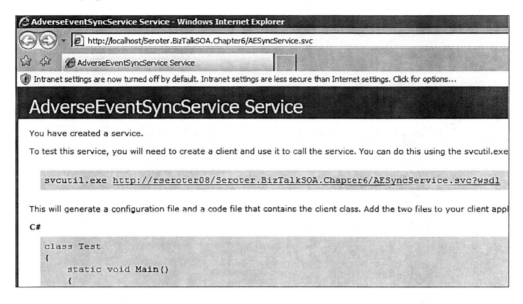

Building a client-side asynchronous experience

Now that our synchronous service is up and running, let's see how we interact with it from the client perspective. Go ahead and add a new **Console Application** project to our existing Visual Studio.NET solution. Right-click the new project and choose to **Add** a new **Service Reference**. After plugging in the URL of our IIS-hosted service, resist the temptation to immediately click the **Ok** button. Instead, let's visit the options we get after clicking the **Advanced** button.

Under the **Client** heading, notice a checkbox labeled **Generate Asynchronous Operations**. Once that is selected, we should exit out of this window and finish our service reference.

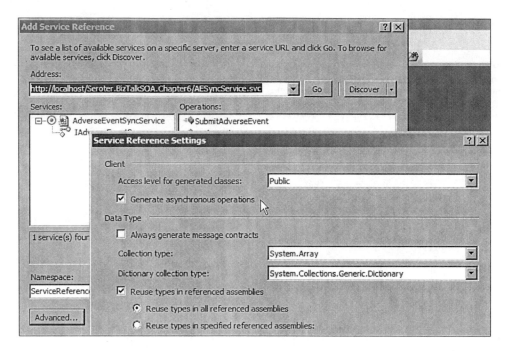

As a result of this wizard, we end up with proxy class and application configuration files. Because I plan on using this same client application over and over again throughout this chapter, I've gone ahead and changed the **Name** attribute of the endpoint configuration in the application configuration file to something more descriptive such as **AESyncEndpoint**. Even though we checked that **Generate Asynchronous Operations** box earlier, absolutely nothing prevents us from calling this service in the traditional synchronous manner that it exposes. Such an example looks like this:

```
class Program
{
  static void Main(string[] args)
  {
      CallSyncServiceSync();
  }
private static void CallSyncServiceSync()
  {
Console.WriteLine("Calling sync service ...");
AdverseEventSyncClient client = new AdverseEventSyncClient("AESyncEnd
point");
```

```
try
    {
AESyncServiceReference.AdverseEvent newAE = new
AESyncServiceReference.AdverseEvent();
    newAE.PatientID = 100912;
    newAE.PhysicianID = 7543;
    newAE.Product = "Cerinob";
    newAE.ReportedBy = AESyncServiceReference.ReportedByType.Patient;
    newAE.Category = AESyncServiceReference.AECategoryType.
      InjectionSoreness;
    newAE.DateStarted = new DateTime(2008, 10, 29);
AESyncServiceReference.AdverseEventAction result =
                client.SubmitAdverseEvent(newAE);
Console.WriteLine("Service result returned ...");
Console.WriteLine("Should the patient reduce dosage? {0}",
    result.doReduceDosage.ToString());
client.Close();
Console.ReadLine();
    }
catch (System.ServiceModel.CommunicationException)
  { client.Abort(); }
  catch (System.TimeoutException) { client.Abort(); }
  catch (System.Exception) { client.Abort(); throw; }
}
```

As we've discussed earlier, while there is no problem with this pattern per se, we've limited the ability to do anything else until that statement returns a response. What if there is significant logic to determining the appropriate action for an adverse event? What if a nurse actually needs to review the event prior to disseminating a course of action?

There are a couple ways to perform client-side asynchronous calls, but I'd like to highlight the one just added for the .NET Framework 3.5. The classic mechanism which uses the `IAsyncResult` object is still perfectly valid, and technically the only way you can go if you exploit the `ChannelFactory` directly. But, if you are using the proxy class, and want the cleanest route, then the new `eventing` capability in .NET 3.5 is a great choice.

If we dig into the service reference's **Reference.cs** file, we will find a generated statement that reveals a new client side event.

```
public event System.EventHandler<SubmitAdverseEventCompletedEventArgs>
SubmitAdverseEventCompleted;
```

Our client code can now register a handler for this event, and have it fire when the service response is eventually returned. The client no longer needs to wait until after executing the service request to continue processing other items. What does this look like in our client code?

```
class Program
{
  static void Main(string[] args)
  {
      //CallSyncServiceSync();
      CallSyncServiceAsync();
  }

private static void CallSyncServiceAsync()
        {
Console.WriteLine("Calling sync service (async) ...");
AdverseEventSyncClient client = new AdverseEventSyncClient
  ("AESyncEndpoint");

  try
  {
AESyncServiceReference.AdverseEvent newAE = new
  AESyncServiceReference.AdverseEvent();
newAE.PatientID = 100912;
newAE.PhysicianID = 7543;
newAE.Product = "Cerinob";
newAE.ReportedBy = AESyncServiceReference.ReportedByType.Patient;
newAE.Category = AESyncServiceReference.AECategoryType.
  InjectionSoreness;
newAE.DateStarted = new DateTime(2008, 10, 29);

client.SubmitAdverseEventCompleted += new EventHandler<SubmitAdverse
    EventCompletedEventArgs>(client_SubmitAdverseEventCompleted);

  client.SubmitAdverseEventAsync(newAE);

  client.Close();
  }
  catch (System.ServiceModel.CommunicationException) { client.Abort();
}
  catch (System.TimeoutException) { client.Abort(); }
  catch (System.Exception) { client.Abort(); throw; }

  for (int i = 0; i < 10; i++)
  {
```

```
    Console.WriteLine("Doing other important things ...");
    }
    Console.ReadLine();
}
static void client_SubmitAdverseEventCompleted(object sender,
SubmitAdverseEventCompletedEventArgs e)
    {
Console.WriteLine("Service result returned ...");

Console.WriteLine("Should the patient reduce dosage? {0}",
    e.Result.doReduceDosage.ToString());

Console.ReadLine();
    }
}
```

There are a number of interesting things to note here. See that I registered a
completed event handler, called the asynchronous version of the service operation,
and closed my proxy class. Also see that the event handler has a strongly-typed
argument that knows about the data members of my service result. This is the
result of the client execution:

```
file:///C:/BizTalk/Projects/Seroter.BizTalkSOA.Chapter6/Seroter.BizTalkSOA.Chapter6.ServiceClient/b...  _ □ X
Calling service ...
Doing other important things ...
Doing other important things ...
Doing other important things ...
Doing other important things ...
Doing other important things ...
Doing other important things ...
Doing other important things ...
Doing other important things ...
Doing other important things ...
Doing other important things ...
Service result returned ...
Should the patient reduce dosage? True
```

Critical Point

Be completely aware that this technique only simulates
asynchronous behavior on a natively synchronous service.
You are still beholden to service timeouts and other characteristics
of a typical synchronous execution.

Working with server-side asynchronous services

As I just mentioned, the above technique is simply a way to call synchronous services in a non-blocking fashion. What if you want to design and expose a truly asynchronous service? This is quite easy task in WCF. In our existing WCF service library project, I added a brand new class to hold the asynchronous service. This interface has the following definition:

```
[ServiceContract(Namespace = "http://Seroter.BizTalkSOA.Chapter6")]
public interface IAdverseEventAsync
{
    [OperationContract(IsOneWay=true)]
    void SubmitAdverseEvent(AdverseEvent NewAE);
}
```

The `IsOneWay` attribute is the key to forcing a truly asynchronous service.

Having a service operation simply return `void` is not the same as making that operation asynchronous. While that may give the impression of a exploiting a "fire-and-forget" pattern, in fact the client executing the code is interacting with a request/response operation and must still wait until the service completes before progressing further.

Next, we need a new service class which implements this interface. Once that is in place, we must revisit our WCF service host project and add a new `.svc` file whose directive points to our just-created service class. All that's left is to update the web configuration file for the service host container by adding an entry for the new service.

This client application call is completely asynchronous. If I added a thirty second delay in the service implementation or threw an exception in the service code, the client would still move ahead immediately after the operation was invoked. However, the operation DOES wait until a successful connection to the server has been achieved and the appropriate HTTP 200 code is returned. Once the client is assured that service infrastructure is up and running, it will continue processing. Understand that this means that the caller has no real assurance that the operation is completed successfully, so this may not be appropriate for scenarios where critical data is passed, or guarantees of once-only delivery is required.

Using asynchronous services in BizTalk with WCF

BizTalk Server natively promotes an asynchronous messaging pattern and readily embraces an event driven architecture. What BizTalk adds to the standalone WCF patterns we've seen above is the injection of a message broker. This middle layer loosely couples the enterprise systems on both ends of the service call while enabling a new set of messaging capabilities not available in standard service implementations.

Consuming asynchronous services

Consuming asynchronous services from within BizTalk Server is an especially straightforward task. However, the huge caveat is: BizTalk Server 2009 cannot execute WCF services whose `isOneWay` flag is set to true. Wait, so doesn't that mean that BizTalk does NOT support asynchronous services? For me, it's a matter of perspective. BizTalk CAN still consume WCF services in an asynchronous manner from orchestration processes. Let's see how.

First modify the existing `IAdverseEventSync` interface to include an operation that returns no data.

```
[OperationContract]
void UpdateAdverseEvent(AdverseEvent modifiedAE);
```

For my implementation of this service, I included a processing delay of thirty seconds, and write a message to the machine's `Application Event Log` afterwards. To make sure our service host reflects this new operation, rebuild the service library and service host container projects.

Next, add a new BizTalk Server Project to the existing Visual Studio.NET solution. Create a new schema that represents the canonical Adverse Event entity. Mine looks like this:

At this point we need to reference the existing WCF service so that we can acquire the metadata necessary for BizTalk to consume it. Remember that we don't do **Add Service Reference** for BizTalk projects, but rather, **Add Generated Items** and choose **Consume WCF Service**.

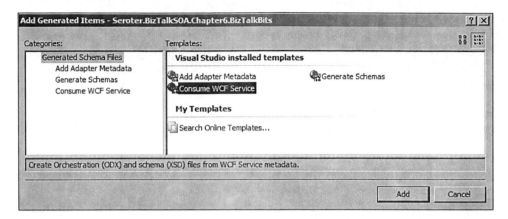

After plugging in the WCF service URL to the wizard, we end up with the schemas we are seeking. We will have to transform the Adverse Event data from the canonical format to the service-specific structure, so add a new BizTalk Map which performs this task.

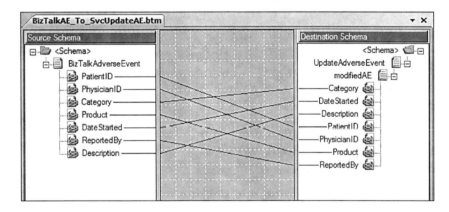

Finally, let's design an orchestration that takes in the canonical message, transforms it to the service format, calls the service, and writes a message to the machine's **Application Event Log**. The orchestration that I built is arranged like this:

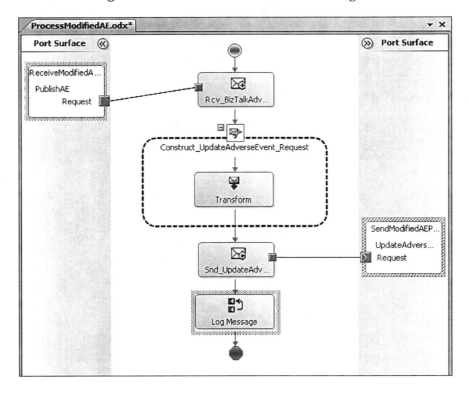

A key thing to note: I created my own one-way orchestration send port because the orchestration port type auto-generated by the **BizTalk WCF Service Consuming Wizard** is a two-way port that handles both the request message and empty response acknowledgement. In my case, I don't want to wait for that response and prefer to simply continue my workflow process. In essence, I am telling BizTalk Server to treat this service invocation asynchronously.

At this point, we can build and deploy the BizTalk project. In the **BizTalk Administration Console**, we create the receive port/location necessary to pick up the canonical schema format. As we decided to abandon the auto-generated type for our orchestration send port, the auto-generated bindings (which are also request/response) are equally unusable. So, define a new static one-way send port that utilizes the **WCF-WsHttp** adapter. The values in this adapter configuration should match your service. This means that the address URI should match, the SOAP Action should be properly set, and the security settings are in sync with the service's expectations.

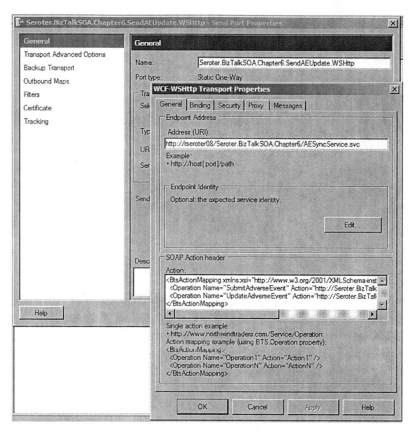

After binding the orchestration to the new ports, and starting all relevant components, the solution can be tested. Remember that our synchronous service has a thirty second delay inside. So if this orchestration behaves like a typical service client (i.e., waiting to proceed until the service completes) we would not expect to see the orchestration's final log message prior to the log message of the service. However, that's not what happens in our just-built scenario. Testing what we've built above, we can clearly see that the orchestration completes 30+ seconds before the service finishes its processing.

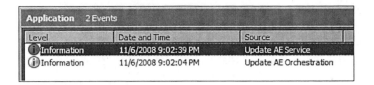

So what does it gives us? Remember how BizTalk works. Our one-way orchestration port means that the orchestration is publishing to the bus and moving on. It's now up to the send port to successfully deliver the message. The send port still sees the service as synchronous and won't complete its processing (and thus delete the message from the MessageBox) until the service returns its acknowledgement. The send port behaves in a "store and forward" fashion where the message is persisted until transmitted successfully.

What if we throw an exception from our service? By default, the send port message will become suspended, but the error does not flow back to the orchestration. It completes without knowing that an exception occurred. What if we WANT the orchestration to catch business exceptions? We could turn **Delivery Notification** on for the orchestration's send port which means that the orchestration waits for confirmation that the physical send port successfully delivered its message. However, this doesn't work as you might expect, as the orchestration still progresses to its next step immediately after the message leaves the orchestration. The safest way for the orchestration to catch any service exception is to switch back to the request/response pattern and apply **Scope** shapes which catch targeted or general exceptions.

Exposing asynchronous services

Exposing BizTalk processes through asynchronous channels is also a clear-cut task. Once again, you cannot expose WCF service from BizTalk that have the **isOneWay** attribute set to **True**. There is no option in the **BizTalk WCF Service Publishing Wizard** to do so. However, because of the loosely coupled nature of BizTalk's messaging engine, a straightforward `void` service behaves in a similar fashion to a true one-way service.

Let's start out with a very basic orchestration that takes in our canonical Adverse Event schema and then purposely causes an exception. In my case, I perform a "divide by zero" calculation. Notice that one-way orchestration receive ports do not have the option to attach a **Fault Message**. On two-way ports, because we know the caller is expecting a response, we can define a specific fault message to return instead of expected result data.

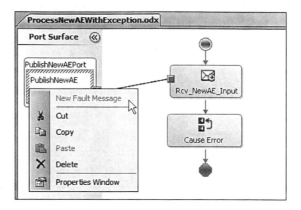

Once our BizTalk project is redeployed, we should walk through the **BizTalk WCF Service Publishing Wizard** in order to produce a service on-ramp for this orchestration. Construct a new service and endpoint for the **WCF-WSHttp** adapter and manually assemble the service contract by choosing the **Publish schemas as WCF service** option.

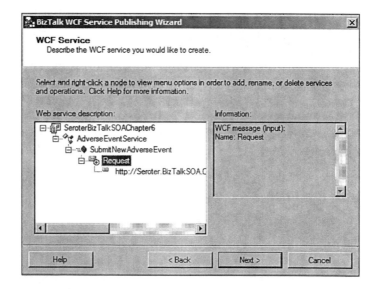

Now this service is technically a request/response service. We can verify this by looking at the resulting WSDL for the service and observing that our `PublishNewAE` operation has both a request and response message. However, it is critical to understand that as far as the service is concerned, its operation is completed when the message reaches the MessageBox, not after (all) subscribers are done with it. Therefore, the service client only needs to wait until the message is published and is not impacted by actions of downstream subscribers.

To prove this, all we have to do is call this service. Before we can do that, let's bind our orchestration to the receive port that was auto-generated by the **BizTalk WCF Service Publishing Wizard**. After starting the receive location and orchestration, we can reference this service from our previously-built console client application. Let's add a new **Service Reference** to the console application and point to the fresh WCF service we just built (if you so desire, nothing prevents you from choosing the advanced option of generating client-asynchronous proxy objects). We can call this service just like any other WCF service:

```
private static void CallBizTalkSyncService()
  {
Console.WriteLine("Calling BizTalk sync service ...");
AdverseEventServiceClient client = new AdverseEventServiceClient
    ("BizTalkAESyncEndpoint");
  try
  {
BizTalkAdverseEvent newAE = new BizTalkAdverseEvent();
  newAE.PatientID = "100912";
  newAE.PhysicianID = "7543";
  newAE.Product = "Cerinob";
  newAE.ReportedBy = "Patient";
  newAE.Category = "Injection Soreness";
  newAE.DateStarted = new DateTime(2008, 10, 29).ToShortDateString();
  client.SubmitNewAdverseEvent(newAE);
Console.WriteLine("Service result returned ...");
client.Close();
Console.ReadLine();
  }
catch (System.ServiceModel.CommunicationException) { client.Abort(); }
  catch (System.TimeoutException) { client.Abort(); }
  catch (System.Exception) { client.Abort(); throw; }
}
```

Sure enough, the service completes successfully, while the BizTalk Administration Console reveals a suspended orchestration resulting from the orchestration exception. So if subscriber exceptions don't flow back to the client application, does that mean that nothing bubbles back to this WCF client as a result of an asynchronous service invocation? What you'll find is that any error encountered while physically publishing the message results in an exception flowed back to the client. For instance, if the web site hosting the service is unavailable, or a receive location is offline, you will see that error in the client application. If no subscribers are found, or a subscriber has any issue processing the message, these errors stay local to the BizTalk Server.

So while BizTalk does not expose truly asynchronous services, the fact that the service operation only extends to MessageBox publication means that in essence, the messages are of a "fire-and-forget" fashion. How the messages are processed is not the concern of the publisher, and BizTalk shields the service caller from these details.

Getting results from asynchronous invocations

In many cases, the "fire-and-forget" nature of asynchronous communication may be applied only to prevent client blocking, not because there is no desire to find out the result of the service call. The options for retrieving service results depend heavily on the types of service clients and expected availability of both ends of the service transactions.

Ideally, you'd want your service client to be able to make outbound calls and also host inbound ones. This sort of solution where both the client and service can send messages to each other independently is called a **duplex service**. In this fashion, our client could make an asynchronous call, and the service could deliver an out-of-band response event that the client would handle accordingly. However, this approach is neither interoperable nor accommodating to clients and services that are online at different times.

A service designer who is most interested in supporting the widest range of consumers will offer both polling and service callback options. For the polling scenario, the service updates an agreed upon repository upon completion, and it remains the client's responsibility to poll this repository to discover the service output. This repository could be a database, file system, queue, or even a URL in the case of the service building a "resource" as a completion output and the service client issuing RESTful calls for said resource. Polling also works well in cases where we don't know if both the service and client are online at the same time. By using an intermediary repository, the service could be unavailable, but its resulting output is residing in a location accessible by the client at any time.

The problem with polling is that it's both unpredictable and expensive. By unpredictable, I mean that the client cannot know whether the result will come back in one second, three seconds, or thirty seconds, and therefore must have an algorithm to poll at distinct times and hope for the best. It's expensive because the client must inevitably waste processing cycles polling for something that may or may not return in a timely fashion. While not optimal for performance, this mechanism works well in cross-platform scenarios where providing generic access to shared repositories is straightforward.

Client callbacks are a solid choice when both the client and service are online simultaneously and both ends of the service transaction use WCF as their service technology. WCF has hidden much of the complexity of this technique and exposed a powerful way to alert users to results of asynchronous processing.

Building WCF services that support client callbacks

WCF has rich support for client callbacks and efficiently handles service response events. What you need in order to support duplex patterns is a service contract that requires sessions, and one of the two available duplex bindings in WCF: **NetTcpBinding** and **WSDualHttpBinding**. Duplex bindings are designed for scenarios where you want to open a two-way communication between endpoints and potentially send numerous messages both ways. However, this technique also fits the bill if you simply want a single result returned from an asynchronous invocation. Let's take a look at how to set up this exchange pattern to accomplish the following scenario:

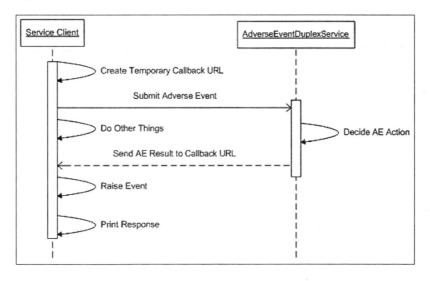

First of all, we need new service interfaces to accommodate our duplex scenario. Our first interface represents the service operation called by the client, and the second interface represents the client operation invoked by the service.

```
public interface IAdverseEventDuplex
    {
        [OperationContract(IsOneWay = true)]
        void SubmitAdverseEvent(AdverseEvent NewAE);
    }
public interface IAdverseEventDuplexCallback
    {
        [OperationContract(IsOneWay=true)]
        void AEResult(AdverseEventAction aeAction);
    }
```

Now that we have the interfaces, we need to decorate the primary service interface with the attributes necessary to support the WCF client callback capability. Specifically, we need to apply both a session requirement and `callback contract` to the service. The callback contract references an interface that must be implemented by the service client.

```
[ServiceContract(
        Namespace = "http://Seroter.BizTalkSOA.Chapter6",
        SessionMode=SessionMode.Required,
        CallbackContract=typeof(IAdverseEventDuplexCallback))]
public interface IAdverseEventDuplex
{
  [OperationContract(IsOneWay = true)]
  void SubmitAdverseEvent(AdverseEvent NewAE);
}
```

Our subsequent service implements the `IAdverseEventDuplex` interface. Notice that we extract the client's callback mechanism from the `OperationContext` object and then proceed to execute the client's `AEResult` function.

```
[ServiceBehavior(InstanceContextMode=InstanceContextMode.PerSession)]
public class AdverseEventDuplexService : IAdverseEventDuplex
{
 public void SubmitAdverseEvent(AdverseEvent NewAE)
 {
   System.Diagnostics.EventLog.WriteEntry("Duplex Service", "New AE
received");

   AdverseEventAction aeAction = new AdverseEventAction();
   aeAction.PatientID = NewAE.PatientID;
   aeAction.Product = NewAE.Product;
   aeAction.doAdmitHospital = true;
```

```
    //access callback object
    IAdverseEventDuplexCallback callback =
OperationContext.Current.GetCallbackChannel<IAdverseEventDuplexCallba
ck>();

    //sleep for two minutes
    Thread.Sleep(120000);

    callback.AEResult(aeAction);
  }
}
```

Now that we have a service implementation defined, we can add this to our existing WCF Service host container project. To do this, add a new .svc file and make sure the service directive points to this new service class. Finally, we have to add a new service endpoint in the configuration file associated with this service. I used the **WsDualHttpBinding** so that we can see how to do callbacks over the HTTP protocol. Our duplex service is now hosted by IIS 7.0 and available for browsing and execution.

On the client side, we need to create a class that implements the anticipated callback interface, and pass that class as context to the duplex service. First, we add a service reference to the duplex service hosted in IIS 7.0. Because this is a duplex service with a callback contract, the client proxy constructor now accepts an additional parameter:

```
public AdverseEventDuplexClient(
InstanceContext callbackInstance, string endpointConfigurationName) :
base(callbackInstance, endpointConfigurationName) {}
```

Notice that an `InstanceContext` is now part of the constructor signature. This acts as the pointer back to the client object that will be executed when the callback occurs. In our client code, we need to first create a class which implements the callback interface we defined earlier.

```
class AECallbackHandler : IAdverseEventDuplexCallback
{
  public void AEResult(AdverseEventAction aeAction)
  {
    Console.WriteLine(
      "AE result for patient {0} says it is {1} that they should be
admitted to a hospital",
      aeAction.PatientID,
      aeAction.doAdmitHospital.ToString());
    Console.ReadLine();
  }
}
```

At this point we have all that we need to call our service and receive an asynchronous response. The code needed to execute our service operation looks like this:

```
private static void CallDuplexService()
  {
Console.WriteLine("Calling duplex service ...");

//create instance context
InstanceContext context = new InstanceContext
    (new AECallbackHandler());
AdverseEventDuplexClient client = new AdverseEventDuplexClient
    (context, "AEDuplexEndpoint");
try
  {
AdverseEvent newAE = new AdverseEvent();

  newAE.PatientID = 100912;
  newAE.PhysicianID = 7543;
  newAE.Product = "Cerinob";
  newAE.ReportedBy = ReportedByType.Patient;
  newAE.Category = AECategoryType.InjectionSoreness;
  newAE.DateStarted = new DateTime(2008, 10, 29);

  client.SubmitAdverseEvent(newAE);

Console.WriteLine("Doing other things ...");

//Reader TODO; pick where to close this proxy AFTER callback
    is received
//client.Close();

Console.ReadLine();
  }
  catch (System.ServiceModel.CommunicationException) { client.Abort();
}
  catch (System.TimeoutException) { client.Abort(); }
  catch (System.Exception) { client.Abort(); throw; }
}
```

We created an InstanceContext object which references our new AECallbackHandler class and pass that object into the proxy constructor. Once we execute our SubmitAdverseEvent operation (which if you recall has isOneWay set to True), we are free to do anything else we wish while waiting for the asynchronous response message.

What is happening behind the scenes? When using the **WsDualHttpBinding**, you actually end up with your service client briefly acting as a service host as well. That is, after you call the primary operation, a temporary endpoint is hosted by our client application. The HTTP address of this endpoint is passed along with the initial request so that the service knows where to send the response to. We can demonstrate this technique in two ways. First, we can add an extended delay to our service implementation which extends beyond the standard service timeout window. This proves that we are not making a pseudo-asynchronous call, which actually relies on a synchronous pattern. The second way to verify this concept is to turn on WCF diagnostics (applied by configuring the **Diagnostics** node of the client's configuration file via the WCF Service Configuration Editor) and watch the traffic that moves between the client and service. In fact, we can observe that our service request message has its temporary callback address stored in the `ReplyTo` node sent to the service.

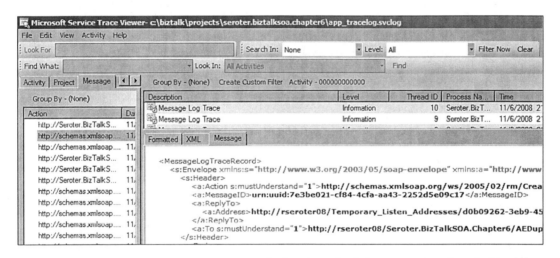

Callbacks in WCF are a very powerful way to transmit data between clients and services in both directions.

BizTalk support for client callbacks

BizTalk has mixed support for WCF-based callbacks. On the receiving side, BizTalk does not have an explicit adapter for the **WsDualHttpBinding**, but does have "hidden" support for this WCF feature. When sending messages to services, BizTalk does not support duplex communication. However, there are mechanisms for mirroring this behavior as well.

First, let's look at the scenario where BizTalk is the service consumer. This is where BizTalk Server's capabilities shine and enable the most flexible and interoperable ways for services to send data back to calling clients. What are we really trying to accomplish? In essence, we want a service to tell the client that something happened well after the initial connection was concluded. In a straight WCF scenario, the core challenge is devising a way to transmit data in a non-client-blocking and WCF-compliant way. In the loosely-coupled, server-side BizTalk environment, we have two ways to retrieve data from services.

First off, BizTalk can call a service, get back a token, and then poll for changes stored within an agreed upon repository. The token is needed so that we can poll for our unique result. Think of getting back a Federal Express tracking number when shipping a product and using that tracking number to poll their website for status updates. Within an orchestration, a loop can be set up which polls the repository (such as database, SOAP endpoint, RESTful HTTP resource) at an agreed upon interval, and only proceeds once the expected result is returned by the polling instance. This model is perfectly acceptable, but it does force the orchestration to wastefully poll when the repository has yet to be updated by the service.

The better way to receive callbacks into BizTalk is to rely on BizTalk adapters, which natively accept a "push" from the service. This could be a BizTalk WCF service endpoint which is executed by the target service, or something more rudimentary such as BizTalk listening for a file or receiving an email. In those cases, an orchestration is bound to this callback receive location and only proceeds once the data is absorbed by the BizTalk adapter. This provides the BizTalk with a wide range of options for receiving responses to asynchronous service invocation.

What about BizTalk Server 2009 acting as the service provider for others? In this case, we can also exploit all the native BizTalk adapters when sending callback information to client applications. For instance, a service client can instantiate a BizTalk orchestration and expect a response once the process is complete. Because the client does not know when BizTalk will finish the workflow, they want to exploit a transport mechanism that will reach them whether they are online or offline. In that case, the client puts an email address in the request message header, and BizTalk utilizes dynamic send ports to send the expected email acknowledgement once the long-running process is complete. You essentially have the entire BizTalk adapter stack at your disposal when choosing how to send notifications back to service clients.

How about actually using the WCF duplex bindings to receive messages into BizTalk and send a later response? On the surface, this doesn't seem particularly easy. There is no BizTalk adapter for the **WsDualHttpBinding** and no way to define a callback contract in a receive location or orchestration. Nonetheless, it is indeed possible to apply the **WsDualHttpBinding** and get duplex behavior from BizTalk Server.

First of all, we need an orchestration that contains a request/response logical port. In my case, I designed an orchestration that takes in our adverse event message, waits for three minutes, and concludes by sending an acknowledgement message. Why the three minute wait? I want to make sure that we are not simply doing a synchronous behavior that looks asynchronous so I'm using a time interval outside the boundaries of the standard service timeout.

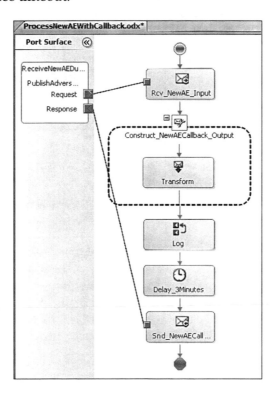

Once this orchestration is built and deployed, we next configure a physical request/response receive port and location. The receive location should use the **WCF-Custom** adapter, which in turn applies the **wsDualHttpBinding**. By using this configuration, we are choosing to host our HTTP endpoint within the in-process BizTalk host service.

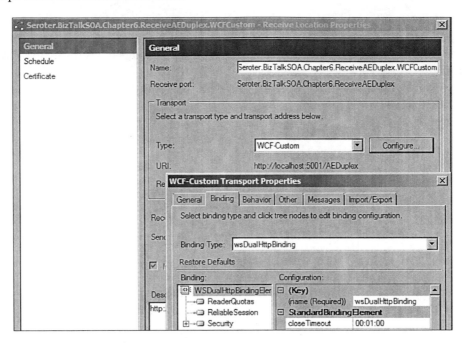

At this point, the BizTalk-based configuration is relatively complete. As I mentioned earlier, we don't have the ability to define the callback contract relationship within BizTalk. Also, the WSDL produced by the **WCF-Custom** receive location does not match the structure produced from a standard WCF service containing callback instructions. So what do we do? The easiest thing to do is define your own WCF contract that represents the BizTalk endpoint and messages.

First, we need data contract representations of the XSD messages circulating within BizTalk Server. Fortunately for us, WCF's svcutil.exe tool can take XSD schemas and generate corresponding WCF data contracts. For instance, the following command produces a class file corresponding to our adverse event schema:

```
svcutil BizTalkAdverseEvent_XML.xsd /dconly
```

Pitfall

The /dconly command in the svcutil.exe tool only works on schemas where the ElementFormDefault value is set to Qualified. Hence, this is yet another good reason to namespace qualify all of your BizTalk schemas.

Once we have class files for both our request and callback schemas, we next need the actual interface definition for the interaction. I defined one interface for the outbound request, and then a callback interface that handles the response from BizTalk.

```
[ServiceContract(
  Namespace= "http://Seroter.BizTalkSOA.Chapter6.BizTalkBits.
BizTalkAdverseEvent_XML",
  CallbackContract=typeof(IBizTalkAdverseEventDuplexCallback),
  SessionMode = SessionMode.Required)]
 public interface IBizTalkAdverseEventDuplex
 {
  [OperationContract(IsOneWay = true, Action = "PublishAdverseEvent")]
  void PublishAdverseEvent(BizTalkAdverseEvent BizTalkAdverseEvent);
    }

 public interface IBizTalkAdverseEventDuplexCallback
 {
  [XmlSerializerFormat]
  [OperationContract(IsOneWay = true, Action =
"PublishAdverseEventResponse")]
   void AEResult(BizTalkAdverseEventAction BizTalkAdverseEventAction);
}
```

What we have here is a typical service contract that supports callbacks. A few key items of note: first, the namespace applied to the service contract is the value used for the XML payload. Thus, I used the namespace value of the inbound schema. Secondly, the name of the parameter in the PublishAdverseEvent operation signature will be the name of the root node in the message. Hence, I chose to name the parameter after the data type to ensure a properly built schema. Thirdly, the callback operation requires the XmlSerializerFormat directive for its response from BizTalk. Without explicitly switching from the default DataContractSerializer, the callback parameter will not be properly interpreted. Finally, the SOAP action of the callback operation must be equal to the name of the initial operation with a Response suffix. So which values in this contract do **not** matter to BizTalk? The interface names and operation names are completely irrelevant. Feel free to use values that best describe the interaction taking place.

Before we use this contract in our client code, we should set up the appropriate endpoint in the client application's configuration. In this case, our endpoint contract is the one constructed above, the binding is the **wsDualHttpBinding**, and the address should match the value specified by our in-process receive location.

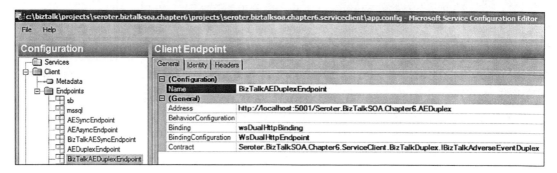

Now we can dive into our client code. Because we don't have a proxy class available, we'll need to dive into the lower-levels of WCF and interact directly with our channel. In this case, we capitalize on the `DuplexChannelFactory` object which enables us to assign the instance context containing the callback object.

```
private static void BizTalkAEDuplexEndpoint()
  {
Console.WriteLine("Calling BizTalk duplex service ...");

//create instance context
InstanceContext context = new InstanceContext
    (new BizTalkAECallbackHandler());

//need to use factory since don't have proxy available
DuplexChannelFactory<IBizTalkAdverseEventDuplex> factory =
    new DuplexChannelFactory<IBizTalkAdverseEventDuplex>
    (context, "BizTalkAEDuplexEndpoint");
IBizTalkAdverseEventDuplex channel = factory.CreateChannel();

  try
  {
BizTalkAdverseEvent newAE =
  new BizTalkAdverseEvent();
  newAE.PatientID = "100912";
  newAE.PhysicianID = "7543";
  newAE.Product = "Cerinob";
  newAE.ReportedBy = "Patient";
  newAE.Category = "InjectionSoreness";
  newAE.DateStarted = new DateTime(2008, 10, 29).ToShortDateString();
  newAE.Description = "none";

channel.PublishAdverseEvent(newAE);
```

```
//Reader TODO; pick where to close this proxy AFTER callback is received
//((IClientChannel)channel).Close();
//factory.Close();
Console.WriteLine("Doing other things ...");
Console.ReadLine();
    }
catch (System.ServiceModel.CommunicationException)
    { ((IClientChannel)channel).Abort(); }
catch (System.TimeoutException) { ((IClientChannel)channel).Abort(); }
catch (System.Exception) { ((IClientChannel)channel).Abort(); throw; }
}
```

Much like our earlier duplex example, we have a class (`BizTalkAECallbackHandler`), which implements our callback contract and deals with the operation invocation in the proper manner.

So is this it? Not quite. When we transmit a message from the client, our BizTalk bus throws an exception. Because we are not using WCF message contracts (which are typically created by service references) but rather data contracts to make our request, the payload is wrapped with the operation name (`PublishAdverseEvent`). The problem is, BizTalk Server doesn't have any message type or subscriptions that match that root value.

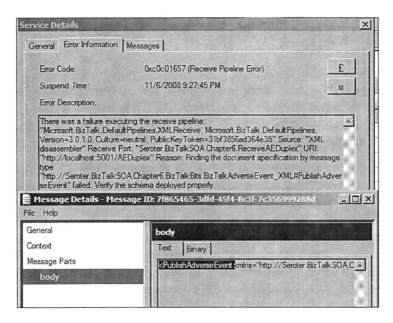

This is where a very handy WCF adapter capability comes to the rescue. If you can recall, the **Messages** tab of the adapter configuration enables us to specify where to find the body of the inbound message. Typically we keep the default value of **Body,** which simply yanks out the structure contained in the SOAP message body element. For this situation, we need to dig a bit deeper and pull out the node beneath the SOAP body's root element. This is accomplished by setting the **Path** value, which in our case looks like this:

```
/*[local-name()='PublishAdverseEvent']/*[local-name()='BizTalkAdverse
Event']
```

 Notice that the parameter in this adapter is called **Path** and not "XPath". This is on purpose. This XML search string only works in a forward fashion so the complete XPath universe is not available. That is, you cannot execute XPath commands that take a gander up and down the XML node tree.

With this change in place, we can now publish messages to BizTalk, and rely on the receive location to maintain the necessary duplex session while waiting for the orchestration to respond. While fairly hidden from public view, BizTalk does indeed support this interesting WCF binding and makes it possible to design rich callback scenarios between WCF service clients and BizTalk Server.

Using queues within asynchronous scenarios

Queue-based technology is an underrepresented but powerful way to exchange data and events between disconnected clients. WCF has full support for Microsoft's queuing implementation (MSMQ) and BizTalk has an adapter specifically targeted at the **netMsmqBinding** WCF binding.

Why introduce yet another layer in your service communication? BizTalk has queuing logic, so what benefit do we get by having our service client send a message to an external queue that BizTalk acts upon? First of all, you get delivery assurance in the case of the service being offline. As you are not travelling over an inherently unreliable transport like HTTP, you can be confident that your message will arrive only once at its destination because of the intermediary queue. Also, a queue enables you to implement a level of soft throttling by allowing the queue to get pummeled by inbound requests but allow the service to process them at its leisure.

What we will demonstrate here is how to put MSMQ on both ends of a BizTalk solution. That is, the client application calls a BizTalk WCF endpoint that uses MSMQ as its transport, and when processing is complete, BizTalk sends its concluding message to a service over a MSMQ channel.

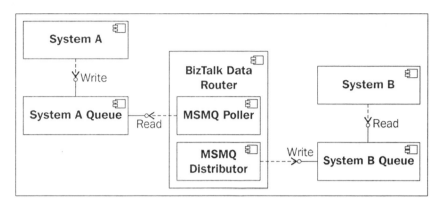

As with all other WCF bindings, the developer's interactions with MSMQ are fairly transparent and do not actively impact the client code. A developer does not need to understand any of the plumbing behind MSMQ and only need to flip the appropriate binding switches to use the queuing transport.

Before building any BizTalk bits, how about we create the actual queues that our solution will use. To access the MSMQ panel in Windows Server 2008, we visit the **Server Manager**, expand the **Features** node, and highlight the **Messaging Queuing** node. Here we can create two private transactional queues that will house our information while in transit between client and service.

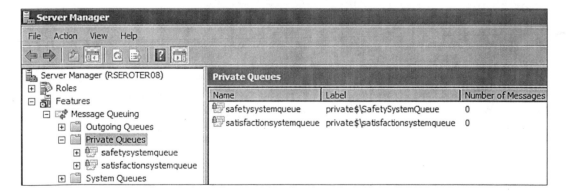

Now we erect the terminating service, which publishes a final acknowledgement message to a dedicated queue. For our scenario, we have a customer satisfaction system that is interested in knowing when adverse events have been resolved. This system wants to send surveys to those who have interacted with our company and gauge their opinions of our efficiency. The first step to building our service requires building our interface contract. We will keep it fairly simple.

```
[ServiceContract(Namespace = "http://Seroter.BizTalkSOA.Chapter6")]
public interface ISatisfactionSystem
{
    [OperationContract(IsOneWay = true)]
    void ProcessClosedAE(ClosedAE closedAE);
}

[DataContract(Namespace = "http://Seroter.BizTalkSOA.Chapter6")]
public class ClosedAE
{
    [DataMember]
    public string AEID { get; set; }
    [DataMember]
    public string Product { get; set; }
    [DataMember]
    public string ResolutionDescription { get; set; }
    [DataMember]
    public DateTime CloseDate { get; set; }
}
```

I've highlighted the fact that service operations used on MSMQ service endpoints must be designated with a one-way messaging pattern. This is the rare example of endpoint selection playing a primary role in contract design.

Critical point:

Earlier I mentioned that BizTalk Server 2009 does not support truly asynchronous services that have their IsOneWay flag set to true. That's not entirely true. WCF service contracts associated with the MSMQ transport require that the IsOneWay flag is equal to true, and BizTalk readily supports that. Hence, unlike other WCF bindings, the MSMQ binding requires you to be aware of which transport you are planning to use when designing the contract.

Next, our contract needs to be implemented by an actual service. In this case, our service will simply write a notification in the machine's event log when a message has been received from the queue.

```
class SatisfactionSystemService : ISatisfactionSystem
{
    public void ProcessClosedAE(ClosedAE closedAE)
    {
        System.Diagnostics.EventLog.WriteEntry("Satisfaction System
Service", "Adverse Event Closed Event Received for case " + closedAE.
AEID);
    }
}
```

Finally, we have to host our service. In this case, we can once again exploit our existing WCF Service project and add a new individual service (.svc file) to it. After this is in place with the appropriate service directive, we simply need to append a new service endpoint in our configuration file.

The MSMQ service endpoint is configured using the **netMsmqBinding** with the path to the private queue as the service address. As we are hosting our service within IIS 7.0, we do not need a separate MEX endpoint for MSMQ, but rather, can simply apply a standard HTTP metadata behavior to our service.

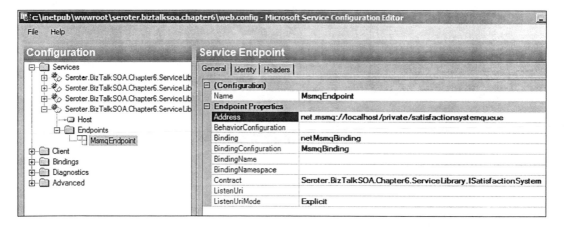

The final part of this service is the deployment. After building the service, we should confirm that the **Net.Msmq Listener Adapter** Windows service is running, as this is what the **Windows Process Activation Service (WAS)** in IIS 7.0 uses to read from our queue.

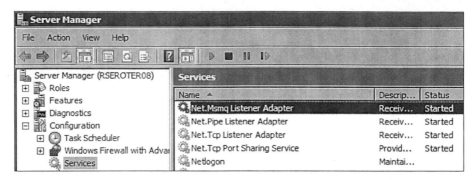

Lastly, we need to specifically enable the MSMQ protocol for our web application. This is accomplished by visiting the **Advanced Settings** of our application in IIS and ensuring that our **Enabled Protocols** contains both **http** and **net.msmq**. We can validate that our configuration is successful by visiting our service URL and seeing our service page displayed.

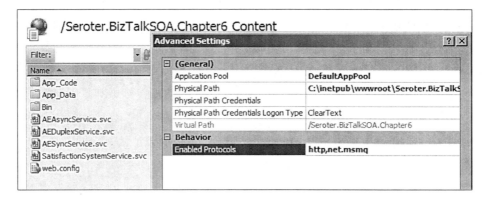

Let's get started building the BizTalk pieces of our application. We start with a new event-style schema representing an adverse event that is considered "resolved" by the primary safety system. The schema contains a few key nodes, which explain the resolution information that the subscriber need to update their system.

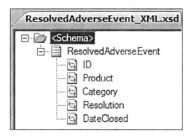

In order to get the artifacts necessary for BizTalk to consume this service, we should choose to **Add Generated Items** to our project and then choose to **Consume WCF Service**. Here we point to the WSDL endpoint associated with our service and end up with the schemas and binding files we sought. We need to map our resolved adverse event from the format received by our service to the structure expected by our destination service.

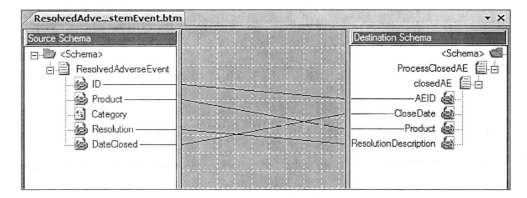

After building and deploying this sample, we need to assemble the necessary messaging ports from within the BizTalk Administration Console. First, import the **BizTalk WCF Service Publishing Wizard**-generated binding to produce our concluding **WCF-NetMsmq** adapter send port. After adding both a "message-type"-based subscription and BizTalk map to the send port, we build a simple FILE receive location to test our destination service. To prove that BizTalk successfully publishes to the queue, we should turn off the IIS 7.0 application pool associated with our service so that the messages are not automatically extracted from the queue by the service. If everything was set up correctly, we should be able to pick up a message, and see BizTalk drop it to the designated queue.

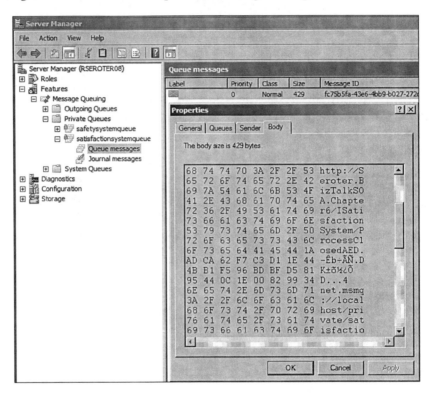

Now that we have BizTalk successfully acting as a MSMQ service consumer, it's time to complete our scenario and promote BizTalk to the status of MSMQ service provider as well. Lucky for us, this requires no additional development activities. Instead, we can switch our inbound receive location from being FILE-based to **WCF-NetMsmq**-based. In this case, we configure the in-process adapter to point to the private queue created earlier in this section.

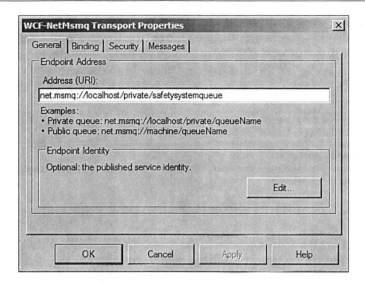

Because we want our upstream service client to interrogate our BizTalk WCF endpoint for metadata, we should generate an IIS-hosted endpoint, which reveals our service contract. To do this, launch the **BizTalk WCF Service Publishing Wizard** and generate a metadata endpoint for our existing **WCF-NetMsmq** receive location.

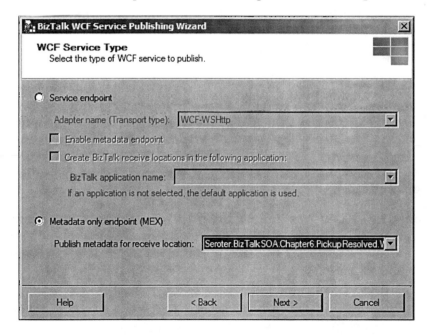

Via the wizard, we want to expose a service with a one-way operation that will publish a message to the queue. If we are successful, a client application will be able to reference the MEX endpoint and import all the objects and configurations necessary to call the BizTalk hosted service. Remember that our MEX WSDL, while hosted as an HTTP endpoint, should show a service address that is MSMQ-based.

```
- <wsdl:service name="SatisfactionSystemService">
  - <wsdl:port name="MsmqEndpoint" binding="tns:MsmqEndpoint">
      <soap12:address location="net.msmq://localhost/private/satisfactionsystemqueue" />
    - <wsa10:EndpointReference>
        <wsa10:Address>net.msmq://localhost/private/satisfactionsystemqueue</wsa10:Address>
      </wsa10:EndpointReference>
    </wsdl:port>
  </wsdl:service>
```

If you recall from earlier BizTalk + WCF discussions, we discovered that a BizTalk receive location needs to be in an **Enabled** status in order for the service to be online. Once again, MSMQ is an exception. Because there is a layer between the client and BizTalk endpoint, our BizTalk receive location (or BizTalk itself!) can be offline and the client application can still confidently distribute messages to the service. Once the BizTalk receive location returns to an active state, messages are read from the queue.

BizTalk has very strong support for MSMQ, and in scenarios with very disconnected clients possessing volatile uptime or specific throttling requirements, an intermediary queue offers a convenient way to reliably transfer data between systems.

Summary

Asynchronous patterns offer a valuable means for interacting with services. While synchronous services are very easy to use and excel at functions with immediate responses, these types of services also cause long-term scalability issues and require client blocking. Asynchronous services promote a more event-driven design and the technological advances in callback mechanisms mean that we can embrace this pattern with confidence.

In this chapter, we've seen how BizTalk Server 2009 exploits asynchronous messaging through its adapters and orchestration. Coming up next, we look at how to create rich service-oriented orchestrations that can take advantage of the rich data flowing through the BizTalk bus.

7
Orchestration Patterns

Of all the things I've done, the most vital is coordinating the talents of those who work for us and pointing them toward a certain goal.
-Walt Disney

So far, we've looked at how to use BizTalk Server to design both service endpoints and contracts, as well as exploit the powerful BizTalk messaging bus to support asynchronous messaging patterns. Now it's time to investigate how to incorporate service implementation patterns using BizTalk Server's orchestration engine. While an optional component of any BizTalk solution, orchestration enables a rich set of scenarios that pure messaging-only solutions are incapable of accommodating. Similar to the previous chapters in this book, this discussion will assume a base knowledge of BizTalk orchestration so that we can jump right into the implementation of occasionally complex concepts.

In this chapter, you will learn:

- Why orchestration matters
- "What it means for an orchestration to utilize "MessageBox direct binding"
- How to take advantage of dynamic service ports
- The way to support multiple initiating message exchange patterns from within a single orchestration
- How to chain orchestrations together in a loosely-coupled fashion
- The role of orchestration transactions in compensating service exceptions
- How to construct a basic mechanism for doing complex event processing

Why orchestration?

At its core, orchestration is an executable business process that acts upon messages passing through the service bus. In the BizTalk world, orchestration has both a design-time and runtime aspect. At design-time, a developer uses a predefined palette of activities, which are linked together to form a business process. The runtime orchestration engine is a server service which coordinates all aspects of orchestration execution ranging from starting up and terminating orchestrations to load balancing and monitoring the orchestration processing health.

In many cases, a purely messaging-oriented solution is exactly what our situation calls for. However, we often need the flexibility to introduce a long-running, stateful interception of messages which may contain business logic, control flow, data processing, exception handling and transactions. This is the value of orchestration. What is the value of orchestration in a service-oriented architecture? Let's look at some of the key value-add scenarios:

- **Service abstraction**: One of the greatest ways to exploit orchestration is to create new services by aggregating existing ones. Instead of requiring clients to call a chained series of system services in order to accomplish an overarching business task, we can create an orchestration which provides a single interface to the clients and orchestrates the set of system services itself. Even if there is only a single system service, we can use orchestration to provide a more abstract and generic interface that hides system-specific service details.

- **Orchestration as service**: Business processes can be decomposed from large flows to more modular, reusable bits. Instead of creating a monolithic orchestration which rigidly enforces a complex business process, we can look for opportunities to break that process apart and in essence, create new orchestration "services" which perform encapsulated, discrete tasks. These orchestrations can be reused by other processes or service interfaces, thus maximizing our investment in process modelling.

- **Orchestration containing process, not logic**: It may be tempting to enclose logical calculations alongside the process flow that makes up an orchestration. However, orchestration is not a replacement for writing services and components that perform business algorithms. We should treat orchestration as the coordinator of a process, not as the origin of all information needed by the process. This means that flow control calculations should be externalized in segmented locations such as the Business Rules Engine, external services, or custom-built components whenever possible. An orchestration isn't yet another place to stash code, but rather a mechanism for executing agile business processes. However, a case may arise where a bit of business logic is appropriate in an orchestration, so don't treat this pronouncement as a hard-and-fast rule, but rather, as a broad recommendation!

What is MessageBox direct binding?

The easiest way to link orchestration with messaging endpoints is to create logical ports in orchestrations and bind them to physical ports at runtime. A developer using this technique will know for sure that an orchestration will exchange messages with the appropriate ports. However, this mechanism of orchestration communication is more point-to-point oriented than event driven. What if relevant messages for an orchestration could arrive via multiple receive ports? Or how about trying to anticipate all the possible parties interested in a message that your orchestration is sending out?

The tight coupling produced by binding orchestration ports to physical ports is not the most service-oriented way to design orchestration communication. Instead, MessageBox direct binding is the cleanest way to sever the one-to-one relationship between the messaging and orchestration architectural layers. The way it works is that the "activating" receive shape that instantiates the orchestration maintains a subscription based on the message type in combination with any "filter" applied to the receive shape. ANY message that hits the MessageBox and meets this subscription criterion will get delivered to this orchestration. For any "non-activating" receive shape (such as receive shapes present elsewhere in the orchestration), the subscription is based on the message type and a correlation set made up of additional subscription attributes.

The greatest benefit of this technique is that orchestrations can absorb messages that match specific data criteria instead of focusing on the data publisher. When sending messages on MessageBox direct bound ports, we get the benefit of broadcasting messages without identifying an individual target. As we'll see later in this chapter, there are cases where you want to use MessageBox direct binding but still need to target a specific consumer and this is entirely possible.

How do you apply MessageBox direct binding? When creating a new orchestration receive port, you get the option of choosing a target binding. In the book so far, we've typically used a **Specify later** binding, which allows us to hook up logical and physical ports at deployment time. However, notice that we also have the option to choose **Direct** binding from this orchestration port creation wizard.

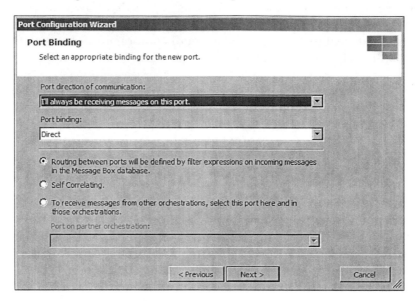

When creating orchestration send ports, we get a similar experience when choosing direct binding.

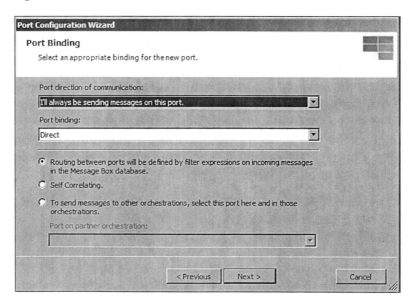

For orchestrations that use direct bound ports, you will see a much different "binding" view in the BizTalk Administration Console. Specifically, you'll notice that there are no ports to bind! The only activity required is the binding of the orchestration to a specific host.

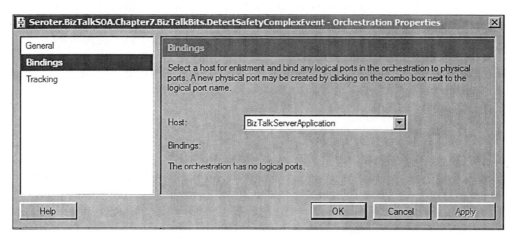

Throughout this chapter, we'll make heavy use of MessageBox direct bound ports in order to demonstrate this technique in a variety of scenarios.

Pitfall

What's the downside of MessageBox direct bound ports? For one, careless usage can lead to unanticipated messages reaching your orchestration or worse, infinite loops. Consider an "activating" receive which is direct bound solely on the message type (i.e., no additional filter applied). If you decide to send this same message out of your orchestration later on (via ANY type of port binding), you will unexpectedly find that this original orchestration starts up all over again! The proper application of direct binding requires forethought of subscription criteria and situational modelling of instantiation scenarios.

Using dynamic service ports

In all the BizTalk solutions we've built so far in this book, the focus was on static ports with URIs set immediately after the code was deployed. However, there exist a number of legitimate cases where BizTalk does not know where to distribute a message until additional runtime-only context is provided. For example, when you configure a send port with an SMTP adapter in BizTalk Server, you are required to explicitly provide the recipient's email address. Any time this port is invoked, that particular email address is applied. But what if the corresponding message could be emailed to any of a number of addresses? You could choose to set up a series of static send ports and summon each one individually based on decision logic from the orchestration. However, this is not a particularly flexible mechanism as it requires changes to the orchestration whenever an email target is added or removed. A better strategy is to apply dynamic ports and perform a runtime query of the endpoint address. We could look up the email recipient (via Business Rules, custom component, message value) and set that value in a single spot within the orchestration. When changes to the recipient list are necessary, the only thing that must undergo a change is the user lookup mechanism and not the orchestration itself.

Defining the service

Let's demonstrate how this would work in a situation with services. As we saw in the previous chapter on asynchronous programming, a service client may invoke a service and expect a response well after the initial connection has been closed. To truly be loosely coupled and support multiple callers, our solution should not hard-code the return address of the service inside the invoked orchestration. Instead, to encourage reusability, this orchestration should extract a reply to value from the message itself and dynamically set the return destination that it will use.

For this scenario, BizTalk will accept data in, process it, and send a notification to an awaiting service when processing is complete. Our first step is to define these services that are anticipating a message from BizTalk. There is a simple contract which expects a status update to be sent to the service endpoint.

```
[ServiceContract (Namespace="http://Seroter.BizTalkSOA.Chapter7")]
public interface IAdverseEvent
{
  [OperationContract]
  void UpdateAEStatus(AdverseEventStatus status);
}
[DataContract]
 public class AdverseEventStatus
 {
   [DataMember]
   public string AE_ID { get; set; }
   [DataMember]
   public AEStatusCode StatusCode { get; set; }
   [DataMember]
   public string Comments { get; set; }
}
public enum AEStatusCode
{
   Received,
   Pending,
```

```
        DataError,
          InReview,
          Resolved
    }
```

I've gone ahead and created a pair of service classes which implement this interface and write differing messages to the machine's **Application Event Log**.

```
public class AdverseEventService : IAdverseEvent
{
  public void UpdateAEStatus(AdverseEventStatus status)
  {
    EventLog.WriteEntry(
      "AE Client Application #1 (HTTP)",
      "Status for AE " + status.AE_ID + " is " +
        status.StatusCode.ToString());
  }
}
```

Next we need to create a **WCF Service** Website project in Visual Studio.NET and define a pair of .svc files whose Service directive points to the service class(es) we just created. Our new service requires a valid application configuration, so I created service definitions that utilized an HTTP endpoint for one service and a **NetTcpBinding** endpoint for the other. As you may recall from the previous chapter, we do not need to specify an address (or base address) for our services when they are hosted by IIS 7.0. I also added a metadata behavior to both so that BizTalk can interrogate the service for its contract.

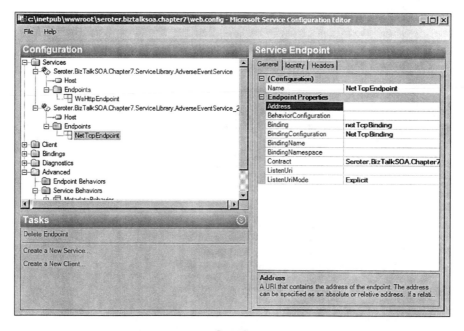

Configuring IIS/WAS to host the service

Once our service has been successfully built, we have to remember to add the **NetTcp** protocol to the IIS web directory. Remember that we do this by viewing the **Advanced Settings** of our virtual directory and setting the **Enabled Protocols** to the desired values.

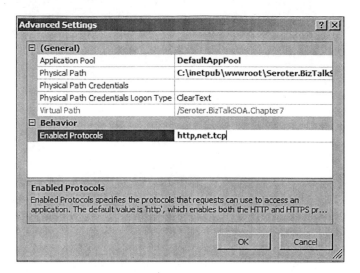

Building the BizTalk solution

Once these services are in place, we should next build the actual message that our BizTalk process will accept. Throughout this chapter, I will be using a modified version of the **Adverse Event** message we created in the previous chapter. This version of the message is structured as so:

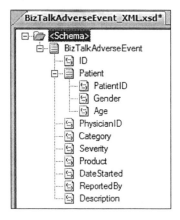

For this scenario, I've designed a new schema (`BizTalkAdverseEventWithCallback`) that includes the `BizTalkAdverseEvent` schema. This schema is comprised of a `Header` and `Message` element. The `Header` is made up of values BizTalk requires to successfully execute a callback, while the `Message` record is made up of the included `BizTalkAdverseEvent` schema.

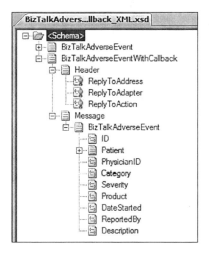

Notice that I've distinguished the `Header` fields, so that I can easily extract them from within my orchestration. Now we're ready to build an orchestration that takes in this message and sends a response to the service interface specified in the message header.

After accepting the initial `BizTalkAdverseEventWithCallback` message into the orchestration, we next set a series of orchestration variables equal to the callback attributes present in the inbound message.

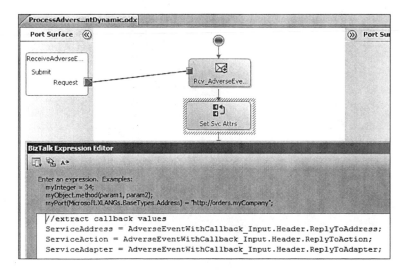

Before we can continue, we must auto-generate the items needed to call the service. Now, because every destination service will conform to the single WCF contract, we can point to either of the two services we built, get its service schema, and be confident that we can send this message to any possible endpoint that applies the same service contract. We utilize the **BizTalk WCF Service Consuming Wizard** to query our service and extract the necessary files. Once we have our schema generated, we should distinguish the StatusCode element so that we are able to set its value from within the orchestration itself.

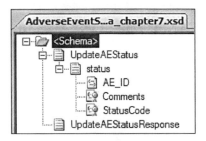

A BizTalk map is required in order to instantiate this service response message. In our case, we only need to map the ID of the adverse event from the source schema to the destination.

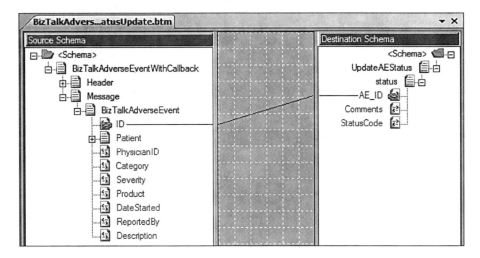

Back in our orchestration, we drop a **Construct**, **Transform**, and **Assignment** shape onto the design surface. Directly below that trifecta, we should add a **Send** shape that is responsible for sending our service response message. Before configuring our message construction operations, we need to create the dynamic port that the orchestration will use to transmit the final message. Add a new configured port to the orchestration and on the **Port Binding** tab of the wizard, our direction should be set to **I'll always be sending messages on this port** and the port binding set to **Dynamic**. When you have a dynamic port in an orchestration, you are expected to set the address of the endpoint before the port is executed.

Returning to our **Construct** shape, we set the **Message Constructed** property of the **Construct** shape equal to the message type of the service response message. Within the **Transform** shape, we pick the map we just created above. The real fun happens in the **Assignment** shape that is directly below the **Transform** shape. Here I first set the StatusCode element of the outbound message, and set four critical context attributes. First, we set WCF-specific attributes WCF.Action and WCF.SecurityMode to values that match the service endpoint. Next, we set transport-specific attributes including the actual endpoint address and which adapter BizTalk should use.

```
AdverseEventStatus_Output.parameters.status.StatusCode = "Received";

//ServiceAction is the orchestration variable
AdverseEventStatus_Output(WCF.Action) = ServiceAction;

AdverseEventStatus_Output(WCF.SecurityMode) = "None";

//uses orchestration variables
SendDynamicAEStatusUpdatePort(Microsoft.XLANGs.BaseTypes.Address) =
ServiceAddress;

SendDynamicAEStatusUpdatePort(Microsoft.XLANGs.BaseTypes.
TransportType) = ServiceAdapter;
```

You may not be as familiar with setting the `Microsoft.XLANGs.BaseTypes.`
`TransportType` attribute as typically, dynamic port adapters are determined based
on the prefix contained in the endpoint URI. For instance, setting the `Microsoft.`
`XLANGs.BaseTypes.Address` equal to `FILE://C:\temp` or `mailto:user@domain.`
`com` enables BizTalk to automatically determine which adapter to use (in this
example, FILE and SMTP). For HTTP-based endpoints, simply prefixing a URI with
`http://localhost/MyService` does not specify which adapter (SOAP, HTTP, WCF)
should be applied. Hence, we explicitly added a directive to help BizTalk choose the
proper endpoint adapter.

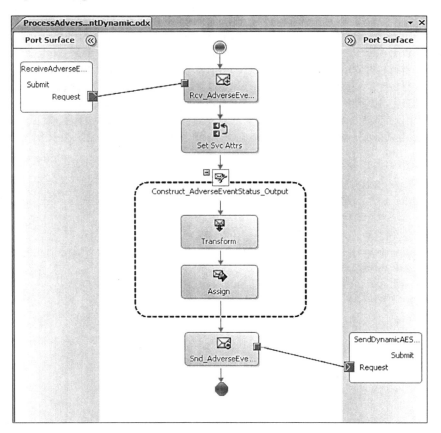

Configuring the BizTalk solution

Once our BizTalk project is completed (including the addition of an orchestration
receive port to accept inbound messages), we deploy it. During the deployment
process, a new auto-generated dynamic send port is created. We should confirm
this by visiting the **Send Ports** section of our application in the BizTalk
Administration Console.

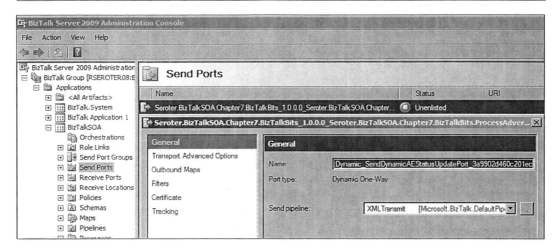

After creating a valid input receive location, we should send instance files into our orchestration and confirm that our two different service endpoints get called depending on the header values of the input message. Sending in multiple instance files (two with HTTP callbacks and one with a TCP callback address) yields the following result in my Event Log:

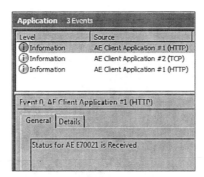

Dynamic ports are a great way to loosely couple the endpoints from your orchestration and rely on message-based context data (or external lookups) to determine the exact destination.

Supporting dual initiating message exchange patterns

Back in Chapter 4, we looked at Message Exchange Patterns (MEP) and evaluated differences between them. We concluded that asynchronous patterns can be more service-oriented and loosely coupled than synchronous patterns. However, there are cases where you want a single business process to accommodate invocation by either mechanism. In certain scenarios, the caller has no interest in the outcome, but in other situations, the caller requires resolution about the service outcome. You could choose to build two distinct processes, which support each distinct MEP, but that is fairly inefficient and challenging to maintain. What if we want to build a BizTalk orchestration with the least amount of effort required that can be invoked either synchronously or asynchronously?

Building the BizTalk solution

In keeping with our "drug product safety" theme, this scenario works with a "product complaint" schema. A product complaint is typically an issue that a customer has with the packaging, appearance, or reaction to the drug. The schema we are using looks like this:

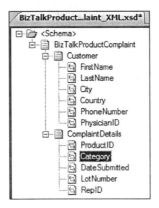

The follow-up message for a product complaint submission should contain a tracking number, assigned case agent identifier and a status.

Now, let's build the orchestration. Because we are going to support both asynchronous (one-way) and synchronous (two-way) service clients, our orchestration needs to be even more loosely coupled from its endpoints than normal. That is, instead of binding to a specific receive port at runtime, we are going to use MessageBox direct binding in order to abstract away the service endpoint as much as possible.

The orchestration begins by receiving a product complaint and executing a bit of pre-defined logic. In our amazingly simplistic case, our robust product complaint handling consists of a message being written to the Application Event Log. I can only assure you that actual biotechnology companies apply a bit more rigor to these types of input.

We must connect this **Receive** shape to an orchestration port whose **Port Binding** tab is set to **I'll always be receiving messages on this port** and its port binding is **Direct** with **Routing between ports will be defined by filter expressions on incoming messages in the Message Box database**.

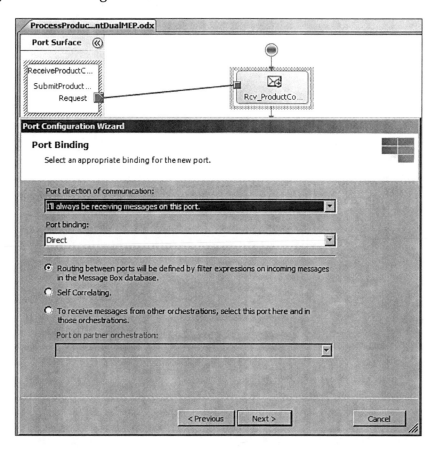

The question is, how do we know that this orchestration consumer is waiting for a response (synchronous) or not? Lucky for us, the BizTalk receive port stamps messages with a unique set of properties when those message are participating in request-reply operations. At the end of our orchestration, we have a **Decision** shape, where we check to see if this orchestration was executed by a synchronous caller. The following conditional statement is the basis for the decision:

```
BTS.EpmRRCorrelationToken exists ProductComplaint_Input
```

The EpmRRCorrelationToken is what the MessageBox uses to associate a response message with the port instance waiting to send a result to a caller. I exploited the exists orchestration function which returns a Boolean indicating whether the particular context property is present in the designated message.

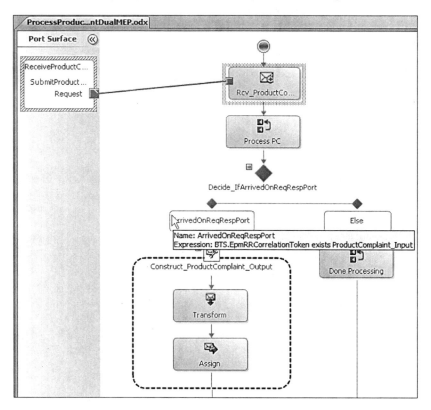

So if the message did arrive via a request-reply messaging port, the lefthand side of the **Decision** shape gets executed. After transforming the `BizTalkProductComplaint` message to the corresponding `BizTalkProductComplaintResponse` message, we have a bit more manipulation of the message left to do. Specifically, we must copy all the context values from the source message to the destination (which copies the `EpmRRCorrelationToken` into the target message) and set the Boolean `BTS.RouteDirectToTP` to `true`. The `RouteDirectToTP` is used by the MessageBox to look for messages to route back to request-reply ports and the `EpmRRCorrelationToken` directs the MessageBox to WHICH port is waiting for a result.

```
ProductComplaint_Output(*) = ProductComplaint_Input(*);
ProductComplaint_Output(BTS.RouteDirectToTP) = true;
```

Finally, we send the response message out of the orchestration using a MessageBox direct bound port. We want to make sure that all the context properties necessary for request-reply routing are properly promoted in our outbound message. The only way to ensure this is to apply a "forced promotion" trick. That is, create a new correlation set that contains: `BTS.CorrelationToken`, `BTS.EpmRRCorrelationToken`, `BTS.IsRequestResponse`, `BTS.ReqRespTransmitPipelineID`, and `BTS.RouteDirectToTP`. On the send port that distributes this outbound message to the MessageBox, set the **Initializing Correlation Sets** to the set we just created. By doing this, we can be assured that these routing-critical values are visible to the BizTalk engine.

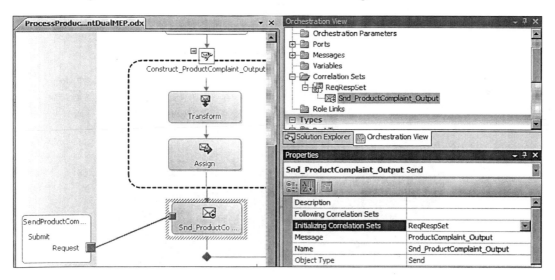

Our orchestration is now built to support dual invocation, but let's prove it. First, we need to generate two service endpoints via the **BizTalk WCF Service Publishing Wizard**. These services are built using the **Publish schemas as WCF service** option and are identical except for the fact that one service expects a response while the other does not.

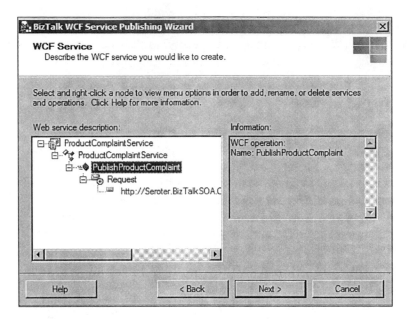

Configuring the BizTalk solution

After deploying our BizTalk project (and binding the orchestration to the target host), we are able to test our orchestration. To do so, I've created a new Visual Studio.NET console application that maintains service references to both the one-way and two-way BizTalk WCF service endpoints. When calling both services, we observe the following results:

```
file:///C:/BizTalk/Projects/Seroter.BizTalkSOA.Chapter7/Seroter.B
Calling one-way service ...
Call complete ...

Calling two-way service ...
Call complete ... response status is Received
```

Sure enough, we've enabled our orchestration to support dual MEPs while not requiring us to butcher our business process or create redundant orchestrations. Note that we could have also decided to put an abstraction layer above our business process orchestration in the form of wrapper orchestrations, which each handle synchronous and asynchronous callers, respectively. This pattern would eliminate any hint of routing logic from the core orchestration, but would also introduce additional layers to manage.

Chaining orchestrations using business rules

In Chapter 4, we talked about how to chain orchestrations together. The simplest way to do so (from a developer's perspective) is to use the **Start Orchestration** or **Call Orchestration** shapes and explicitly invoke one orchestration from another. While this strategy is easy to develop and allows for transfer of more than just message data (such as variables, ports), it's also a very tightly-coupled and inflexible way to connect stages of a business process. Ideally, you should pursue a route of Message Box direct binding which enables fully encapsulated, reusable orchestrations that can be invoked by a wide number of clients (for example, services or other orchestrations).

What if your business process consists of a number of discrete steps that are subject to change over time? That is, let's assume a process by which an inbound "adverse event" must pass through a set of business logic and human review stages prior to commitment into the enterprise system. As I see it, you have three possible solutions to this situation:

- Put the entire process into a single orchestration. On the plus side, there is only one artifact to maintain, but on the downside, this process must maintain a rigid structure with no capacity to accommodate isolated change.

- Use the **Call Orchestration** or **Start Orchestration** shapes to link each separated stage of the process in a sequential manner. This is a better option because we have isolated each process into more management pieces, but we are still engaged in tight-coupling with less optimal means for supporting a reordered or enhanced sequence of steps.

- Completely wall off each orchestration from the next and rely on MessageBox direct binding and a dynamic lookup to choose what the next step of the process should be invoked. Each orchestration acts as a distinct service with clear boundaries which awaits a chunky message consisting of the entire context needed to make a decision. This model also supports common "repair and resubmit" patterns where messages that fail at a discrete step can exit the process, undergo correction, and return to the flow.

Building the BizTalk solution

Let's look at how to construct this optimal third option. Our adverse event process currently contains three steps:

1. Receive and log the inbound adverse event.

2. Apply a set of business rules to categorize the adverse event.

3. Evaluate the current work queue and assign the proper case agent to follow up on the adverse event.

As we analyze the business process further, we may find that additional steps may be injected into this flow, or the flow may become less sequential and have the option of taking a variety of twists and turns.

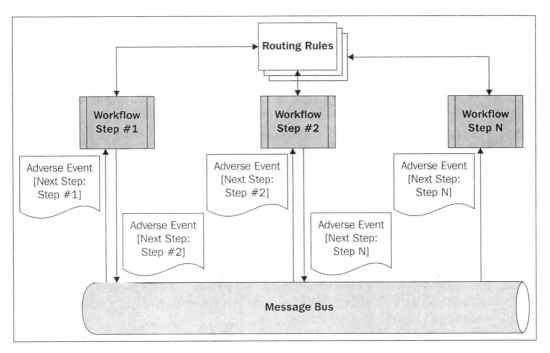

First, we need the schema which not only describes the adverse event, but also contains the means for routing this adverse event from orchestration to orchestration. Similar to the earlier demonstration of dynamic ports, our message should be comprised of a header and a body. In this case, the `header` is actually the message bus routing instructions, and the body is the included (reused) adverse event schema.

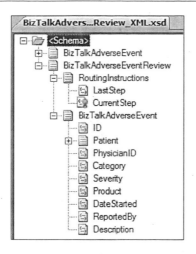

Now it would be foolish to expect our service client to know or care about the internal routing procedures of our BizTalk solution, so we don't want to reveal this particular (non-abstract) schema to the outside world. Instead, our process should accept the standard adverse event message, and a map responsible for instantiating our routing-friendly message should be applied at the receive port tier. This map sets the **CurrentStep** routing instruction to the first stage of adverse event processing (**Initial Receive**).

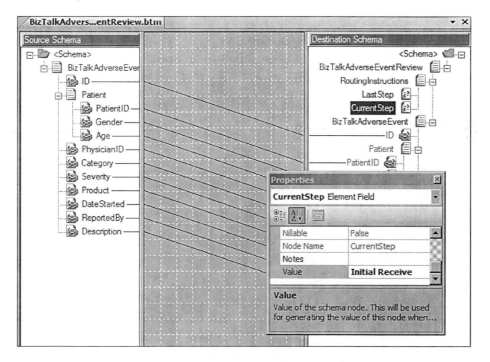

Because we are using MessageBox direct binding to control process flow, we will need to promote the routing instruction node expected by our orchestration filters.

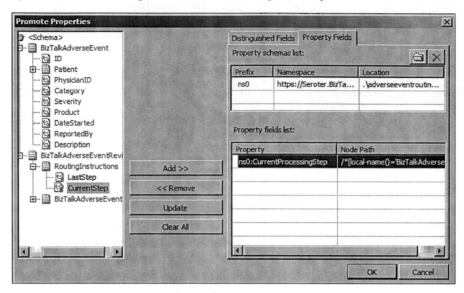

Before we start building our set of orchestrations, we need to devise a scheme for electing which step to execute after the current one. We want this information stored outside the orchestration(s) itself so that future changes to the flow do not require updates to existing components. This scenario cries out for the BizTalk Business Rules Engine (BRE). The BRE enables us to store logical conditions in a centrally managed and accessible storage medium that can be updated independently of components that rely on it.

Upon opening the Microsoft Business Rules Composer application, we choose which artifacts serve as the "facts" for our rule set. In this case, the `BizTalkAdverseEventReview` schema has all the information we need. I like using friendly references to my XML nodes instead of XPath statements, so I went ahead and created a BRE vocabulary that replaces XPath references with English language snippets.

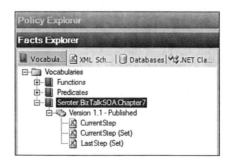

Next, we must define the rules that BizTalk will apply when a particular stage of the broader workflow process is reached. In this simple case, I look at what the previous state was, and set the next one. In a real-world example, you'd most likely apply a bit of additional logic to see which particular path you need to follow instead of blindly and sequentially moving from one stage to the next. From the image below, you can see that I have defined three rules that shuffle the adverse event between the available process steps.

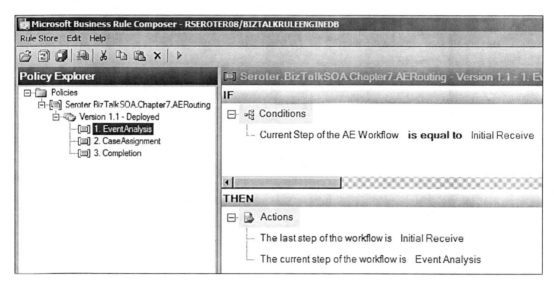

The great thing about the BRE is that the individual rules that make up a rule set are completely hidden from the calling application. A consumer of rules may only invoke a policy and does not explicitly identify which rules in a policy to call. In this manner, it would be amazingly simple to reorder existing steps or add completely new ones while not requiring any changes to rule consumers.

Now that we have our data schema, a property schema and a set of routing rules, we are ready to build the orchestrations that make up our overarching business process. In the first orchestration, the topmost **Receive** shape should accept the `BizTalkAdverseEventReview` message type and have a filter which restricts the receipt to only messages set for an **Initial Receive** state. We immediately connect this shape to an orchestration receive port that is set to receive direct bound messages.

After walking through any logic specific to this processing step, we must next call our BRE policy in order to stamp this message with its updated routing instructions. While it is possible to call the BRE from code, it's much simpler to apply the **Call Rules** orchestration shape and choose the policy and corresponding input message.

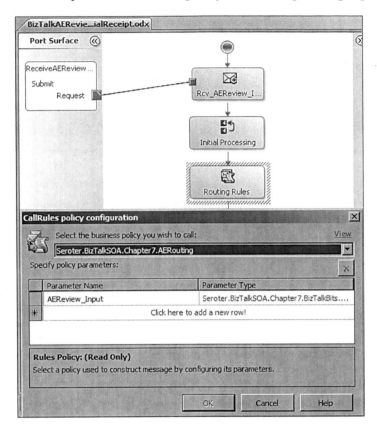

Pitfall

Be aware that by passing a message through the BRE, the original message is actually copied and a "new" message is returned. This is important because all pre-existing context values are stripped from the messages departing the **Call Rules** shape. If you had a value in the message context that is required by downstream consumers, make sure to add those values back to the message before shipping it out of the orchestration.

Finally, we send the message back to the MessageBox via a direct bound send port. The additional two orchestrations all closely resemble this one, except for two key differences: each has a distinct `filter` on the activating receive shape, and each writes a different message to my **Application Event Log**. When we build and deploy this solution, we still must create an initial on-ramp receive location to accept messages into the bus and have to remember to apply our routing-friendly map to the appropriate receive port. When everything is in place, we send in an adverse event message and acknowledge the completeness by watching the Event Log results.

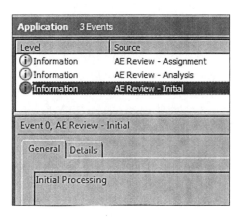

When you are looking to decompose workflow processes into more manageable sub-parts, consider the best possible options for the virtual re-composition that occurs at runtime. Designing this solution in a loosely-coupled, rules-driven fashion will require additional forethought and planning but in return you get a more future-oriented process that accommodates change.

The role of transactions in aggregated services

One of the principles of SOA that we discussed earlier in this book is the concept of abstraction. That is, shielding service clients from all sorts of implementation details with which they should not be concerned. One way to promote abstraction is through the use of aggregate services. Instead of having a service client call a series of required services that result in a new customer being added to a system, we should instead expose a single `CreateCustomer` operation that internally navigates the set of necessary system services. BizTalk orchestration is practically built for this situation. By injecting a stateful, cross-domain processing engine, our solution can coordinate a wide range of activities that our initiating service client never knows about.

However, one challenge with aggregating services in a single business process is figuring out how to effectively wrap these disconnected services into a single participating transaction. While BizTalk Server 2009 implements the idea of atomic transactions within orchestrations, this feature does not behave as you might suspect. In a truly atomic transaction, all the enclosed operations either complete successfully or else none of them do. It is a means to prevent partial updates or anything that might leave the target system(s) in an inconsistent state. That said, a middleware solution can only provide a certain level of atomicity. In the case of an error within the orchestration's atomic transaction, changes to orchestration variables and messages are reversed, but the actual calls to adapter endpoints do not automatically get rolled back. Logistically, this makes sense. How do you reverse a message to the email adapter? How about calling a stateless web service? BizTalk Server integrates with a host of applications and protocols that don't share a common transaction scheme. This is where the concept of **compensation** arises. Within an orchestration **Scope** shape, we explicitly define a compensation action that should be executed in the case that this previous successfully transaction needs to be rolled back. We can put any orchestration shape necessary into a compensation block if it helps us effectively reverse the effect of the transaction.

Defining the service

So, how do we correctly implement transactions in an aggregate service? What we want to do here is create a composite service that comprises three individual services. If any of these services fail, then any previously committed changes must be rolled back. In this case, I use the term *services* to represent a business service versus just being a WCF service. That is, the three services we want to aggregate are:

- Send an email to the initiator of an adverse event indicating receipt of their message
- Insert the adverse event into a tracking system
- Send the adverse event to an investigator who reviews, categorizes and validates the adverse event

All of these operations must succeed, or else previously committed operations must be compensated. Both the second and third action has a WCF service component. We need a service operation that is able to insert into our destination system and a service that assigns the adverse event to an investigator. Our WCF service contract looks like this:

```
[ServiceContract(Namespace = "http://Seroter.BizTalkSOA.Chapter7")]
public interface IAdverseEventReview
{
    [OperationContract]
```

```
  string InsertNewAdverseEvent(AdverseEvent newAE);
  [OperationContract]
  void DeleteAdverseEvent(string aeID);
  [OperationContract]
  void PublishAEForInvestigation(AdverseEventCase newAECase);
}
[DataContract]
public class AdverseEvent
{
  [DataMember]
  public string AE_ID { get; set; }
  [DataMember]
  public string ProductCode { get; set; }
  [DataMember]
  public string PatientId { get; set; }
  [DataMember]
  public string PatientGender { get; set; }
  [DataMember]
  public int PatientAge { get; set; }
  [DataMember]
  public string AECategory { get; set; }
  [DataMember]
  public string AESeverity { get; set; }
  [DataMember]
  public DateTime AE_Onset { get; set; }
  [DataMember]
  public string AdditionalNotes { get; set; }
}

[DataContract]
public class AdverseEventCase
{
  [DataMember]
  public string AE_ID { get; set; }
  [DataMember]
  public string CaseID { get; set; }
  [DataMember]
  public string Product { get; set; }
  [DataMember]
  public AEStatusCode Status { get; set; }
}
```

Notice that I added a service operation that also deletes data from the adverse event system. I plan on executing this operation only in the case of compensating for a previously successful insertion. After all three of these service operations are implemented, we add them to the pre-existing WCF Service project and host the endpoints in IIS 7.0 as HTTP services.

Building the BizTalk solution

Back in our BizTalk project, we have to add a reference to this service in order to get access to the artifacts we need to successfully call each operation. Absent any worries about transactions, our straightforward aggregate orchestration should resemble the following figure.

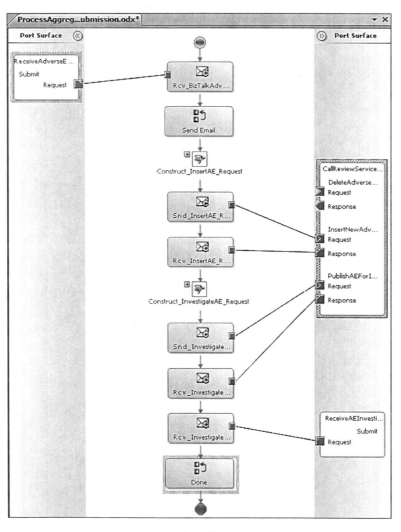

Notice that our "investigator service" expects a response (outside the synchronous service call) that describes the final assessment of the investigator. This is done by initializing a correlation set (on the adverse event ID property) when the investigator service is called, and following that correlation set when the subsequent out-of-band response is returned.

Now let's add some transactions. In order for an orchestration to contain transactions, the orchestration itself must be marked as transactional. This is done by clicking on any whitespace in the orchestration designer, finding the **Transaction Type** property and setting it equal to a value such as **Long Running**. Wrap the **Send Email** Expression shape in an atomic transaction (using a **Scope** shape) and add a compensation section by right-clicking the scope and choosing **New Compensation Block**. For this example, I put an additional **Expression** shape in the compensation block which writes a message to my Event Log.

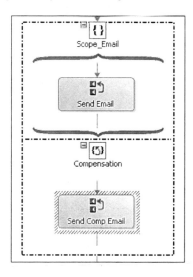

Next, we wrap the `InsertNewAdverseEvent` WCF service operation into a long-running transaction. After the service call is completed, we should set the ID of the adverse event to a member variable for later access. For this section's compensating action, we take the saved adverse event ID and pass that into the `DeleteAdverseEvent` WCF service operation.

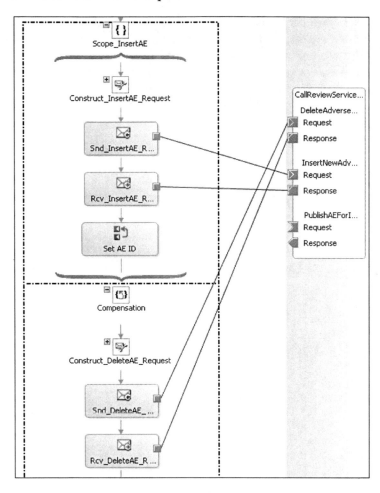

Because the investigator review is the last step of the process, there is no compensating action for the long-running transaction enclosing this operation. However, we do want to look at the result of the investigator review; and if they find this adverse event to be illegitimate, then we should throw an exception because this service operation has, in essence, failed.

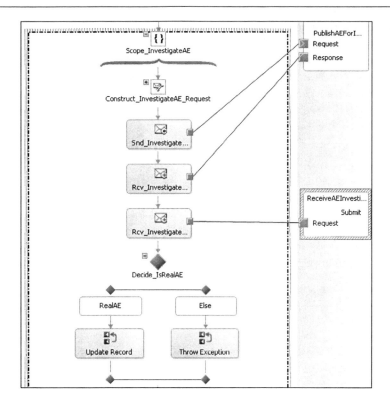

We want all three of these actions to behave as one, so next we will wrap all three transactions into one large long-running transaction.

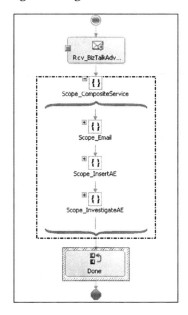

Add a single **Catch Exception** block to the outermost transaction. This will catch any exceptions thrown by the contained transactions. Now, we could choose to put two **Compensate** shapes in this exception block in order to explicitly execute the compensation block of the first two transactions. However, that strategy is hard to maintain when there are many nested transactions. Instead, put a single **Compensation** shape in the exception block, and choose **the transaction of the outermost scope** to compensate. What we are saying by doing this is that all the transactions contained within the outermost transaction should have their compensation logic fired in reverse execution order. This is much simpler than calling out each individual compensation block.

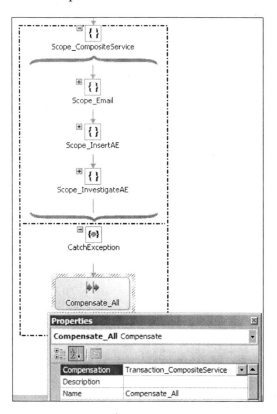

After we build, deploy, and bind this orchestration, we send in an initial request and watch our scenario play out. If we send an investigator response indicating a false adverse event, we are able to observe each compensation block being called in the reverse order of execution.

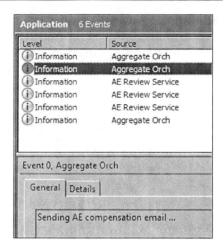

Critical point:

Be especially careful in long-running transaction scenarios when you choose to reverse a service operation that you called previously. Changes made to a given system may spawn an entire set of processes (such as new record means workflow instantiated) that might not get notified of a later change to the source record. Evaluate these scenarios prior to blindly deleting a record that you created at an earlier part of a transaction.

BizTalk Server 2009 provides solid support for modeling cross-domain transactions, but the usage of such transactions requires a fair amount of upfront design and consideration. However, to truly architect composite services, transactions need to become a familiar part of your orchestration arsenal.

Building a Complex Event Processing solution

Complex Event Processing (CEP) is a fascinating concept that has been around for a number of years now. Tim Bass of the Complex Event Processing blog (http://www.thecepblog.com/) nicely describes CEP as:

> *Complex event processing (CEP) is an emerging network technology that creates actionable, situational knowledge from distributed message-based systems, databases and applications in real time or near real time.*

Simply put, we take individual event streams, and use existing knowledge to correlate items that are related and can tell a bigger story. These events could be infrastructure focused or business focused within a messaging environment. Systems typically disseminate events that are contextual to the local system, but when you take a step back and observe the array of message types produced by your system catalog, you have the opportunity to identify patterns and model more complex aggregate events. Taken individually, the registration of a doctor in a drug trial, the request for a series of drug samples, and the un-registration of a doctor from a drug trial are all part of day-to-day operations. However, taken together, this combination of events in a short time window (such as twelve hours) may indicate that a physician is trying to fraudulently obtain drug samples. CEP is all about looking for patterns across diverse event streams in order to acquire business knowledge we didn't have previously.

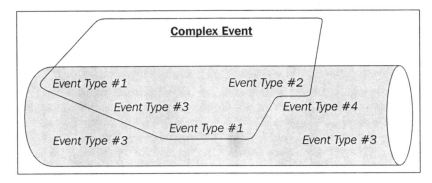

Critical point:

I'm not delusional enough to sell you BizTalk Server as a CEP technology. CEP is typically made up of many aspects such as event data analysis, adaptive business process management, process refinement, flexible pattern matching, and rich visualizations. While BizTalk server can fulfil some of these requirements (with the help of Business Activity Monitoring as well), it does not approach the dedicated offerings in the CEP space. My goal in including this demonstration is to introduce you to a few CEP concepts from a BizTalk perspective, not mislead you into believing that BizTalk Server represents the best that CEP has to offer.

Building the BizTalk solution

So how do we perform complex event pattern matching in a BizTalk solution? Let's take a look at one implementation scenario. Throughout this chapter we've worked with adverse events and product complaints. That means we have a lot of interesting events travelling through our message bus that may be able to tell us things well before our data mining platform gets around to it. For instance, nearly all therapeutics have known risks and warnings. This is why most television commercials spend more time explaining the sometimes cringe-worthy side effects than telling you what the drug actually does. With proper input from both the scientific and business arms of our company, we can model a complex event made up of seemingly unrelated individual events. Here, we try to find adverse events and product complaints, which when combined with a short time window, reveal a potential safety event.

Let's take a look at the components we need to effectively make this scenario come alive. We have "event listener" orchestrations which subscribe to particular combinations of fields for a given message. Each of these acts as a singleton so that a particular "count" of occurrences can be monitored. For instance, if we define a particular safety event as the receipt of more than ten adverse events with a particular profile in a twenty four period, we need a singleton orchestration to keep track of the count for that period of time. If an event listener orchestration meets its threshold, then a canonical `BizTalkComplexEventParameter` message is created and published directly to the MessageBox. A single "complex event" orchestration is listening for combinations of events that signify the specific safety signal being monitored. Specifically, if this complex event orchestration receives three distinct `BizTalkComplexEventParameter` messages that match a pre-defined subscription, then we know instantly that we have a safety concern on our hands and should email the appropriate parties to investigate further.

Constructing the event schemas

Let's go ahead and build this out. First, I've defined a property schema containing all the relevant adverse event or product complaint attributes that can be combined to signal a composite event.

Next, we have to take our existing `BizTalkAdverseEvent` and `BizTalkProductComplaint` schemas and promote the corresponding values from our property schema.

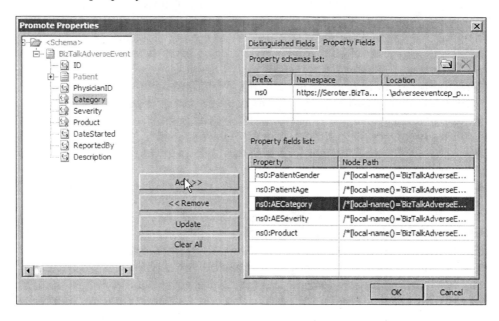

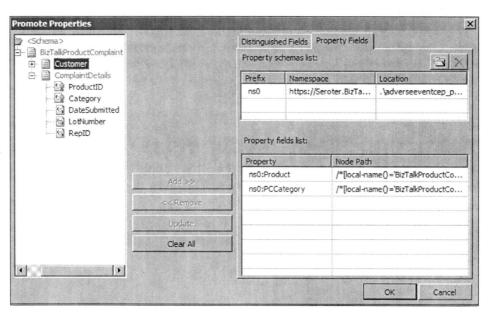

Now we create the `BizTalkComplexEventParameter` schema which represents the generic format for any complex event parameter published by the event listener orchestrations. It contains only three fields: one to hold the name of the broader complex event that this event parameter corresponds to, the data entity that this pertains to (for example "adverse event" or "product complaint") and a structured description of the aggregate event detected.

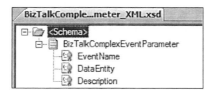

Building Pattern Matching Orchestrations

At this point, we are ready to build our first "event listener" orchestration. I've decided that I'm looking for any adverse event for a specific product where there is severe bleeding occurring in men over sixty five years of age. I'm specifically watching for a minimum of three occurrences of this particular event in a five-day period. So to start the necessary orchestration, we need a receive shape listening for our standard `BizTalkAdverseEvent` message on a direct bound orchestration receive port. In order to satisfy the particular event matching, this activating receive shape requires a filter on it.

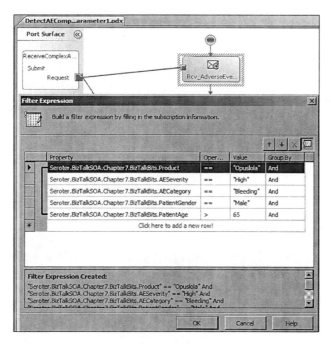

This orchestration will act as a singleton so that I can listen for a particular count of events in a given time period. Therefore, I need to instantiate a correlation set for our singleton to adhere to. In my case, the correlation set is on the adverse event category, severity and product.

Critical point:

While ideally our correlation set would encapsulate ALL the attributes of the orchestration filter, an orchestration can only be enlisted with a maximum of three correlation properties. Hence, you either need to limit your filter size, or maintain a decision shape in the singleton to filter out any unwanted messages.

After adding an expression shape that instantiates a variable indicating how many events we are listening for, we need to add a **Loop** shape, which carries on until the event threshold is achieved. Inside the loop, we have another receive shape which listens for the `BizTalkAdverseEvent` message and follows the previously instantiated correlation set.

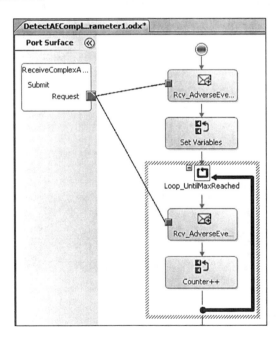

Because our correlation set has fewer properties than our filter, we need to add a **Decision** shape within the loop which only increments our counter if the remaining two filter criteria (patient age and patient gender) are equivalent to the inbound message.

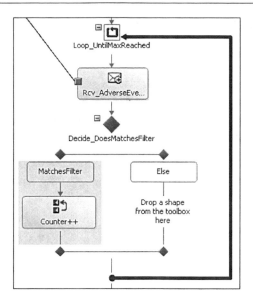

Earlier we stated that this aggregate event has a specific time window. To produce this effect, our **Loop** shape needs to be encapsulated by a long-running transactional **Scope** shape whose timeout value corresponds to our event window.

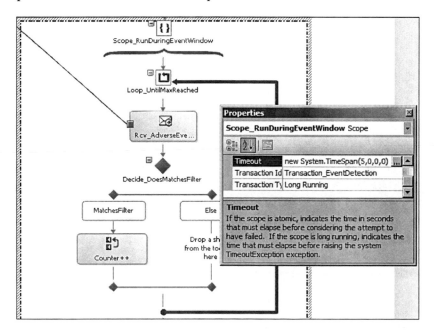

If the specified number of events are not received before the timeout occurs, this orchestration tears down, and starts up again upon receipt of the next event that matches the initial criteria.

Pitfall

What I've built here is a fairly rigid batched window of time. A great CEP solution would have sliding windows and provide enough sophistication to detect events that span ANY five-day window, not just five days since the orchestration started. This could potentially be done by introducing a persistent database or other mechanism to allow more flexible monitoring windows.

In the case that we DO encounter the preset number of events, our loop completes and we inflate a `BizTalkComplexEventParameter` message and ship it back to the MessageBox via the direct bound port. In my case, I constructed the message from an XML instance and set the overarching complex event name and entered the specific condition that this orchestration encountered.

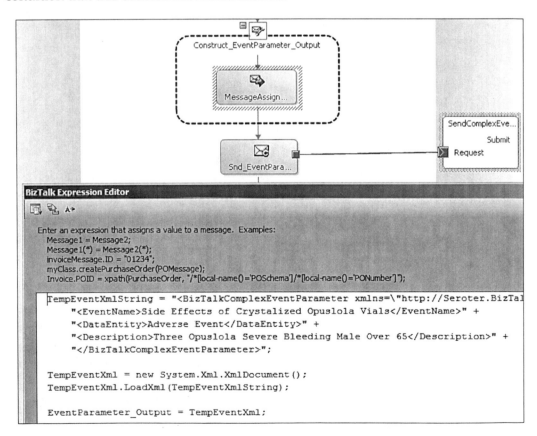

Constructing the complex event orchestration

After creating two more event listener orchestrations (with differing event pattern filters), we are ready to actually implement our higher-level event processor. For this orchestration, because we don't know which event parameter might be encountered first, we need to model the orchestration in a parallel receive fashion. First, I created three messages, all of type `BizTalkComplexEventParameter`. Regardless of which upstream process produced the event message, this orchestration only cares about the abstract event data structure. Next, we need a correlation set on the `EventName` because that's the common aspect of each event parameter that arrives at this orchestration.

Our orchestration flow design starts with a parallel shape containing three branches. Each branch receives a different activating **Receive** shape which initializes the correlation set. So, whichever branch is started first, the others will simply follow the correlation set automatically. The key part of each **Receive** shape is the filter. In my case, the filter corresponds to the master event, and the description of each event parameter.

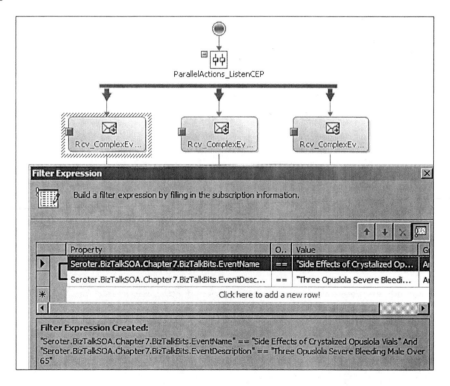

Each branch initializes the same correlation set based on the event name, but each branch possesses a different filter, which matches a distinct aggregate event that occurred. Similar to our earlier orchestrations, this master complex event also has a distinct time window. If we are listening for a complex set of safety events which all occurred in a five-day period, we can wrap our **Parallel** shape in a long-running transactional **Scope**. If a timeout is encountered, then we know that the complex event did not happen in the time window specified and should terminate the orchestration. If all three parallel branches are activated, then we apply whatever logic is necessary to inform personnel about the realization of the complex event.

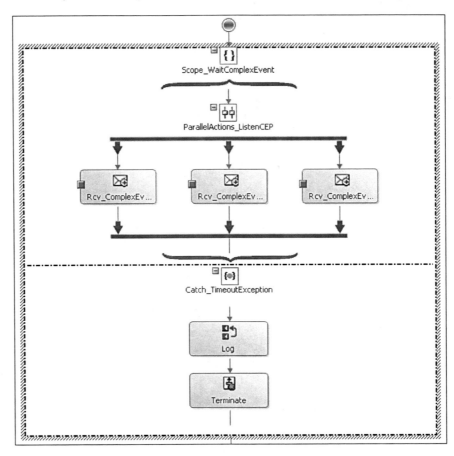

What's interesting is that the attainment of a complex event could actually produce yet another event message that yet another higher-level orchestration is listening for. You can continue to move up the chain from discrete application events to broader system events which eventually play a role in the early warning of a critical business event. Is BizTalk Server 2009 a perfect complex event processing engine? Hardly. For one, it should be easier to listen for intricate combinations of events that don't fit neatly into the rigid orchestration filter predicates. Also, we'd want to have better usage of business rules in our pattern matching algorithm to enable more agile updates stemming from process analysis. However, if you are using BizTalk Server as your messaging engine, you can certainly use patterns like the one demonstrated here to detect compound business events that were not previously captured from the many event streams passing through your bus.

In many of these cases, I pulled loop constraints and timeout values from hard-coded variables. If at all possible, consider using the BRE or any other external store to persist these values. As another example of a metadata repository, the BizTalk SSO store allows the secure storage of key/value pairs. Using an externally maintained (secure) metadata repository provides greater agility when conditions change and you need an agile process to accommodate it.

Summary

In this chapter, we looked at a variety of orchestration usage scenarios that exploit BizTalk in a service-oriented fashion. Through the use of dynamic ports and direct binding, we can create very loosely-coupled processes that are capable of reuse. By not directly connecting a batch of related orchestrations, but rather relying on external routing rules, we make our orchestration act like encapsulated services whose execution sequence can be determined on the fly. Finally, we saw that there are creative ways to listen in on the traffic of the message bus and seek out aggregate business events that may provide early warning insight into critical business conditions.

In the next chapter, we'll look at how to take these service-oriented BizTalk artifacts and effectively version them so that new capabilities can be supported while causing minimal impact to existing clients.

8
Versioning Patterns

There is nothing permanent except change.

-Heraclitus

Up until this point, we have looked at how to design and build many of the core components of a service-oriented architecture using BizTalk Server 2009. One of the most prominent aspects of SOA is the capacity to support change. This chapter focuses on how to change service components while introducing the least amount of impact to existing clients.

In this chapter you will learn:

- The importance of versioning your SOA solution
- Which components of an SOA may undergo versioning
- Strategies for versioning schemas
- How to version endpoints
- How to version long-running orchestrations
- Ways to lengthen the life of production services and delay the need to explicitly introduce changes

Why versioning?

When I talk about *versioning* I don't mean simply updating code and pushing out an updated set of libraries to target locations. A traditional, monolithic application is typically updated by rebuilding the entire solution and deploying the complete package to desktops or servers. This makes deployments fairly burdensome but on the plus side, the developers are fairly confident that the changes being made only affect entities within the discrete application boundaries.

A solution based on an SOA pattern is much easier to deploy because functional modules may stand alone if principles of encapsulation and loose coupling are correctly applied. Changes made to a single service shouldn't necessarily impact every component of the application and force a massive redeployment of the entire system. However, this flexibility comes at a cost. Unlike classic applications with discrete boundaries, SOA applications have components with a potentially disparate set of clients outside of the initially deployed "application" boundary. A service developer cannot know for sure who all of the clients for a given service are, and therefore must treat future modifications differently than developers working in monolithic applications. Specifically, service developers need to apply changes through distinct new versions while keeping existing versions in a frozen state.

So true *versioning* means that multiple distinct versions are accessible simultaneously instead of simply overwriting the existing code base. This is vitally important because those who rely on a particular service have built and tested their applications around specific behavior and SLA present at a specific point in time. We must be careful to not to impact these existing clients in ways that fundamentally changes their contract with our service. Herein lies the challenge: we need to provide a level of continuity to existing clients while at the same time providing new or modified capabilities to clients that need them.

A "version" of a component is typically comprised of both a major and minor version indicator. As a rule of thumb, the minor version is incremented for backwards compatible changes while the major version is reserved for breaking changes. What is a backwards compatible change as it relates to services? Backwards compatible changes are ones that produce no ill-effect or altered behavior for existing clients. For example, switching a message parameter from being required to optional does not require service clients to alter any portion of their application. There may be functional implications that clients have to address in future releases of their own application, but a change of this type doesn't fundamentally alter the service contract. In another case, adding new service operations to an existing contract is considered a backwards compatible change. Clients who used the existing contract are not impacted by the addition of new operations to the contract.

Major version updates are applied for breaking changes. For instance, if the service has a new parameter added to an existing service operation, then the client's contract is broken and their application will probably raise an exception. Similarly, adding non-optional elements to the schema of the message being transmitted by the service will result in a breaking change. That is, if I added a new required field to a schema, clients built against the original contract will obviously not be able to satisfy this new requirement without rebuilding their application.

> **Pitfall**
>
> Even though the addition of new optional elements is typically considered a non-breaking change, some clients may still fail to adjust to this change if they use an aggressive XML/XPath strategy for reading response messages and rely on nodes being present a specific position in the tree. If the client expects the "Name" node to be the fourth node from the root and the response message now contains new (optional) nodes preceding the "Name" node, the client will encounter an error. This risk highlights the need for using a strong unit testing tool like BizUnit so that you can automate the testing of positive and negative cases.

In an architecture where reusable services are the goal, a pattern of versioning instead of "rebuild + redeploy" is key to long-term success.

What service aspects may undergo changes?

In an SOA solution, there are four key areas which are subject to change: contract, address, binding, and implementation.

Let's take a look at the contract. As we've discussed back in Chapter 4, contracts explain what operations the service exposes, and the types of messages and exchange patterns supported by this service. So as you can imagine, there are cases when all of those items are subject to change. A widely-used service, which provides an abstraction of business functionality is likely to be extended with new operations and capabilities. For example, when first created, a service may have operations for publishing both new and changed invoices. Some time later the service adds the capability to query and return existing invoices. Users may then request the capability to only return the status of a given invoice. Over time, our service has additional operations added while keeping the existing operations in place.

Similarly, a contract may adopt new versions of messages or entire new messages altogether. Inevitably, data schemas will undergo some changes as new fields are required or tighter restrictions are added to existing fields. When those modifications are made, our service contract must reflect the reality of new message types that future operations can exploit. If you're willing to make a breaking change, then these updated messages can be applied to existing operations. However, breaking changes can be difficult to detect, so this reiterates the need for unit testing of all aspects of the service-oriented solution.

If a service needs to undergo significant changes, one of the best items to version is the address itself. This way, client using an original version of the service have no opportunity to accidentally collide with new or changed features and messages. By putting service changes at an entirely new URI, you are creating the ultimate "opt-in" scenario for clients.

As a WCF service matures, it's definitely realistic that the binding will require changes. It's possible to introduce either breaking changes or backwards compatible changes to a service binding depending on what is modified. Adding behaviors pertaining to data processing within the WCF server stack versus the transmission of data over the wire can often be backwards compatible. For instance, we can add custom behaviors that perform message instrumentation, exception handling, or output caching without directly affecting service consumers. However, changing binding attributes or behaviors impacting security schemes, service timeout, or encoding strategy will result in a breaking change for the client application.

Finally, we can clearly expect the actual implementation logic of the service to mature over time. These can be incremental, backwards-compatible changes that address bugs, extend exception handling routines, or introduce processing efficiencies through caching. While many of those types of changes would not require service clients to be notified, it is critical to evaluate any change made to service implementation to determine whether or not it changes the behavior of the service in any way. Just because the interface doesn't change, it doesn't mean that the service hasn't undergone a functional modification that will cause the service to execute its logic in a way the client does not expect.

In order to maintain the confidence of service clients, we need to have a well-defined versioning and unit testing strategy that evaluates changes made to contracts, endpoints, bindings, and implementation and clearly articulates how to introduce such changes to your service layer.

How to version schemas

Schemas define the messages that travel between our service endpoints and represent a core aspect of the service contract. As the need arises to reshape our schema to fit changing business needs, it's critical to understand the impact our choices have and strategies for minimizing impact on existing consumers.

What if we have an existing BizTalk schema exposed via WCF service to client applications and decide to reorganize the underlying node structure of the schema? Or, what if we chose to remove existing schema elements and add new required ones? From our earlier discussion, this would seem to be a blatant breaking change. However, if you perform a vanilla exposure of a BizTalk schema as a service, these types of schema changes do NOT cause an immediate runtime exception in the client application, which is bound to earlier service versions.

In the beginning of this book, we talked about the fact that BizTalk receive locations are inherently "type-less". That is, they aren't explicitly tied to a specific schema format. Similarly, the BizTalk WCF service endpoints are not strongly typed to a particular message. This differs from the classic SOAP adapter service endpoints where the designated schema was converted to a serializable .NET type and tightly bound to the service interface. If we updated a BizTalk-generated ASP. NET service with a new schema, then any legacy callers would receive errors about the now-invalid data being sent over the wire. For the BizTalk WCF services, you can technically publish ANY object to a given endpoint. The metadata associated with a WCF endpoint is purely reference data and not a binding part of the service interface. Let's prove that this is the case.

I've created a **Product** schema that we'll be using throughout this chapter. Each product, or drug in our case, has attributes such as what it is used for, how often it should be taken, which countries have approved its use, and any critical safety issues to be aware of.

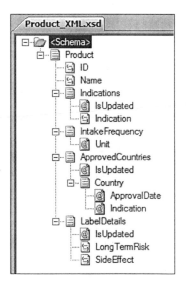

We then create a WCF service by exposing this schema as part of an asynchronous service contract.

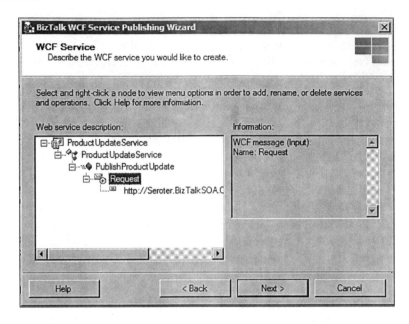

After starting up the corresponding receive location (and creating an associated send port, which spits our message to the file system), our client application is able to reference this service endpoint and interrogate its current metadata. Based on the types generated, our client builds up the product object and calls this service with the following code.

```
private static void CallProductUpdateV1()
{
Console.WriteLine("calling V1 service");

ProdUpdateSvc.ProductUpdateServiceClient client =
    new ProdUpdateSvc.ProductUpdateServiceClient("ProdUpdateService");

  try
  {
ProdUpdateSvc.Product prodInput = new ProdUpdateSvc.Product();
  prodInput.ID = "1234";
  prodInput.Name = "Watsonastic";

ProdUpdateSvc.ProductIndications prodIndications =
    new ProdUpdateSvc.ProductIndications();
  prodIndications.IsUpdated = true;
  prodIndications.Indication =
      new string[] { "Oncology", "Immunology" };
```

```
    ProdUpdateSvc.ProductIntakeFrequency intakeFrequency =
        new ProdUpdateSvc.ProductIntakeFrequency();
    intakeFrequency.Value = "60";
    intakeFrequency.Unit = "Days";

    ProdUpdateSvc.ProductApprovedCountries approvedCountries =
        new ProdUpdateSvc.ProductApprovedCountries();
    approvedCountries.IsUpdated = true;
    ProdUpdateSvc.ProductApprovedCountriesCountry[] approvedCountry =
        new ProdUpdateSvc.ProductApprovedCountriesCountry[2];
    approvedCountry[0] =
        new ProdUpdateSvc.ProductApprovedCountriesCountry();
    approvedCountry[0].ApprovalDate = DateTime.Parse("12/22/2001");
    approvedCountry[0].Indication = "Oncology";
    approvedCountry[0].Value = "USA";
    approvedCountry[1] =
        new ProdUpdateSvc.ProductApprovedCountriesCountry();
    approvedCountry[1].ApprovalDate = DateTime.Parse("08/10/2004");
    approvedCountry[1].Indication = "Immunology";
    approvedCountry[1].Value = "Germany";
    approvedCountries.Country = approvedCountry;

    ProdUpdateSvc.ProductLabelDetails labelDetails =
        new ProdUpdateSvc.ProductLabelDetails();
    labelDetails.IsUpdated = true;
    labelDetails.LongTermRisk = new string[] { "heart disease" };
    labelDetails.SideEffect = new string[] { "headache", "exhaustion" };

    prodInput.Indications = prodIndications;
    prodInput.IntakeFrequency = intakeFrequency;
    prodInput.ApprovedCountries = approvedCountries;
    prodInput.LabelDetails = labelDetails;

    client.PublishProductUpdate(prodInput);

Console.WriteLine("V1 service completed");

    client.Close();
Console.ReadLine();
    }
    catch (System.ServiceModel.CommunicationException)
        { client.Abort(); }
    catch (System.TimeoutException) { client.Abort(); }
    catch (System.Exception) { client.Abort(); throw; }
}
```

After confirming that our service works as expected, we can go ahead and change our existing Product schema. I switched the `Indication` field to the `ID` data type and made the `Indication` property of the `Country` node an `IDREF` data type. This forces a tighter restriction that says that only indications that this product is approved for can be associated with a given country's usage. I continued changing the schema by adding a new required element (`Competitors`) and renaming an existing element (`Name` to `ProductName`).

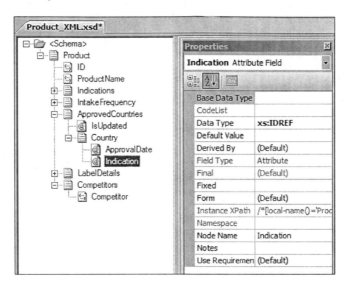

So in theory, these are all breaking changes. I've added restrictions to existing elements, added required elements, and changed the name of an existing element. After deploying the changes to the BizTalk Server (and not updating our service contract), and calling our original service again, we see that everything behaves exactly as it did before. If we walk through the **BizTalk WCF Service Publishing Wizard** again and overwrite our previous service with a new one (and make no changes to our client), we can still call our service with no errors. If we choose to update our service reference in the client application, THEN we are forced to address the contract changes represented in the generated .NET client types.

What does all this mean? Unless you apply data verification in a WCF adapter behavior or in the receive pipeline, there is nothing preventing clients from publishing out-of-date or malformed messages to the bus. More importantly from a client perspective, they are now not getting the same service behavior that they are used to getting. In my opinion, this is an essential reason why having a well-articulated (and practiced!) schema versioning strategy will go a long way towards preventing service data mismatches. If it is your policy to never deploy changes to a schema without explicitly versioning the schema (and service), you'll be in a good position to establish a consistent experience for service consumers.

So how do you exactly version a schema? Your first thought may be to set the **Document Version** attribute that is part of the root schema node in the BizTalk Editor. However, this attribute is only an informational schema annotation and has no discernable impact on the processing of messages themselves by the parser. Similarly, the XSD standard itself defines a "version" attribute on the root `<schema>` element but again there is no semantic meaning attached to this value, and, it is not supported in the BizTalk Editor environment.

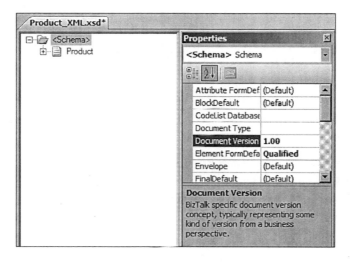

The next choice is to explicitly add a `Version` attribute or element to your schema structure. While this method allows us to make MessageBox routing decisions based on the message version (assuming that you promote the node), it is still a content parameter and thus subject to client entry error and does not convey the true impact of changing a schema.

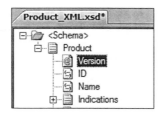

Versioning a schema through the namespace is the preferred mechanism. If you recall, the unique identifier for any message in BizTalk is typically the schema namespace plus the root node name. No two schemas should have this same combination of values or else you run the risk of parser confusion within BizTalk Server. Because of the overall scope of the namespace, it is a prime candidate to communicate the version of a given schema. There are two choices I'd recommend when inserting version information into a namespace:

- **Numerical values**: It is perfectly acceptable to represent the schema version using the traditional numerical attributes like so:

  ```
  http://Seroter.BizTalkSOA.Chapter8/v1
  ```

  You can also decide to represent minor versions:

  ```
  http://Seroter.BizTalkSOA.Chapter8/v1/1
  ```

- **Date driven approach**: Instead of applying numerical values that denote no enterprise context, you can also use date as the namespace version indicator.

  ```
  http://Seroter.BizTalkSOA.Chapter8/20081212
  ```

  For many organizations, these dates would provide context to schema readers and associate the schema with major software milestones within the company.

There is no right-or-wrong choice between these two options. The numerical values provide greater granularity to designate major and minor changes while the date-driven approach works well for enterprise services that are aligned with software platforms and organizational milestones. My only advice here is to pick a namespace versioning mechanism and apply it consistently across all schemas.

I'd be remiss if I didn't raise a warning about the impact of changing namespaces. If you are a seasoned BizTalk developer, you know that it's a real pain in the neck to accommodate namespace changes. Why? The schema namespace seeps into a myriad of locations within a BizTalk project:

- Schemas and imported/included references
- Maps and any custom XSLT within the map
- Pipelines and pipeline components
- Generated service metadata
- Business rules
- Orchestrations that contain custom Xpath statements
- Helper components that execute against orchestration messages as XML documents

Changing namespaces should not be a task undertaken lightly. To that point, I'd recommend only changing namespaces (and thus versioning) for major versions only. Minor versions that are assured to be backwards compatible do not need to have their schemas explicitly versioned.

 Where possible, try and eliminate the namespace portion of any XPath query you have to execute within maps, pipelines, or orchestrations. If you simply use the `local-name()` function in your queries, then a namespace change with not break your existing XPath queries (assuming the queried node still exists following the schema update).

Schemas are arguably the most critical part of any BizTalk solution, and correctly applying versioning patterns to these schemas will enable your services to maintain their contractual agreements in a predictable way.

How to version endpoints

The service endpoint is the gateway to the service. Clients who design, develop, and test against services on that endpoint expect consistent behavior. While there are non-breaking changes that we can introduce to our BizTalk WCF endpoints (for example, instrumentation), we want to follow good practices when preparing to introduce new or modified capabilities to our service endpoints.

Let's look at an example here. Assume that we have a business process applied to the Product schema through the use of BizTalk orchestration. Our orchestration takes apart each section of the product and inserts or updates the relevant data into downstream systems.

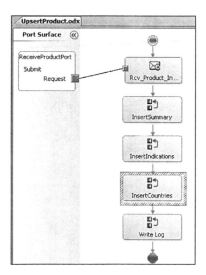

After deploying this orchestration, we bind its logical receive port to the WCF service receive port we've created earlier in this chapter. When the business units come calling and ask for **Manufacturing Locations** to be added to the product schema, we can apply namespace versioning and create a new orchestration that works with the updated schema type.

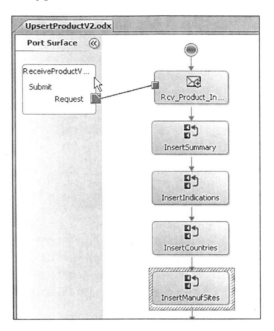

We need an additional endpoint to accommodate this new schema + orchestration combination. While we could attempt to reuse the existing endpoint or worse, overwrite it, we would rather leave our existing static endpoint and create a new distinct URI for service consumers. When we walk through the **BizTalk WCF Service Publishing Wizard** this time, we should choose to NOT create a receive location for the service.

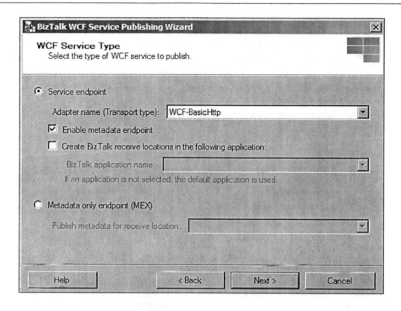

Once the service is created by the wizard, we should go to our existing receive port (that accepts the original product schema) and add a new receive location. This new receive location points to the latest service endpoint associated with the modified product schema.

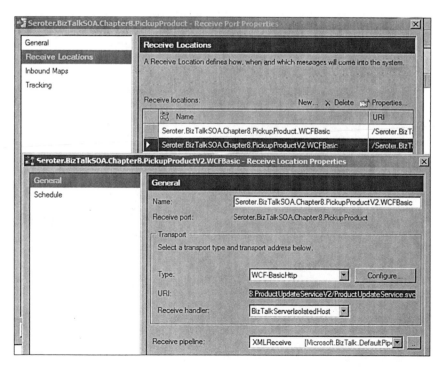

The new orchestration can now bind its logical receive port to this physical one. But won't the orchestrations get confused? Now I've bound two orchestrations to the same receive port which in turn accepts two different types of messages. If we look at the subscriptions maintained by our orchestrations, we see that each one, while bound to the same receive port, is seeking a different message type.

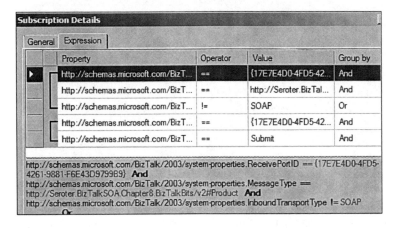

 Instead of using the BizTalk WCF Service Publishing Wizard to create a mirror image of the original WCF service which only differs by URI, consider versioning the service itself by altering the namespace of the service. This way, you can establish a distinct service definition which can be managed as a separate asset than the previous service version.

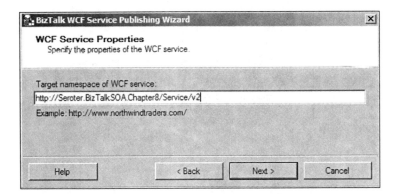

You may have looked at that last example and wondered "why create a whole new orchestration instead of trying to reuse and modify the old one?" In that example, the new orchestration is not introducing breaking changes to original clients but simply taking new data (if available) and adding to a system. So, it is indeed a candidate for reuse. But how do we insulate our original service clients who are not ready (or willing) to upgrade their service contract to take advantage of the new schema? One word: maps.

BizTalk maps offer us a powerful way to satisfy existing contracts while not sacrificing progress necessitated by business demand. For the solution above, we still need the two receive locations so that we persist two distinct service URIs. However, we want to ONLY maintain a single orchestration. To accomplish this, let's create a new map that takes the first version of the product schema and maps it to the second version.

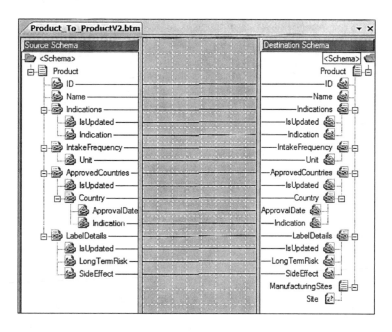

After deploying the updated assembly, we now apply this to the single receive port, which holds both receive locations. Remember that maps are applied based on message type, so this map will only be applied to the messages arriving via the original receive location.

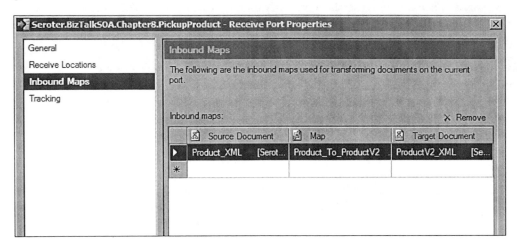

Now when we call either service endpoint, we see that only the latest orchestration gets executed. Using this strategy, we can provide full continuity to legacy clients.

This principle also applies when talking about distributing messages to target systems through BizTalk send ports. In some cases, you will have an update to a canonical schema (and possibly the orchestration that operates on it) but certain downstream systems are not yet ready to consume the new standard entity. Once again, BizTalk maps to the rescue. We can apply maps to our send ports so that we gracefully downcast our new internal entities to the classic format expected by clients slow to change.

Creating endpoints for custom WSDLs

If we wish to use custom WSDL files instead of allowing BizTalk to define the metadata description, there are two ways to create endpoints that accommodate this. As we have seen in Chapter 5, you can define a WSDL document and associate it with a particular WCF receive location through the **externalMetadataLocation** setting of the **Metadata** behavior. But how do we create the actual endpoints that use this WSDL?

The first choice is to exploit the **WCF-Custom** adapter and select an HTTP-based binding, which in effect enables BizTalk to act as a HTTP service host. There is no need to walk through wizards or create IIS services while still getting the advantages of the HTTP binding.

If you do wish to still have a service hosted in IIS 7.0, you can do one of two things. First, you can copy an existing BizTalk-generated service and rename the service file (.svc) and web application/directory. There is risk in getting this wrong, so you have the second option of creating a brand new endpoint. Because we don't want our service to produce any auto-generated description, we want to walk through the **BizTalk WCF Service Publishing Wizard** and select the **WCF-CustomIsolated** adapter and deselect the **Enable Metadata endpoint** option.

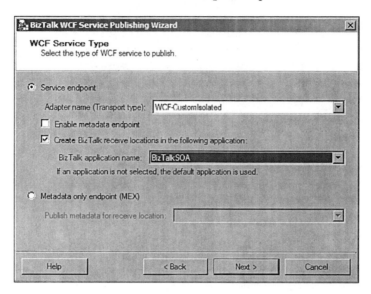

While we should choose to create a service from schemas, what we do on the following wizard pane is virtually irrelevant. The ONLY thing that matters here is the message exchange pattern, which influences the type (one-way or request-response) of receive location generated for this endpoint. Why does the rest (service name, operation name, message type) not matter? Remember that services generated by BizTalk for the WCF adapter have no contract logic embedded in the service itself. All we want is physical endpoint that we can connect our custom WSDL to. Once the wizard completes, we can go into the generated project and remove the **App_Data** folder which contains bits used for metadata generation. Finally, we can go into the receive location produced by the wizard and add a **Metadata** behavior with the **externalMetadataLocation** pointing to our externally managed WSDL.

 Using external WSDLs as a service's metadata source is a clean way to make backwards-compatible changes to services without doing the error-prone steps involved with overwriting a service via the **BizTalk WCF Service Publishing Wizard**.

Let's say that we want to expose a service interface based on our `Product` schema and host that service using in-process HTTP via the **WCF-Custom** adapter. When creating the WSDL, we could make the (poor) choice of copying the XSD content of that schema directly, or, we could reference the existing schema file. I created a WSDL file that along with a copy of the `Product` schema, is hosted in IIS 7.0.

```
<?xml version="1.0" encoding="utf-8"?>
<wsdl:definitions name="ProductService"
    targetNamespace="http://Seroter.BizTalkSOA.Chapter8"
    xmlns:wsdl=http://schemas.xmlsoap.org/wsdl/
    xmlns:soap="http://schemas.xmlsoap.org/wsdl/soap/"
    xmlns:tns="http://Seroter.BizTalkSOA.Chapter8"
xmlns:bizsoa="http://Seroter.BizTalkSOA.Chapter8.BizTalkBits/v1"
    xmlns:xsd="http://www.w3.org/2001/XMLSchema">

  <!-- declare types-->
  <wsdl:types>
     <xsd:schema targetNamespace="http://Seroter.BizTalkSOA.Chapter8.
BizTalkBits/v1/Imports">
       <xsd:import schemaLocation="http://rseroter08:80/Product_XML.
xsd" namespace="http://Seroter.BizTalkSOA.Chapter8.BizTalkBits/v1" />
     </xsd:schema>
  </wsdl:types>

  <!-- declare messages-->
  <wsdl:message name="PublishProductRequest">
    <wsdl:part name="part" element="bizsoa:Product" />
  </wsdl:message>
  <wsdl:message name="EmptyResponse" />

  <!-- declare port types-->
  <wsdl:portType name="PublishProduct_PortType">
    <wsdl:operation name="PublishNewProduct">
      <wsdl:input message="tns:PublishProductRequest" />
      <wsdl:output message="tns:EmptyResponse" />
    </wsdl:operation>
    <wsdl:operation name="PublishUpdatedProduct">
      <wsdl:input message="tns:PublishProductRequest" />
      <wsdl:output message="tns:EmptyResponse" />
    </wsdl:operation>
  </wsdl:portType>

  <!-- declare binding-->
  <wsdl:binding name="PublishProduct_Binding" type="tns:
PublishProduct_PortType">
     <soap:binding transport="http://schemas.xmlsoap.org/soap/http"/>
     <wsdl:operation name="PublishNewProduct">
```

```
        <soap:operation soapAction="PublishNewProduct"
style="document"/>
        <wsdl:input>
          <soap:body use ="literal"/>
        </wsdl:input>
      </wsdl:operation>
      <wsdl:operation name="PublishUpdatedProduct">
        <soap:operation soapAction="PublishUpdatedProduct"
style="document"/>
        <wsdl:input>
          <soap:body use ="literal"/>
        </wsdl:input>
        <wsdl:output>
          <soap:body use ="literal"/>
        </wsdl:output>
      </wsdl:operation>
    </wsdl:binding>

  <!-- declare service-->
  <wsdl:service name="PublishProductService">
    <wsdl:port binding="PublishProduct_Binding" name="PublishProductP
ort">
      <soap:address location="http://localhost:8087/Seroter.
BizTalkSOA.Chapter8.ProductServiceCustom"/>
    </wsdl:port>
  </wsdl:service>
</wsdl:definitions>
```

If I need to make a small, backwards-compatible change to the schema associated with this service, the only thing I need to do is copy the **Product_XML.xsd** file to the web directory housing the WSDL file. That's much cleaner than walking through the error-prone wizard.

Pitfall

Be careful to only use operations of the same message exchange pattern within a single WSDL referenced by a receive location. A receive location is set up as either one-way or request-response and won't be able to accommodate a mix of MEPs.

The other useful aspect of a hand-built WSDL is that we can add new operations to our service with little effort. If we are using the same messages available in the WSDL (or even want to add references to new types), all we need to do is add a new operation to our PortType and Binding nodes in the WSDL.

> **Pitfall**
>
> Back in WSDL 1.1, you were able to do overloading of service operations. That is, you could have multiple operations named "PublishProduct" and have each one define a different parameter. This is great for keeping an operation name and providing newer messages in each copy. However, this capability was removed from the WSDL 2.0 specification. While WCF currently supports the WSDL 1.1 standard, the SOAP Basic Profile 1.1 additionally disallows operations with the same name existing within the same port definition. Regardless, overloading should be avoided in service-oriented design as you want your contract to have clear usage scenarios and limit confusion by consumers.

Versioning long-running orchestrations

Orchestrations can be built to operate in a stateful, long-running fashion. This introduces a host of powerful service aggregation and coordination capabilities. However, it would appear to be quite difficult to ever find the right time to introduce a new version of such an orchestration. If we always have orchestrations dehydrated and waiting for messages, how can we ever hope to bring a new version online?

In this scenario, we want to initiate a manual review of any product label changes introduced by the upstream systems. First then, we need a new schema representing a product label review.

Next we need a property schema that holds a pointer to the unique `review change ID` that this review schema retains during long-running processes.

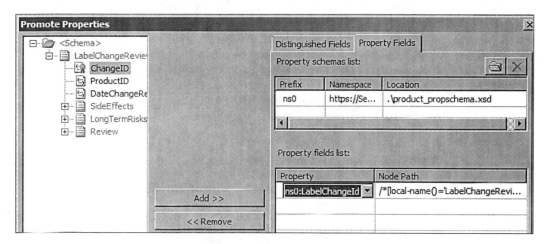

In order to inflate this review message, we need a map that takes the data from our **Product** schema and maps it to the review schema.

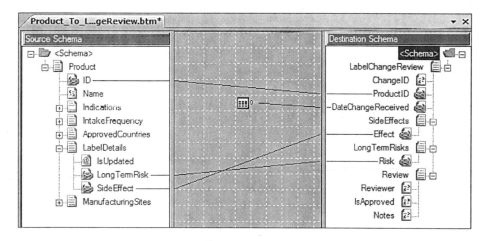

Because we'll be explicitly versioning our BizTalk assembly, I want to separate our new orchestrations from the various messages it uses by placing the orchestrations in a different assembly than the schemas and maps. Our workflow, not the underlying schemas, will undergo changes. After a new BizTalk project is added to the solution and the existing BizTalk project is referenced, we create a new orchestration that has messages defined for the `Product` message that starts the orchestration, and the review messages that are transmitted in and out of the orchestration.

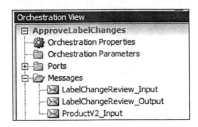

In this orchestration, the `Product` message arrives, the review message is constructed and review ID assigned, the review message is sent out, and at a later time returned back to the waiting orchestration. The response message is then evaluated to see if the reviewer approved or denied the label change.

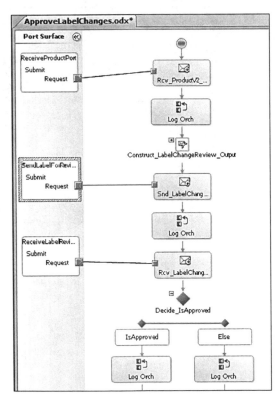

I've defined an orchestration variable that holds the "version" of this orchestration. Each **Expression** shape uses this variable when printing its status to the machine's Application Event Log. After creating the appropriate correlation type and set, and setting the necessary "initializing" and "following" attributes of the orchestration send and receive shapes, we can deploy this orchestration.

When we run this orchestration we can see all of the "version 1.0" designations. Before versioning our orchestration, let's initiate one more instance, but leave it in a dehydrated state while it waits for the label review message to come back into BizTalk.

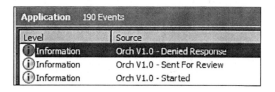

Back in Visual Studio.NET, we now should change the actual assembly version of this project. To do this, we visit the project properties, and look on the **Application** tab for the **Assembly Information** button. Clicking this reveals a set of assembly parameters, including version. I changed my **Assembly Version** to 2.0.0.0.

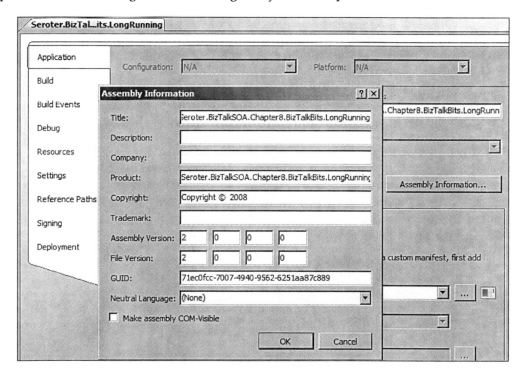

Next I changed my internal orchestration variable so that we know that the "version 2.0" orchestration is being executed when messages are written to the Event Log.

If I had wanted to be extremely clever, instead of manually setting the value of my "version" orchestration variable, I'd use an Expression shape at the top of my orchestration and set that variable's value to:

```
System.Reflection.Assembly.GetCallingAssembly().
GetName().Version.ToString(4)
```

This technique uses reflection to determine the version of the active assembly and would leave us with one less manual task when building a new version of an orchestration.

After deploying this project, we can see its distinct version designation by looking at the **Resources** section of this application in the BizTalk Administration Console.

Looking in the **Orchestrations** section of this application in the BizTalk Administration Console, we see our currently running orchestration, and our new unbound, unenlisted one.

We want to bind this new orchestration to the same ports used by the original orchestration and then unenlist the original and enlist the new one. We do this so that any new messages arriving to BizTalk Server will only start with the new version of this orchestration and do not accidently run the out-of-date process. If we send a new message in, we see the version 2.0 notifications in the **Event Log**.

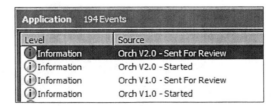

Critical point:

As a best practice, we really should unenlist an old orchestration version and enlist a new orchestration programmatically within a single transaction. This helps minimize the window when no orchestration subscriptions exist. See the BizTalk Help documentation topic entitled **Deploying and Starting a New Version of an Orchestration Programmatically** (http://msdn.microsoft.com/en-us/library/aa562027.aspx) for more details. In an ideal case, you should stop the inbound receive location to be 100% sure that no messages will come in during the orchestration switch-over.

Now what happens to our dehydrated orchestration associated with the version 1.0.0.0 assembly? If you recall, we unenlisted this orchestration, thus taking it out of regular usage by BizTalk. If we conclude this orchestration by sending back our associated product label review, which orchestration will it complete with? As you would hope, the original orchestration is still used when the product label review message returns to BizTalk.

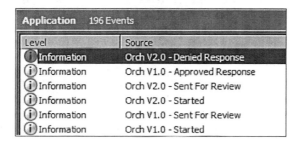

This is important to note. Even though the orchestration is unenlisted and virtually invisible to BizTalk now, we get continuity so that the process that was agreed upon when this message was first received is the same process that brings resolution to the message. How is this possible? The unenlistment of our old orchestration removes any activation subscriptions (which prevents new instances of the old orchestration from starting up), but retains any existing subscriptions such as those anticipating a correlated response. Therefore, messages arriving into BizTalk will be accurately routed to the correct version of the running orchestration instances. If the new orchestration version picked up where the old one left off, we'd inevitably run into both business and technical issues.

As you can see, BizTalk Server has fairly clean support for versioning even the longest of running orchestration.

Techniques for delaying change

Throughout this chapter (and hopefully the entire book!) we've been looking at building loosely-coupled services that accommodate flexibility and change. This includes direct bound ports that loosely coupled the messaging and orchestration layers, transforming messages at the edges to enable internal progression of components, applying explicit versioning attributes to schemas and much more. Here I'd like to investigate two ways to build solutions for volatile situations where change is constant and adaptability is vital.

Flexible fields

First, let's talk about situations where we want to future-proof parts of our schema that seem to be likely candidates for extension. In essence, we want to create a sort of "flex field" that enables us to stash additional information message into the message even though there aren't explicit schema fields to hold that information. This is done through the use of the xsd:any element type. On example of using this is on an Address node where we want to allow parts of the organization to place country-specific or custom addressing attributes into the message without requiring us to create named elements just for them.

How about we build an actual example of this concept? I've created a new version of my Product schema (and changed the namespace to reflect this fact) and added a DescriptionDetails node. Here I have a named element for the actual Description text, but have decided to also add a generic placeholder for details about this product that may only be relevant for a short time or for a specific audience. The any node allows any namespace and skips any attempt to match the contents to a particular schema.

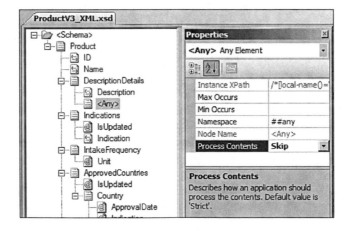

A bit earlier in this chapter we handcrafted a WSDL file that we applied to an in-process HTTP receive location. Let's go ahead and extend that WSDL now in order to accommodate our new message type and operation and bypass the **BizTalk WCF Service Publishing Wizard**. Our WSDL requires multiple small changes:

- New namespace reference on the root node.

  ```
  <wsdl:definitions name="ProductService"
  ...
  xmlns:bizsoa3="http://Seroter.BizTalkSOA.Chapter8.BizTalkBits/v3">
  ```

- New type which references our (copied) schema that now resides on the web server.

  ```
  <wsdl:types>
   ...
   <xsd:schema targetNamespace="http://Seroter.BizTalkSOA.Chapter8.
  BizTalkBits/v3/imports">
     <xsd:import schemaLocation="http://rserot08:80/ProductV3_XML.
     xsd" namespace="http://Seroter.BizTalkSOA.Chapter8.BizTalkBits/
     v3" />
   </xsd:schema>
  </wsdl:types>
  ```

- New message that points to the schema type needed.

  ```
  <wsdl:message name="PublishProductV3Request">
      <wsdl:part name="part" element="bizsoa3:Product" />
  </wsdl:message>
  ```

- Addition of operation to the WSDL port type definition.

  ```
  <wsdl:portType name="PublishProduct_PortType">
      ...
      <wsdl:operation name="PublishProductV3">
        <wsdl:input message="tns:PublishProductV3Request" />
        <wsdl:output message="tns:EmptyResponse" />
      </wsdl:operation>
  </wsdl:portType>
  ```

- New operation in the WSDL binding.

  ```
  <wsdl:binding name="PublishProduct_Binding" type="tns:
   PublishProduct_PortType">
      ...
      <wsdl:operation name="PublishProductV3">
        <soap:operation soapAction="PublishProductV3"
         style="document"/>
        <wsdl:input>
          <soap:body use ="literal"/>
  ```

```
        </wsdl:input>
        <wsdl:output>
          <soap:body use ="literal"/>
        </wsdl:output>
      </wsdl:operation>
    </wsdl:binding>
```

Once our WSDL is up to date, our service client can add/update its service reference to the WSDL. When we attempt to inflate the `Product` object in our client code, we can see that the `DescriptionDetails` member has a string-based attribute for `Description` and an `XmlElement` attribute to hold the generic content.

```
/// <remarks/>
[System.CodeDom.Compiler.GeneratedCodeAttribute
[System.SerializableAttribute()]
[System.Diagnostics.DebuggerStepThroughAttribut
[System.ComponentModel.DesignerCategoryAttribut
[System.Xml.Serialization.XmlTypeAttribute(Anon
public partial class ProductDescriptionDetails

    private string descriptionField;

    private System.Xml.XmlElement anyField;
```

In the code, I've built up this block of XML which we will add to the `Product` object. It represents data about an advertising campaign for the product that will only be included in messages for a 45 day period. Instead of forcing the schema to be versioned over and over again to accommodate temporary data needs, we can place this data into our generic placeholder.

```
StringBuilder adBuilder = new StringBuilder();
    adBuilder.Append("<MediaBuy>");
    adBuilder.Append("<Agency>Demattia Partners</Agency>");
    adBuilder.Append("<StartDate>01/22/2009</StartDate>");
    adBuilder.Append("</MediaBuy>");

XmlDocument adDoc = new XmlDocument();
    adDoc.InnerXml = adBuilder.ToString();

product.DescriptionDetails.Any = adDoc.DocumentElement;
```

When this client calls the service, we can see that BizTalk receives the message and our temporary block of XML is nestled into the rest of the structure in a valid way.

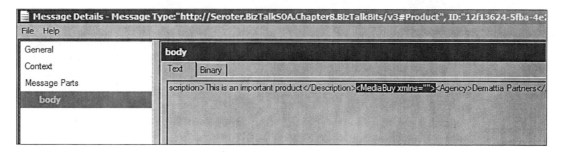

This technique should not be a substitute for proper versioning of schemas. That is, you shouldn't place a xsd:any node at the end of every schema just so that you can avoid making changes in the future. A strongly-typed schema is a valuable commodity in the enterprise and the flexibility offered by the xsd:any node is no replacement for thoughtful design and diligent versioning.

Generic on-ramps

The previous technique demonstrated how to embed flexible elements into a strongly-typed interface. But what are the options if you want a generic endpoint that can accept any number of different messages? In this scenario, we'll build an on-ramp to BizTalk Server that accepts any message the user provides. However, I'll show how we can encourage the developer to utilize a set of predefined message types when calling this loosely-typed service.

First, we need to build the generic endpoint. There are two options available. First, we can walk through the **BizTalk WCF Service Publishing Wizard** and produce an endpoint. What data type would we use to generate a loosely-typed service? When using the classic SOAP adapter, we could create an orchestration that accepts a message of type System.Xml.XmlDocument and then expose that orchestration as a service. However, this mechanism does not work the same when applying the WCF adapters. So, we should instead create a wrapper schema whose root node has a single child of type any element. However, instead of walking through the wizard to produce such an endpoint, our second choice is to manually update an external WSDL with this wrapper schema and corresponding operation. Let's look at this second option in practice.

In the `wsdl:types` portion of my existing custom WSDL file, we need to add a new schema definition.

```
<wsdl:types>
   ...
 <xsd:schema xmlns="http://Seroter.BizTalkSOA.Chapter8" elementFormDef
ault="qualified" targetNamespace="http://Seroter.BizTalkSOA.Chapter8">
   <xsd:element name="ProductWrapper">
     <xsd:complexType>
       <xsd:sequence>
         <xsd:any namespace="##any" processContents="skip" />
       </xsd:sequence>
     </xsd:complexType>
   </xsd:element>
 </xsd:schema>
</wsdl:types>
```

As you can see, I have a `ProductWrapper` root node and allow any possible XML structure underneath it. Next we need to add the appropriate message declaration to our WSDL.

```
<wsdl:message name="ProductData">
        <wsdl:part name="part" element="tns:ProductWrapper" />
</wsdl:message>
```

Now we need to add our operation to the existing port type section and then update our WSDL binding.

```
<wsdl:portType name="PublishProduct_PortType">
   ...
 <wsdl:operation name="PublishProductData">
  <wsdl:input message="tns:ProductData" />
  <wsdl:output message="tns:EmptyResponse" />
 </wsdl:operation>
</wsdl:portType>
<wsdl:binding name="PublishProduct_Binding" type="tns:PublishProduct_
PortType">
 <soap:binding transport="http://schemas.xmlsoap.org/soap/http"/>
  <wsdl:operation name="PublishProductData">
    <soap:operation soapAction="PublishProductData" style="document"/>
    <wsdl:input>
      <soap:body use ="literal"/>
```

```
    </wsdl:input>
    <wsdl:output>
      <soap:body use ="literal"/>
    </wsdl:output>
  </wsdl:operation>
</wsdl:binding>
```

At this point, we are able to reference our WSDL from a client application and can then publish messages to the endpoint.However, we'd like to encourage developers to use a known set of types so that the message bus doesn't encounter a mess of unknown entities. What we can do is create the schemas the bus should expect, create .NET objects out of those schemas, package the objects into a standalone assembly, and constantly provide fresh versions of these approved data types to our clients.

We start with a pair of schemas that describe the types of messages we expect our generic port to receive.

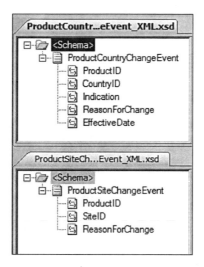

Next, we run the xsd.exe tool to build XML serializable objects for each schema. The command is as follows:

```
xsd /c /n:"Seroter.BizTalkSOA.Chapter8.GeneratedTypes" "C:\BizTalk\
Projects\Seroter.BizTalkSOA.Chapter8\Seroter.BizTalkSOA.Chapter8.
BizTalkBits\ProductSiteChangeEvent_XML.xsd"
```

The resulting two C# class files should then be loaded into their own .NET assembly that can be shared with service clients. The generic service endpoint accepts an `XmlElement` object meaning that our typed classes need to be converted to XML for submission to the service. I wrote a helper function that I included in the assembly which holds the generated types. That helper function looks like this:

```csharp
public static XmlElement ConvertObjectToXml(object inputObject)
  {
     XmlDocument tempXml = new XmlDocument();
     XmlSerializer serializer =
       new  XmlSerializer(inputObject.GetType());
     using (MemoryStream memStream = new MemoryStream())
     {
        serializer.Serialize(memStream, inputObject);
        memStream.Seek(0, SeekOrigin.Begin);
        tempXml.Load(memStream);
      }
     return tempXml.DocumentElement;
}
```

In our service client, we first add a reference to our generic service endpoint. This gives us a service operation, which accepts an `XmlElement`.

```
client.PublishProductData (|
void PublishProduct_PortTypeClient.PublishProductData (XmlElement ProductWrapper)
```

Next, we add a reference to our assembly containing the .NET types generated from the XSD schemas. Our client code inflates one of our strongly-typed objects and applies our helper function in order to cleanly send XML content to our service endpoint.

```csharp
private static void CallGeneric()
  {
Console.WriteLine("calling generic service first");

ProdSvcGeneric.PublishProduct_PortTypeClient client =
    new ProdSvcGeneric.PublishProduct_PortTypeClient
        ("ProdServiceGeneric");

  try
  {
  ProductCountryChangeEvent countryChange =
      new ProductCountryChangeEvent();
  countryChange.CountryID = "90032";
```

```
countryChange.ProductID = "322";
countryChange.Indication = "Oncology";
countryChange.EffectiveDate = DateTime.Parse("12/29/2008");
countryChange.ReasonForChange =
    ProductCountryChangeEventReasonForChange.Approved;

client.PublishProductData(ConversionHelper.ConvertObjectToXml
    (countryChange));

Console.WriteLine("generic service completed");

    client.Close();
Console.ReadLine();
    }
    catch (System.ServiceModel.CommunicationException) { client.Abort(); }
    catch (System.TimeoutException) { client.Abort(); }
    catch (System.Exception) { client.Abort(); throw; }
}
```

Now we can create send ports in BizTalk Server, which subscribe to the message types sent via the generic endpoint. These send ports have subscriptions based on the BTS.MessageType so that we can clearly see that messages arriving via the generic port are treated the same as those coming in via strongly-typed WSDLs.

We're all done, right? Not yet. If you recall, we wrapped our generic payload in a ProductWrapper element. If we call our service as is, we get a suspended message in BizTalk saying that we have no subscriptions matching the inbound message (or an error saying message type not found if the ProductWrapper isn't also a BizTalk schema).

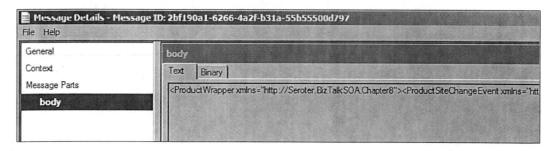

We need to rip off this header element and leave just the meaty center. This is where the new WCF adapters provide an easy solution. The **Messages** tab of the BizTalk receive location configuration allows us to specify the actual body of the inbound message.

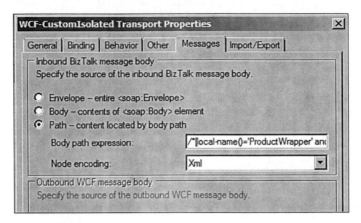

Instead of taking the entire SOAP body node, we can instead use a custom path to grab whatever is below the root node.

```
/*[local-name()='ProductWrapper' and namespace-uri()='http://Seroter.
BizTalkSOA.Chapter8']/*
```

Once this setting is applied, messages arriving to this receive location are appropriately parsed and our target payload is published to the MessageBox.

While a well-defined interface is an important part of a successful, reusable service-oriented architecture, there are cases where volatile business requirements will force a more creative approach for accommodating such cases. What we've seen is that you can create un-typed endpoints while still providing a set of valid objects in a format that can be regularly versioned without changing the service interface itself.

Summary

It can be easy to fall into the lazy trap of simply taking an existing solution, making the changes to the necessary components and overwriting those changes on the production servers.

In this chapter, we looked at strategies for versioning service artifacts and establishing creative ways to build our services to accommodate change. In the next chapter, we start looking at the newest service-oriented capabilities of BizTalk Server 2009.

9

New SOA Capabilities in BizTalk Server 2009: WCF SQL Server Adapter

Do not go where the path may lead; go instead where there is no path and leave a trail.

-Ralph Waldo Emerson

Many of the patterns and capabilities shown in this book thus far are compatible with the last few versions of the BizTalk Server product. So what's new in BizTalk Server 2009?

BizTalk Server 2009 is the sixth formal release of the BizTalk Server product. This upcoming release has a heavy focus on platform modernization through new support for Windows Server 2008, Visual Studio.NET 2008, SQL Server 2008, and the .NET Framework 3.5. This will surely help developers who have already moved to these platforms in their day-to-day activities but have been forced to maintain separate environments solely for BizTalk development efforts.

In addition to infrastructure-related updates such as the aforementioned platform modernization, Windows Server 2008 Hyper-V virtualization support, and additional options for failover clustering, BizTalk Server also includes new core functionality. You will find better EDI and AS2 capabilities for B2B situations and a new platform for mobile development of RFID solutions.

In addition, BizTalk Server 2009's Visual Studio.NET project system integration has been revamped, which means automated builds using MSBuild technology and an improved user experience when setting project properties and adding (any) artifact to BizTalk solutions.

While this most recent release of BizTalk Server is focused primarily on the underlying platform technologies, I'd like to highlight some of the key SOA-friendly features of this release and walk through demonstrations that vividly display those features in action. In this chapter, we will look at the new WCF-based SQL Server adapter and build a set of scenarios that demonstrate its flexibility and reusability.

What is the WCF SQL Adapter?

The BizTalk Adapter Pack 2.0 now contains five system and data adapters including SAP, Siebel, Oracle databases, Oracle applications, and SQL Server. What are these adapters and how are they different than the adapters available for previous version of BizTalk?

Up until recently, BizTalk adapters were built using a commonly defined BizTalk Adapter Framework. This framework prescribed interfaces and APIs for adapter developers in order to elicit a common look and feel for the users of the adapters. Moving forward, adapter developers are encouraged by Microsoft to use the new WCF LOB Adapter SDK. As you can guess from the name, this new adapter framework, which can be considered an evolution of the BizTalk Adapter Framework, is based on WCF technologies.

All of the adapters in the BizTalk Adapter Pack 2.0 are built upon the WCF LOB Adapter SDK. What this means is that all of the adapters are built as reusable, metadata-rich components that are surfaced to users as WCF bindings. So much like you have a **wsHttp** or **netTcp** binding, now you have a **sqlBinding** or **sapBinding**. As you would expect from a WCF binding, there is a rich set of configuration attributes for these adapters and they are no longer tightly coupled to BizTalk itself. Microsoft has made connection a commodity, and no longer do organizations have to spend tens of thousands of dollars to connect to line of business systems like SAP through expensive, BizTalk-only adapters.

This latest version of the BizTalk Adapter Pack now includes a SQL Server adapter, which replaces the legacy BizTalk-only SQL Server adapter. What do we get from this SQL Server adapter that makes it so much better than the old one?

Feature	Classic SQL Adapter	WCF SQL Adapter
Execute create-read-update-delete statements on tables and views; execute stored procedures and generic T-SQL statements	Partial (send operations only support stored procedures and updategrams)	Yes
Database polling via FOR XML	Yes	Yes
Database polling via traditional tabular results	No	Yes
Proactive database push via SQL Query Notification	No	Yes
Expansive adapter configuration which impacts connection management and transaction behavior	No	Yes
Support for composite transactions which allow aggregation of operations across tables or procedures into a single atomic transaction	No	Yes
Rich metadata browsing and retrieval for finding and selecting database operations	No	Yes
Support for the latest data types (e.g. XML) and SQL Server 2008 platform	No	Yes
Reusable outside of BizTalk applications by WCF or basic HTTP clients	No	Yes
Adapter extension and configuration through out of the box WCF components or custom WCF behaviors	No	Yes
Dynamic WSDL generation which always reflects current state of the system instead of fixed contract which always requires explicit updates	No	Yes

Needless to say, the WCF SQL Server Adapter offers significant benefit over the previous SQL Server adapter and introduces a range of new capabilities that are well overdue in the realm of database interaction. In this section, we will look at a few use cases and patterns for this adapter, which best demonstrate the capabilities it provides.

Solution set up

Before we get started building a series of different scenarios, we need to prepare our environment with the database tables and schemas that will be reused over and over again. All of our demonstrations in this chapter deal with batches of biologic materials that we use in our drug making process. These batches of material go through different stages before being ready for shipment.

To get started, I created a SQL Server 2008 database named **BizTalkSOA**, which houses our relevant tables. In all, there are four tables that we will use throughout this chapter:

- **BatchMaster**: This table holds the complete batch description as well as its current state. Note that this table's last column uses an XML data type.

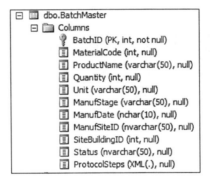

- **BatchDistribution**: This table stores information used by distributors who pick up completed batches.

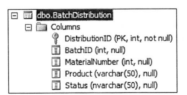

- **BatchDistributionPickup**: This table stores the details of where a batch is physically located.

- **DistributionVehicles**: This table holds information about the fleet of vehicles used to transport batches.

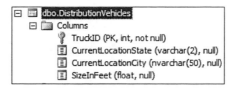

Next, we need a new BizTalk project to hold our enterprise schema that represents a batch of materials. While messages about material batches may arrive to (or depart from) BizTalk Server in diverse formats, this canonical schema is what BizTalk should use internally to represent this enterprise object.

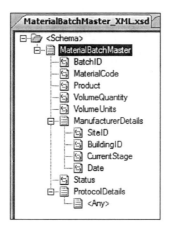

Now we're ready to start building solutions on the SQL Server WCF adapter.

Executing composite transactions

In a normalized database environment, a single canonical data entity often has its data spread across more than one underlying database table. Therefore it's critical to be able to insert data into all relevant tables from within a single transaction. Otherwise, we end up with an inconsistent state across our tables. Ignoring the database-centric ways to ease this burden (such as table views, stored procedures), let's consider how we would update multiple tables at once from BizTalk Server 2009. Specifically, we want to take a material batch canonical message and insert its data into multiple tables. After that, we need to execute a scalar operation against the database in order to find out if any shipping trucks are regionally available for transporting this batch.

First, we need the XML schemas which represent our data source. By installing the WCF LOB Adapter SDK, we get a nice metadata browser built into Visual Studio. NET. We access this from a BizTalk project by right-clicking the project, choosing **Add** then **Generated Items** and selecting **Consume Adapter Service**.

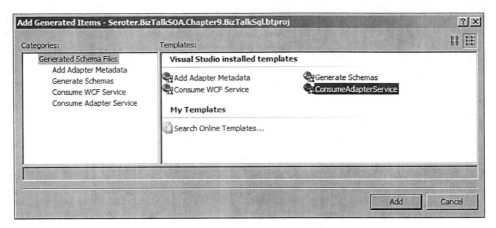

This action opens a new window that provides us the interface to connect to, browse, and select database objects for service interaction. The very first thing we need to do here is choose the **sqlBinding** as the service binding, and then configure a connection string. The simplest working connection string consists of an **Initial Catalog** value for the database, and a valid **Server** name entry. Note that the adapter now uses a connection string in the form of a URI instead of the traditional `Data Source=;Initial Catalog=;User Id=;Password=` style.

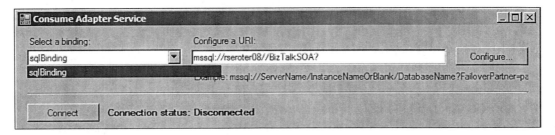

Once a satisfactory connection string is defined, we click the **Connect** button to establish our active connection to the target database. If the connection is successful, we see the category browser stuffed with a set of database object categories.

If you recall from our use case summary earlier, we need to get schemas for two
tables (**BatchDistribution** and **BatchDistributionPickup**) as well as a generic
scalar query. If we click on the root "/" character, we see a range of untyped
generic functions that we may exploit. I've added the **ExecuteScalar** operation
to my desired list of schemas.

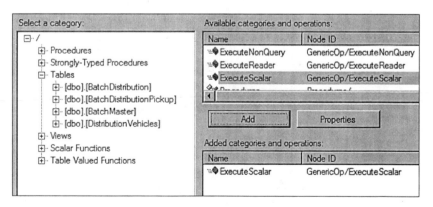

Keeping this window open, we next want to add `Insert` operations for the two target tables. This leaves us with three operations selected in the window.

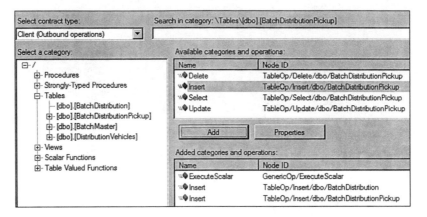

After clicking the **Ok** button at the bottom, we see a series of schemas (and a single binding file) added to our associated BizTalk project in Visual Studio.NET. A pair of `type` schemas are created to represent underlying data types, but the three most important schemas are shown here. There are two schemas for table operations, and one for the generic scalar query.

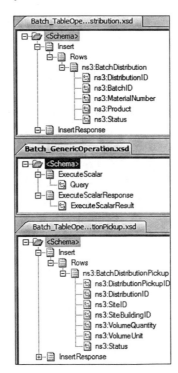

In Chapter 5, we saw how to reuse schemas and build new schemas out of existing types. Now we get to apply that lesson again. The WCF SQL Server Adapter supports the nesting of multiple (cross) table interactions within a single schema, which in turn get executed inside a single transaction. The schema must have two root nodes: one named `Request` and another named `RequestResponse`. The namespace of the schema must be in the format of `http://[PROJECT_NAME].[COMPOSITE_SCHEMA_NAME]`, which means that my schema below has a namespace of `http://Seroter.BizTalkSOA.Chapter9.BizTalkSql.CompositeBatchInsert_XML`. In order to reuse our adapter-generated schemas, we must use the **Import** option and reference both the **BatchDistribution** and **BatchDistributionPickup** schemas.

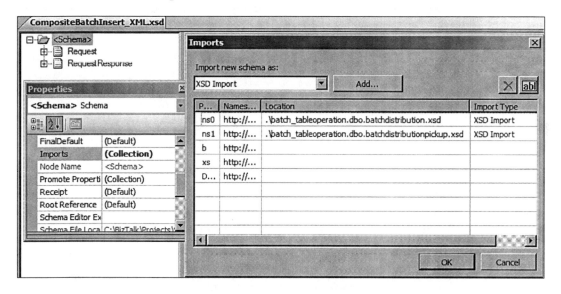

Once the import references are established, we must create records underneath both the `Request` and `RequestResponse` nodes and access the **Data Structure Type** property to find our imported types.

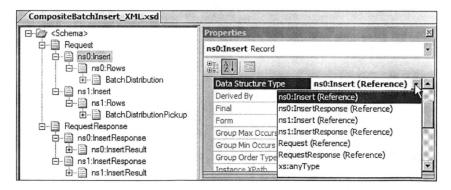

Pitfall

Note that the physical order of the nodes maintains significance to the adapter. In the schema above, the structure of the `Insert` nodes implies that the `BatchDistribution` insert occurs before the `BatchDistributionPickup` insertion. Keep this in mind when dealing with tables that have foreign key relationships or other dependencies on execution order.

With our schemas in place, we must now forge ahead with the orchestration, which processes these messages. To execute the "insert" part of the process, we need a total of three orchestration messages: one corresponding to the inbound "master" message, and two to handle the communication with the adapter.

As you might expect, we need a BizTalk Map in order to get from the "master" schema to the adapter's request message schema. I have used Scripting functoids in this map to create random IDs needed by the destination database.

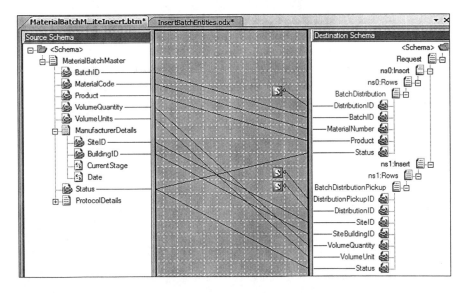

Pitfall

Because you have multiple destination nodes with the same name, you will need to set the BizTalk map grid property **Ignore Namespaces for Links** to **No**. Otherwise, your map will not successfully compile due to namespace confusion.

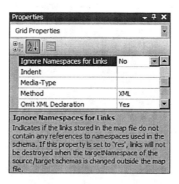

At this point, we can complete our orchestration flow and deploy the BizTalk project. In summary, our orchestration accepts in the Material Batch master message, transforms the message using the map we just created, and then sends that message to a request/response orchestration port. Finally, just for logging purposes, I send the adapter result message back out of the orchestration.

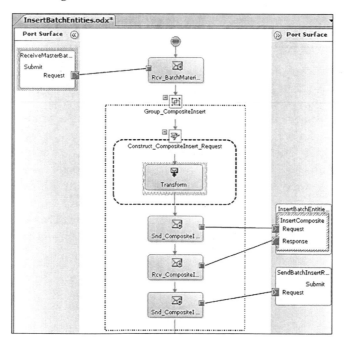

To save ourselves some work, we should import the adapter-generated binding file into our BizTalk application, which results in a new bi-directional send port being created in the BizTalk Administration Console. Now as you might expect, our generated send port has no knowledge of the fact that we are looking to do a composite transaction. If we look at the SOAP actions of the send port, we see entries for inserting into either of two tables, and an entry for the scalar operation.

We need to add an additional entry here, which reflects our composite operation. The new entry is:

```
<Operation Name="InsertComposite" Action="CompositeOperation" />
```

The operation Name must match the orchestration's logical port name, while the Action value must always be equal to CompositeOperation in order for the adapter to correctly process it. The only other item to confirm in this send port is that the binding property **useAmbientTransaction** is set to **True**. The CompositeOperation action is a known keyword for the adapter and signifies that multiple operations are about to be executed within a single transaction. An ambient transaction is the one used by the code being executed, so the **useAmbientTransaction** property ensures that we are wrapping all operations inside the common transaction BizTalk has established.

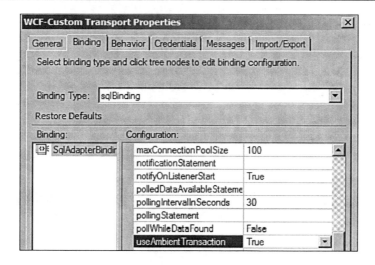

After physical ports are created to receive the initial file and send the logged result, we start the application and send in a material batch master instance. Sure enough, we can see new database entries inserted with matching **DistributionID** values. The XML emitted by the orchestration shows the expected empty result nodes.

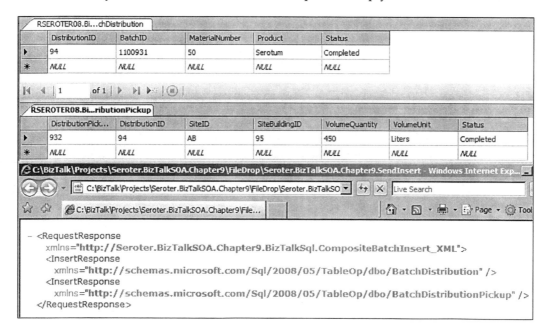

What about adding the "scalar query" aspect to the existing orchestration? To accomplish this, we first add two more orchestration messages that correlate to the existing auto-generated scalar request and response schemas. Next, we need to inflate the query message. We could build this message via code, but I chose to use a BizTalk map. The left side message is irrelevant since I don't use any data from it and only care about a single **Concatenate** functoid in the middle design surface. I utilized this functoid to construct the scalar query. In this very simple case, I hard-coded the query parameters, but clearly a real-life scenario would require us to look up the site where the batch was produced and transmit that location to the functoid.

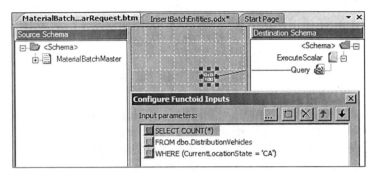

This orchestration now includes flow steps to create the scalar query message, send it to the adapter, and log the response. Because the scalar operation is known in the binding file and is thus part of the existing send port's SOAP action, I made sure to use the correct orchestration port operation name (i.e. **ExecuteScalar**).

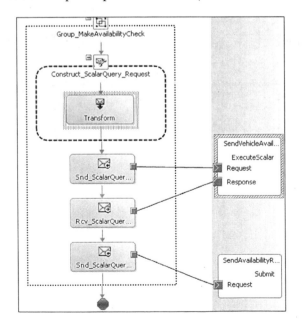

After building, deploying, and binding this orchestration to the necessary ports, I sent another batch message into BizTalk Server and observed the scalar output. Sure enough, I have two records in my database associated with California, and the scalar result reflects that.

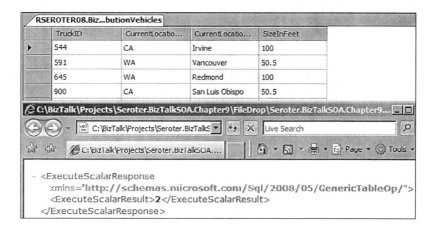

Polling for data

The original BizTalk Server SQL Server adapter supported polling of databases, but we now have a much more full-featured experience than before. For example, in the classic SQL Server adapter, the server-side stored procedures had to be authored with the BizTalk consumer in mind. A FOR XML clause was required in the procedure in order to force the results into a BizTalk-friendly XML format. To see how that experience has been changed, let's look at how to poll our BatchMaster table and yank the relevant records into BizTalk Server.

Once again we return to the **Consume Adapter Service** window. If you remember, we access this by right-clicking our project and choosing to **Add** a **Generated Item**. However, instead of simply setting the target database and server, we must now classify some additional parameters. First we must set the **InboundID** as part of the connection properties. This makes the connection string unique to each poller and is a requirement of the adapter for polling scenarios.

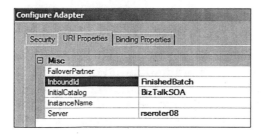

On the **Binding Properties** tab, we have three critical properties. First, we need to tell the adapter we are doing **TypedPolling** (versus untyped polling or classic FOR XML based polling). Next, we set the **PolledDataAvailableStatement** which the adapter uses to figure out if there are any records to pull. This statement should return a numeric count. My statement is:

```
SELECT COUNT(*) FROM dbo.BatchMaster WHERE ManufStage = 'Final'
   AND Status = 'Pending'
```

Finally, we distinguish the actual **PollingStatement** which the adapter uses to return data to BizTalk Server. My polling statement returns all the rows from the table if we've reached the final manufacturing stage. However, to prevent polling the same records over and over again, we want to flag those previously polled records as Read. What's great is that we can combine this with our polling statement and execute this update within the same transaction.

```
SELECT * FROM dbo.BatchMaster WHERE (ManufStage = 'Final') AND (Status
= 'Pending');  UPDATE dbo.BatchMaster SET Status = 'Read'  WHERE
ManufStage = 'Final' AND Status = 'Pending'
```

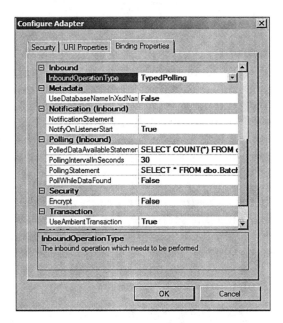

Following the entry of all these connection settings, we return to the **Consume Adapter Service** window and connect to our database. This time, we must switch the **Select contract type** from **Client (outbound operations)** to **Service (inbound operations)**. This is because instead of treating the adapter as a service (and BizTalk as a client), the roles are reversed. Once that switch is made, we see new operations available. Choose the **TypedPolling** option and select **Add**.

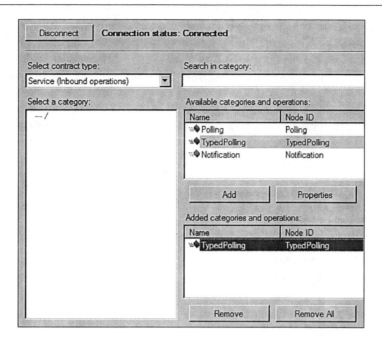

 If you want to confirm that your polling statement is correct, you can highlight the **TypedPolling** operation and click the **Properties** button. This shows you the dyanamically-generated WSDL for the operation, including the data contract returned.

Once this **Consume Adapter Service** window is closed, we end up with a new schema and binding file. The schema shows the typed result set emitted by the polling query. If you recall, our table has a column (**ProtocolSteps**) using the XML data type, and the wizard successfully reads it and interprets it as a string type.

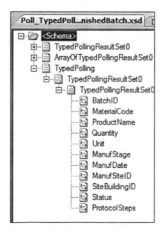

After deploying our new schema, we import the auto-generated binding into our BizTalk application and observe that a new receive port and receive location now exist. The receive location is configured with all of the connection and polling settings we defined in the **Consume Adapter Service** window during metadata browsing. I've also created a send port which simply subscribes to the message distributed by this receive location. Once we turn the receive location on, and confirm that our table holds data in a `pollable` state, we should see the polling result message sent to disk.

```xml
- <TypedPolling
    xmlns="http://schemas.microsoft.com/Sql/2008/05/TypedPolling/FinishedBatch">
  - <TypedPollingResultSet0>
    - <TypedPollingResultSet0>
        <BatchID>1</BatchID>
        <MaterialCode>100</MaterialCode>
        <ProductName>Serotum</ProductName>
        <Quantity>400</Quantity>
        <Unit>Vials</Unit>
        <ManufStage>Final</ManufStage>
        <ManufDate>2/1/2009</ManufDate>
        <ManufSiteID>WA122</ManufSiteID>
        <SiteBuildingID>45</SiteBuildingID>
        <Status>Pending</Status>
      - <ProtocolSteps>
          <![CDATA[ <Step1>ABC</Step1><Step2>DEF</Step2>  ]]>
        </ProtocolSteps>
      </TypedPollingResultSet0>
    </TypedPollingResultSet0>
  </TypedPolling>
```

Using SQL Server Query notification

While database polling is certainly a sufficient way to learn about database changes, it is inherently fraught with inefficiency. In order to guarantee a timely processing of data, I have to set an aggressive polling window, which in turn means that there will be a measurable number of polling operations that return no results. In essence, the database acts as a passive store, which is constantly being harassed with "do you have anything yet" messages. Isn't there a better way?

Enter Query Notification which is a capability now supported by the WCF SQL Server adapter in concert with SQL Server 2008. Query notification is a means for the database server (through the use of SQL Server Service Broker) to communicate state changes to subscribers as they occur. So instead of asking for changes, the database tells you when a particular condition has been detected.

Yet again, we head to the **Consume Adapter Service** wizard to generate schemas. Like the previous demonstration, we have more to add to our initial connection than just the database and server names. On the **Binding Properties** tab, we set the **Inbound Operation Type** to **Notification** and set the **Notification Statement** which expresses our interest in a particular condition. My statement is:

```
SELECT BatchID FROM dbo.BatchMaster WHERE (ManufStage = 'Final') AND
    (Status = 'Pending')
```

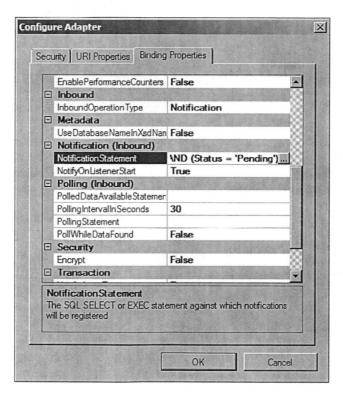

I'm telling the database that I only want insert/update/delete messages when data matching the above condition is impacted. Once our connection properties are adequate, we connect to the target data source and again switch our "client type" from a **Client** to a **Service**. Now we choose **Notification** as a service operation and complete this wizard.

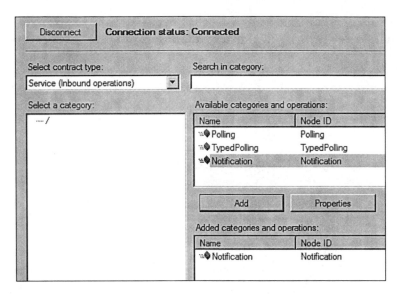

This wizard produces a single schema and a binding file. The schema is almost alarmingly simplistic and contains no context about the data source that changed.

We are meant to absorb this message into an orchestration, and having context about which receive port it came from, query our database for the corresponding messages. For instance, we set up a notification for batches in a final stage of manufacturing. When a batch reaches that stage, this notification message is sent out which simply says data has changed. Knowing that this message arrived from the receive port using a particular notification query, we send a message to the database requesting the records which triggered the notification. The Query Notification process simply tells us "something happened" but it's still our responsibility to ascertain the impact.

That said, we need to generate a schema that lets us "select" from the master batch table so that we are able to extract the impacted records. After once again visiting the **Consume Adapter Service** wizard and choosing the **Select** operation on the **BatchMaster** table, we end up with yet another binding file, and a strongly-typed query schema.

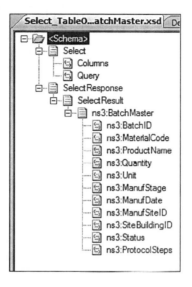

Let's tie all these pieces together now. We need a new orchestration, which accepts the query notification message. Using the distinguished fields on that message, we can determine if we've received a change notification for a message meeting our criteria.

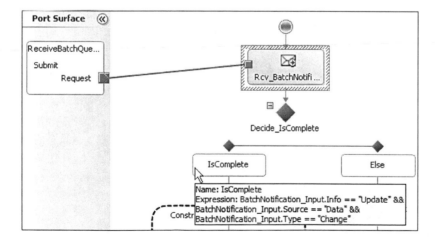

If a change message is encountered, we want to query the **BatchMaster** table and pull back those records of interest. I used a BizTalk map to construct the table query message. Like an earlier demonstration, I disregard the source message and use a single **Concatenate** functoid to produce the where portion of my query (with Columns defaulted to "*"). Note that we want to prevent the retrieval of records that we've read before. Similar to our previously polling demonstration, we will embed an update statement in this request so that immediately after the relevant records are read, they are flagged to prevent a duplicate read.

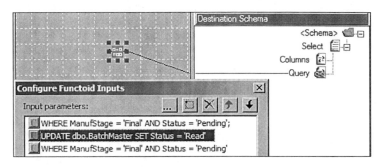

The orchestration flow should now be completed. After receiving the notification, checking the type of change, building a query message, and calling the adapter, we send the response out for logging purposes.

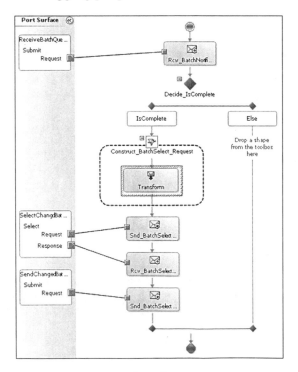

After building and deploying the solution, we import our new binding files into the BizTalk application. As a result, we should have a new receive port and location for query notification, and a new send port for database querying.

Once the orchestration is bound and the ports started, we need to change our database table content in a way that will trigger our notification event. If I take a record in a previous manufacturing state and switch it to `Final`, SQL Server sends a notification and my orchestration reads, marks, and distributes the data.

```xml
- <SelectResponse
    xmlns="http://schemas.microsoft.com/Sql/2008/05/TableOp/dbo/BatchMaster">
  - <SelectResult>
    - <BatchMaster xmlns="http://schemas.microsoft.com/Sql/2008/05/Types/Tables/dbo">
        <BatchID>1</BatchID>
        <MaterialCode>100</MaterialCode>
        <ProductName>Scrotum</ProductName>
        <Quantity>4000</Quantity>
        <Unit>Vials</Unit>
        <ManufStage>Final</ManufStage>
        <ManufDate>2/1/2009</ManufDate>
        <ManufSiteID>WA122</ManufSiteID>
        <SiteBuildingID>45</SiteBuildingID>
        <Status>Pending</Status>
      - <ProtocolSteps>
          <![CDATA[ <Step1>ABC</Step1><Step2>DEF</Step2>  ]]>
        </ProtocolSteps>
      </BatchMaster>
    </SelectResult>
  </SelectResponse>
```

Query notification is a powerful mechanism for making our SQL Server database event driven instead of simply being a passive repository. This opens up a range of possibility on our service bus for establishing more real-time connections and lookups between systems.

While it's great that BizTalk Server can auto-generate schemas for SQL Server artifacts, don't discount the importance of canonical schemas that decouple your processes from the potentially fickle back end data structures. Consider using canonical schemas for your data entities and only map to the auto-generated formats at the edges of the bus.

Consuming the adapter from outside BizTalk Server

One of the benefits of the new WCF SQL Server Adapter that I mentioned earlier was the capability to use this adapter outside of a BizTalk Server solution. Let's take a brief look at three options for using this adapter by itself and without BizTalk as a client or service.

Called directly via WCF service reference

If your service resides on a machine where the WCF SQL Server Adapter (and thus, the **sqlBinding**) is installed, then you may actually add a reference directly to the adapter endpoint.

I have a command-line application, which serves as my service client. If we right-click this application, and have the WCF LOB Adapter SDK installed, then **Add Adapter Service Reference** appears as an option.

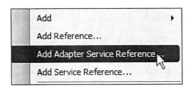

Choosing this option opens our now-beloved wizard for browsing adapter metadata. As before, we add the necessary connection string details and browse the **BatchMaster** table and opt for the **Select** operation.

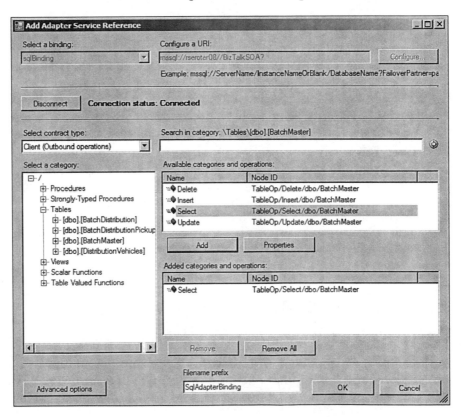

Unlike the version of this wizard that opens for BizTalk Server projects, notice the **Advanced options** button at the bottom. This button opens a property window that lets us select a variety of options such as asynchronous messaging support and suppression of an accompanying configuration file.

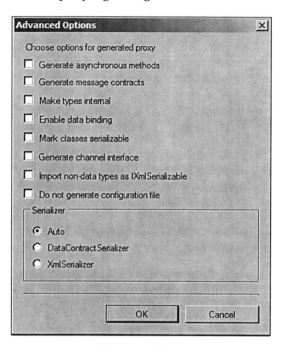

After the wizard is closed, we end up with a new endpoint and binding in our existing configuration file, and a .NET class containing the data and service contracts necessary to consume the service.

We should now call this service as if we were calling any typical WCF service. Because the auto-generated namespace for the data type definition is a bit long, I first added an alias to that namespace. Next, I have a routine, which builds up the query message, executes the service, and prints a subset of the response.

```
using DirectReference = schemas.microsoft.com.Sql._2008._05.Types.
  Tables.dbo;
...
private static void CallReferencedSqlAdapterService()
  {
Console.WriteLine("Calling referenced adapter service");

TableOp_dbo_BatchMasterClient client = new TableOp_dbo_
  BatchMasterClient("SqlAdapterBinding_TableOp_dbo_BatchMaster");
  try
```

```
    {
    string columnString = "*";
    string queryString = "WHERE BatchID = 1";

    DirectReference.BatchMaster[] batchResult =
        client.Select(columnString, queryString);
Console.WriteLine("Batch results ...");
Console.WriteLine("Batch ID: " + batchResult[0].BatchID.ToString());
Console.WriteLine("Product: " + batchResult[0].ProductName);
Console.WriteLine("Manufacturing Stage: " + batchResult[0].ManufStage);

    client.Close();
Console.ReadLine();
    }
    catch (System.ServiceModel.CommunicationException){client.Abort(); }
    catch (System.TimeoutException) { client.Abort(); }
    catch (System.Exception) { client.Abort(); throw; }
    }
```

Once this quick block of code is executed, I can confirm that my database is accessed and my expected result set returned.

Auto-generated IIS-hosted service

The option above is quite easy to use, but does rely on the service client having the **sqlBinding** installed on their machine. That's not a very service-oriented requirement for us to impose on our clients. Instead, we should make this service available through traditional HTTP protocols. We could do this by hand, or, use the handy wizard installed in the WCF LOB Adapter SDK directory.

This wizard takes the SQL Server Adapter and generates a proxy IIS-friendly web service. To access it, right-click your Visual Studio.NET solution file and choose to **Add New Web Site**. If you have **Visual C#** chosen as the **Language**, you should see an option called **WCF Adapter Service**.

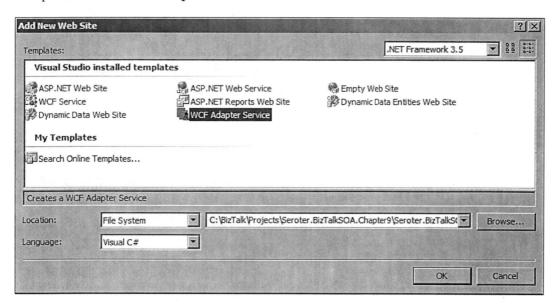

What you get next is a wizard, which walks you through the selection of operations to expose as an HTTP service.

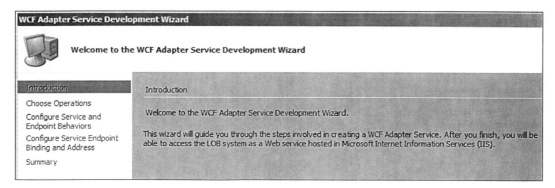

After selecting our connection string, we once again should choose the **Select** operation on the **BatchMaster** table.

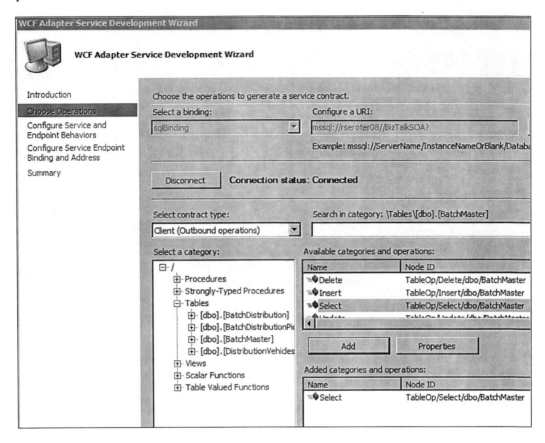

Next, we are asked to provide a subset of the service and endpoint behavior settings. Notice that I've switched **UseServiceCertificate** to **false** which eliminates the requirement to use SSL.

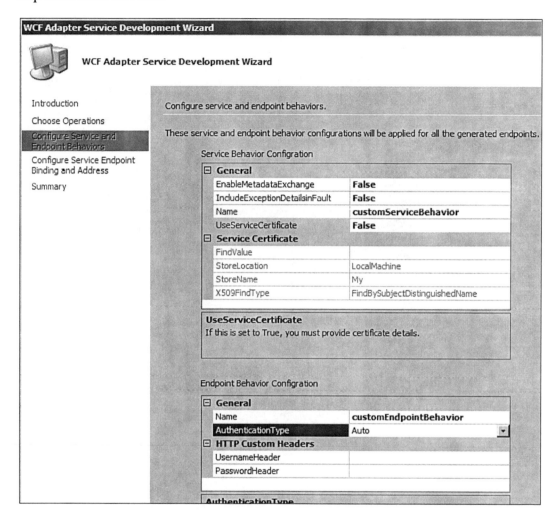

Now we provide additional binding configuration data. I changed the
BindingConfiguration property to use the **None** security setting instead
of **Transport**.

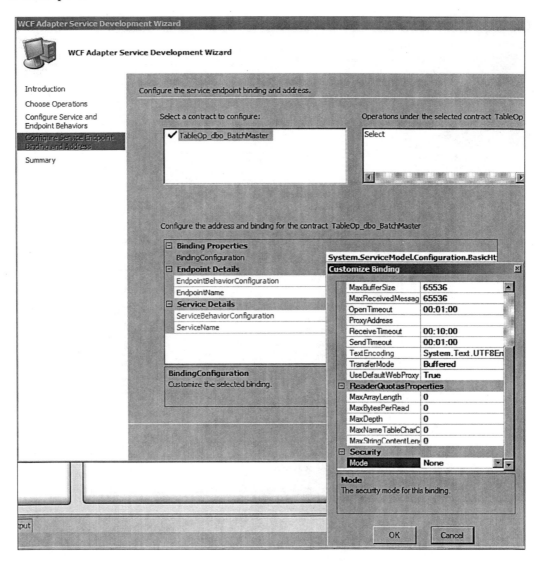

The final **Summary** pane lets us review all of our chosen settings and finally
builds the physical service for us. The wizard didn't completely configure our
service bindings as much as I'd like, so load the generated configuration file
(**web.config**, in this case) into the **WCF Service Configuration Editor**. Specifically,
I added a metadata browsing behavior (to allow WSDL interrogation), and also
set a credential/authorization scheme to use Window integrated security.

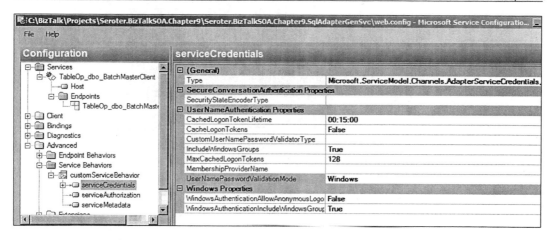

With all of this in place, I added this service to IIS 7.0 and included a traditional WCF service reference to this endpoint from my Visual Studio.NET project. Instead of the client requiring the **sqlBinding** to be installed on the local machine, this service now relies on good old cross-platform basic HTTP communication.

As you can tell here, the client code to call the service is remarkably similar to the code needed by a direct adapter invocation demonstrated previously.

```
private static void CallAutoGeneratedSqlAdapterService()
{
Console.WriteLine("Calling auto-generated adapter service");
AdapterGeneratedSvc.TableOp_dbo_BatchMasterClient client =
  new AdapterGeneratedSvc.TableOp_dbo_BatchMasterClient("TableOp_dbo_
    BatchMasterEndpoint");
try
{
string columnString = "*";
string queryString = "WHERE BatchID = 1";
AdapterGeneratedSvc.BatchMaster[] batchResults =
  client.Select(columnString, queryString);
Console.WriteLine("Batch results ...");
Console.WriteLine("Batch ID: " + batchResults[0].BatchID.ToString());
Console.WriteLine("Product: " + batchResults[0].ProductName);
Console.WriteLine("Manufacturing Stage: " + batchResults[0].
ManufStage);
client.Close();
Console.ReadLine();
}
catch (System.ServiceModel.CommunicationException) { client.Abort(); }
catch (System.TimeoutException) { client.Abort(); }
catch (System.Exception) { client.Abort(); throw; }
}
```

```
c:\ file:///C:/BizTalk/Projects/Seroter.BizTalkSOA.Chapter9/S
Calling auto-generated adapter service
Batch results ...
Batch ID: 1
Product: Serotum
Manufacturing Stage: Final
```

Directly exposing the sqlBinding or auto-generating an HTTP endpoint are both fairly straightforward and easy ways to consume the adapter, but they violate the SOA tenets of loose coupling and abstraction. We require intimate knowledge of our underlying data source and are executing low-level queries against it. Ideally, we should be accessing this service in a more business-service friendly way where both the underlying data source and query plumbing are hidden from view.

Custom built proxy IIS-hosted service

Since the WCF SQL Server Adapter does most of the hard work for us, the least we can do is slap a simple façade on the adapter and abstract the implementation details away from the service clients. We are able to do this by writing a wrapper service which does nothing but front the adapter.

Let's start with a simple WCF contract and data type definition housed in a new Visual Studio.NET class library project. Our wrapper service takes in a batch ID and returns back a MaterialBatch canonical object. Notice no tight coupling to where this data actually resides.

```
[ServiceContract]
public interface IBatchMaster
{
    [OperationContract]
    MaterialBatch GetBatchByID(int batchID);
}

[DataContract]
public class MaterialBatch
{
    [DataMember]
    public int? BatchID { get; set; }
    [DataMember]
    public int? MaterialCode { get; set; }
    [DataMember]
    public string ProductName { get; set; }
    [DataMember]
    public int? Quantity { get; set; }
    [DataMember]
```

```
   public string UnitOfMeasure { get; set; }
   [DataMember]
   public string ManufacturingStage { get; set; }
   [DataMember]
   public string ManufacturingDate { get; set; }
   [DataMember]
   public string SiteID { get; set; }
   [DataMember]
   public int? BuildingID { get; set; }
   [DataMember]
   public string Status { get; set; }
}
```

Just like the previous demo, we add a service reference directly to the WCF SQL Server adapter. Now in our custom service implementation, we call the adapter service using the single parameter passed in from the client.

```
public class BatchMasterService : IBatchMaster
  {
  public MaterialBatch GetBatchByID(int batchID)
  {
  TableOp_dbo_BatchMasterClient client = new TableOp_dbo_
    BatchMasterClient("SqlAdapterBinding_TableOp_dbo_BatchMaster");
  try
  {
  string columnString = "*";
  string queryString = "WHERE BatchID = " + batchID.ToString();
  BatchMaster[] batchResults =
    client.Select(columnString, queryString);
  client.Close();
  if (batchResults.Length > 0)
  {
  MaterialBatch batchResult - new MaterialBatch();
  batchResult.BatchID = batchResults[0].BatchID;
  batchResult.MaterialCode = batchResults[0].MaterialCode;
  batchResult.ProductName = batchResults[0].ProductName;
  batchResult.Quantity = batchResults[0].Quantity;
  batchResult.UnitOfMeasure = batchResults[0].Unit;
  batchResult.ManufacturingStage = batchResults[0].ManufStage;
  batchResult.ManufacturingDate = batchResults[0].ManufDate;
  batchResult.SiteID = batchResults[0].ManufSiteID;
  batchResult.BuildingID = batchResults[0].SiteBuildingID;
  batchResult.Status = batchResults[0].Status;
  return batchResult;
  }
  else
  {
```

```
        return null;
      }
  }
    catch (System.ServiceModel.CommunicationException) { client.Abort(); }
    catch (System.TimeoutException) { client.Abort(); }
    catch (System.Exception) { client.Abort(); throw; }
    return null;
      }
  }
```

Once we're satisfied with this service library, we next create a new **WCF Service**
project in Visual Studio.NET and use the above class as the implementation logic of
the service. This service has both client and service binding configurations because it
receives inbound HTTP requests and calls into the SQL Server adapter through the
sqlBinding binding.

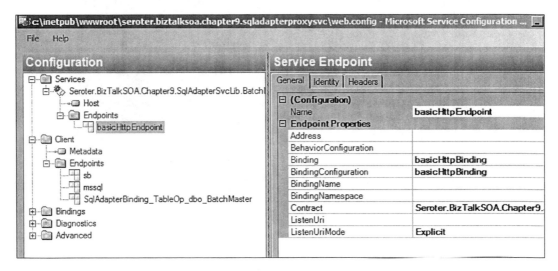

After we add a reference to this new WCF service from within our client application,
we call our application through a much more refined, business-service friendly way.

```
    private static void CallProxySqlAdapterService()
      {
    Console.WriteLine("Calling adapter proxy service");

    AdapterProxySvc.BatchMasterClient client =
        new AdapterProxySvc.BatchMasterClient("basicHttpEndpoint");

      try
      {
    AdapterProxySvc.MaterialBatch batchResult = client.GetBatchByID(1);

    Console.WriteLine("Batch results ...");
    Console.WriteLine("Batch ID: " + batchResult.BatchID.ToString());
```

```
Console.WriteLine("Product: " + batchResult.ProductName);
Console.WriteLine("Manufacturing Stage: " +
   batchResult.ManufacturingStage);

   client.Close();

   Console.ReadLine();
   }
   catch (System.ServiceModel.CommunicationException){client.Abort(); }
   catch (System.TimeoutException) { client.Abort(); }
   catch (System.Exception) { client.Abort(); throw; }
}
```

Once this code is executed, we are able to confirm a successful invocation.

We've seen three ways to call the WCF SQL Server Adapter without the help of BizTalk Server. While it is perfectly valid to expose adapter execution directly to clients, there are long-term service-orientation benefits to putting a small layer of abstraction on top of the native adapter operations.

Summary

In this chapter, we've seen a new way to generate and consume services through the WCF SQL Server Adapter. This new adapter offers us significantly more control over access to our back end database while providing a cleaner metadata browsing and development experience. The reusability of this adapter is compelling and means that a developer well-versed in BizTalk development can seamlessly transfer that data connectivity knowledge to a standard WCF application. Because you can now define SQL Server-based services outside of BizTalk Server, consider whether or not it makes sense to define a particular operation as a standalone service that BizTalk (and others) can consume, or whether you should use the WCF-SQL binding directly within a BizTalk send port. Each situation is different, but it's great to now have such choices.

In the next chapter, we take a look at the new UDDI Server that comes with BizTalk Server 2009.

10

New SOA Capabilities in BizTalk Server 2009: UDDI Services

All truths are easy to understand once they are discovered; the point is to discover them.

-Galileo Galilei

In the previous chapter, we outlined some of the new platform support in BizTalk Server 2009. It seems that Microsoft is reinforcing BizTalk Server's role in a service-oriented architecture by moving their UDDI Services into the BizTalk Server 2009 product. In this chapter, we discuss what UDDI is, and how to use its capabilities in your environment.

What is UDDI?

Universal Description and Discovery Information (UDDI) is a type of registry whose primary purpose is to represent information about web services. It describes the service providers, the services that provider offers, and in some cases, the specific technical specifications for interacting with those services. While UDDI was originally envisioned as a public, platform independent registry that companies could exploit for listing and consuming services, it seems that many have chosen instead to use UDDI as an internal resource for categorizing and describing their available enterprise services.

Besides simply listing available services for others to search and peruse, UDDI is arguably most beneficial for those who wish to perform runtime binding to service endpoints. Instead of hard-coding a service path in a client application, one may query UDDI for a particular service's endpoint and apply it to their active service call. While UDDI is typically used for web services, nothing prevents someone from storing information about any particular transport and allowing service consumers to discover and do runtime resolution to these endpoints. As an example, this is useful if you have an environment with primary, backup, and disaster access points and want your application be able to gracefully look up and failover to the next available service environment. In addition, UDDI can be of assistance if an application is deployed globally but you wish for regional consumers to look up and resolve against the closest geographical endpoint.

UDDI has a few core hierarchy concepts that you must grasp to fully comprehend how the registry is organized. The most important ones are included here.

Name	Purpose	Name in Microsoft UDDI services
BusinessEntity	These are the service providers. May be an organization, business unit or functional area.	Provider
BusinessService	General reference to a business service offered by a provider. May be a logical grouping of actual services.	Service
BindingTemplate	Technical details of an individual service including endpoint	Binding
tModel (Technical Model)	Represents metadata for categorization or description such as transport or protocol	tModel

As far as relationships between these entities go, a Business Entity may contain many Business Services, which in turn can have multiple Binding Templates. A binding may reference multiple tModels and tModels may be reused across many Binding Templates.

What's new in UDDI version three? The latest UDDI specification calls out multiple-registry environments, support for digital signatures applied to UDDI entries, more complex categorization, wildcard searching, and a subscription API. We'll spend a bit of time on that last one in a few moments.

Let's take a brief lap around at the Microsoft UDDI Services offering. For practical purposes, consider the UDDI Services to be made up of two parts: an Administration Console and a web site. The website is actually broken up into both a public facing and administrative interface, but we'll talk about them as one unit.

The UDDI Configuration Console is the place to set service-wide settings ranging from the extent of logging to permissions and site security.

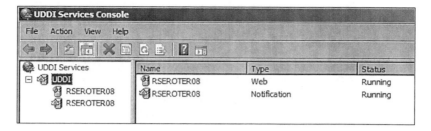

The `site` node (named **UDDI**) has settings for permission account groups, security settings (see below), and subscription notification thresholds among others.

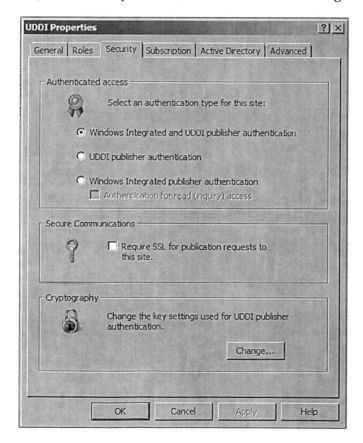

The web node, which resides immediately beneath the parent, controls web site setting such as logging level and target database.

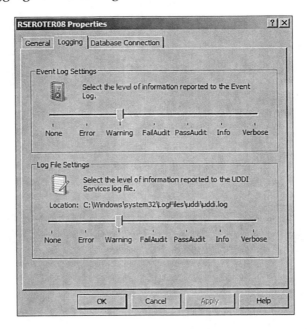

Finally, the notification node manages settings related to the new subscription notification feature and identically matches the categories of the web node.

The UDDI Services web site, found at http://localhost/uddi/, is the destination for physically listing, managing, and configuring services.

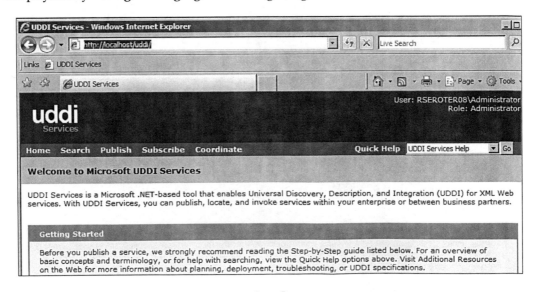

The **Search** page enables querying by a wide variety of criteria including category, services, service providers, bindings, and tModels.

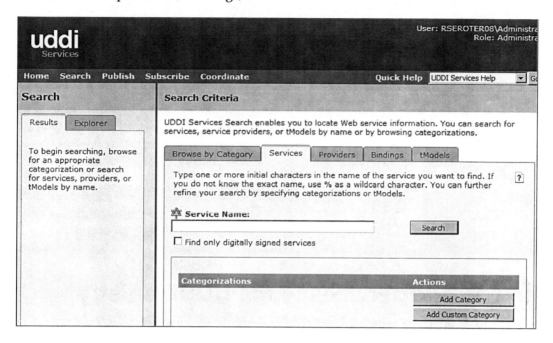

The **Publish** page is where you go to add new services to the registry or edit the settings of existing ones.

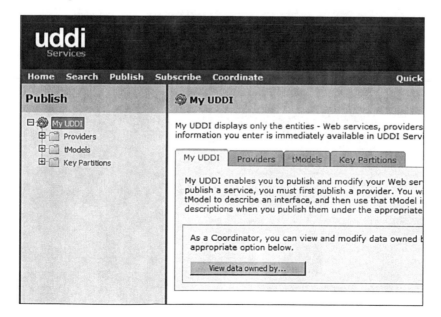

Finally, the **Subscription** page is where the new UDDI version three capability of registry notification is configured. We will demonstrate this feature later in this chapter.

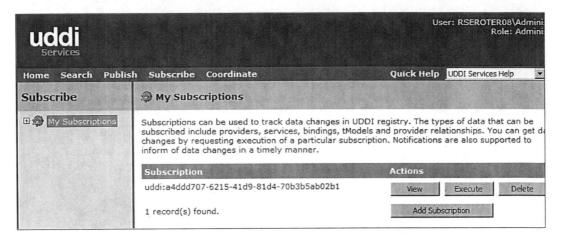

How to add services to the UDDI registry

Now we're ready to add new services to our UDDI registry. First, let's go to the **Publish** page and define our Service Provider and a pair of categorical tModels. To add a new Provider, we right-click the **Provider** node in the tree and choose **Add Provider**.

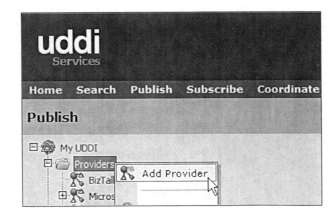

Once a provider is created and named, we have the choice of adding all types of context characteristics such as a contact name(s), categories, relationships, and more.

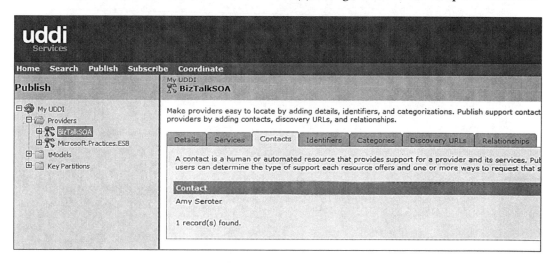

I'd like to add two tModel categories to my environment: one to identify which type of environment the service references (development, test, staging, production) and another to flag which type of transport it uses (Basic HTTP, WS HTTP, and so on). To add a tModel, simply right-click the **tModels** node and choose **Add tModel**.

This first one is named **biztalksoa:runtimeresolution:environment**.

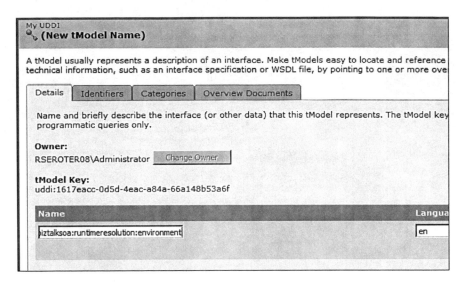

After adding one more tModel for **biztalksoa:runtimeresolution:transporttype**, we're ready to add a service to the registry. Right-click the **BizTalkSOA** provider and choose **Add Service**. Set the name of this service to **BatchMasterService**.

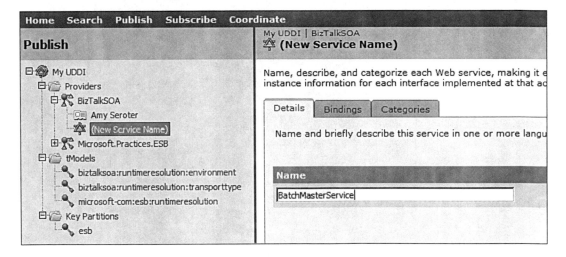

Next, we want to add a binding (or access point) for this service, which describes where the service endpoint is physically located. Switch to the **Bindings** tab of the service definition and choose **New Binding**. We need a new access point, so I pointed to our proxy service created in the previous chapter and identified it as an **endPoint**.

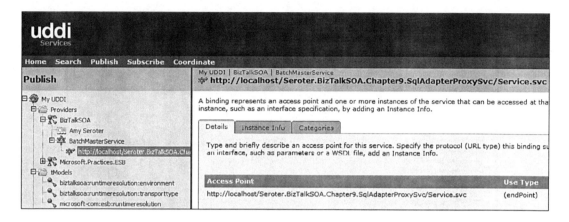

Finally, let's associate the two new tModel categories with our service. Switch to the **Categories** tab, and choose to **Add Custom Category**. We're asked to search for a tModel, which represents our category, so a wildcard entry such as **%biztalksoa%** is a valid search criterion.

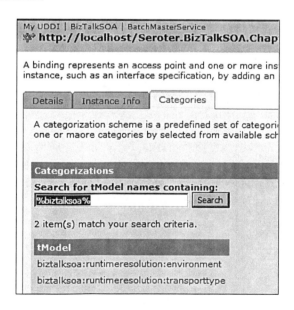

After selecting the environment category, we're asked for the key name and value. The key "name" is purely a human-friendly representation of the data whereas the tModel identifier and the key value comprise the actual name-value pair. I've entered **production** as the value on the **environment** category, and **WS-Http** as the key value on the **transporttype** category.

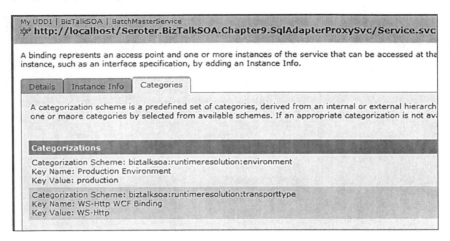

At this point, we have a service sufficiently configured in the UDDI directory so that others can discover and dynamically resolve against it.

Dynamic endpoint resolution via UDDI

Speaking of resolving, how do we actually call into a UDDI directory from code and discover information (including the endpoint) about a service? Let's take a look.

From within our command-line client application, we need to add a reference to the **Microsoft.Uddi.dll**. You should find this at `C:\Program Files\Microsoft UDDI Services\SDK\Microsoft.Uddi.dll`. We'll first look at the scenario where you already know the service key for the service. What is the service key and how do you find that? On the **Details** page of your service in the directory, there is a **More Details** link which opens up a window containing both the UDDI V2 and V3-compatible keys.

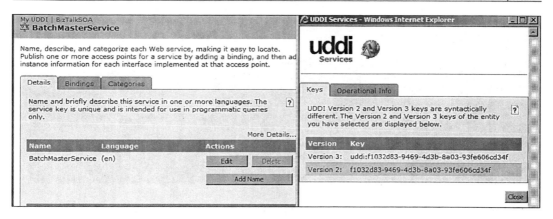

Armed with this exciting piece of information, we're ready to look up our service. In the code below, you should see that I have a reference to the UDDI library, and have created a connection that points to the query service URI provided by the UDDI Services. Next, I ask for the details of the service based on the key and connection I've provided.

```
using Microsoft.Uddi3;
using Microsoft.Uddi3.Extensions;
using Microsoft.Uddi3.Services;

...

UddiConnection conn =
new UddiConnection("http://localhost/uddi/inquire.asmx");
 GetServiceDetail getDetails =
new GetServiceDetail("uddi:f1032d83-9469-4d3b-8a03-93fe606cd34f ");
ServiceDetail details = getDetails.Send(conn);
```

Once we have the service details in response, we are capable of discovering all sorts of things about our service.

```
//add pointer to target service
BusinessService service = details.BusinessServices[0];
Console.WriteLine("Service Name: " + service.Names[0].Text);
Console.WriteLine("Access Point: " +
   service.BindingTemplates[0].AccessPoint.Text);
KeyedReferenceCollection categories =
   service.BindingTemplates[0].CategoryBag.KeyedReferences;
Console.WriteLine("** Categories **");
foreach (KeyedReference catKey in categories)
  {
    Console.WriteLine("Category Name: " + catKey.KeyName);
    Console.WriteLine("Category Value: " + catKey.KeyValue);
  }
Console.ReadLine();
```

The result of this block of code reveals all of the entries we added to our UDDI directory just a short time ago.

```
file:///C:/BizTalk/Projects/Seroter.BizTalkSOA.Chapter9/Seroter.BizTalkSOA.Chapter9.ServiceClientUI...
Calling UDDI key lookup service
Service Name: BatchMasterService
Access Point: http://localhost/Seroter.BizTalkSOA.Chapter9.SqlAdapterProxySvc/Se
rvice.svc
** Categories **
Category Name: Production Environment
Category Value: production
Category Name: WS-Http WCF Binding
Category Value: WS-Http
```

Now what if we don't know the service key? Fortunately for us, the UDDI service API also provides a query interface. If we want to search by service name, or by a set of categories we can.

```
Console.WriteLine("Calling UDDI query lookup service");

UddiConnection conn =
 new UddiConnection("http://localhost/uddi/inquire.asmx");

FindService serviceQuery =
  new FindService("BatchMasterService");
ServiceList queryResult = serviceQuery.Send(conn);
string key = queryResult.ServiceInfos[0].ServiceKey;
Console.WriteLine("Service key: " + key);

Console.ReadLine();
```

When this code runs, we get back a key corresponding to our service in the registry.

```
file:///C:/BizTalk/Projects/Seroter.BizTalkSOA.Chapter9/Seroter.BizTalkSOA.C
Calling UDDI query lookup service
Service key: uddi:f1032d83-9469-4d3b-8a03-93fe606cd34f
```

The query scenario is useful if you want to do runtime resolution of a service within a given environment (say, production) and enable the UDDI administrators to re-point users to available services if the primary service is down. An administrator could perform this task by simply changing UDDI category values.

Building subscription alerts for service changes

One of the new features in UDDI V3 is the ability to subscribe to changes that occur within the UDDI directory. That is, we can build service listeners which act when UDDI objects (providers, services, and so on) undergo revision.

The Microsoft UDDI Service conforms to the official UDDI standard, and thus complies with WSDLs hosted at http://www.uddi.org. So, in order to build a listener service that UDDI Services will consume, create a service library with a service reference to the relevant WSDL on http://www.uddi.org. How do we do this? First, point the WCF svcutil.exe tool at the public WSDL:

```
svcutil http://uddi.org/wsdl/uddi_subr_v3_portType.wsdl /out:
IUDDISubscriber.cs
```

Take the resulting class, and add it to a new class library project in Visual Studio.NET.

Pitfall

The interface generated by the WCF svcutil.exe tool is not completely accurate according to the message sent by Microsoft UDDI Services. Specifically, the generated interface UDDI_SubscriptionListener_PortType has an operation named notify_subscriptionListener whose Action property should be changed to "*". There is no SOAP action defined in the core WSDL so WCF automatically adds one. However, this causes a mismatch when UDDI Services call the WCF service. Once the Action property is modified, the service contract matches the message sent by the UDDI Services.

After adding the necessary project references to **System.ServiceModel.dll** and **System.Runtime.Serialization.dll**, create a new class which implements this contract identified in the public WSDL.

```
public class UDDISubscriberService : UDDI_SubscriptionListener_
PortType
{
  public notify_subscriptionListenerResponse notify_subscriptionListen
er(notify_subscriptionListenerRequest request)
  {
    string requestValues;

    // Open file to write to log
    System.IO.StreamWriter file = new System.IO.StreamWriter("c:\\
UDDILog.txt", true);
```

```
      file.WriteLine("**" + System.DateTime.Now + "**");
      //get UDDI key
      requestValues = request.notify_subscriptionListener.
  subscriptionResultsList.subscription.subscriptionKey;
      //write contents
      file.WriteLine("Subscription key: " + requestValues);
      get_serviceDetail impactedService = (get_serviceDetail)request.
  notify_subscriptionListener.subscriptionResultsList.subscription.
  subscriptionFilter.Item;
      requestValues = impactedService.serviceKey[0].ToString();
      //write contents
      file.WriteLine("Impacted service key: " + requestValues);
      file.WriteLine("*********");
      file.Close();
      notify_subscriptionListenerResponse result = new notify_
  subscriptionListenerResponse();
      result.dispositionReport = new dispositionReport();
      return result;
    }
  }
```

Now we create a new **WCF Service** project and reference this existing service library. After making sure the .svc file points to our referenced library object, and adding a valid endpoint configuration file, view our service in the web browser to ensure that it's up and running.

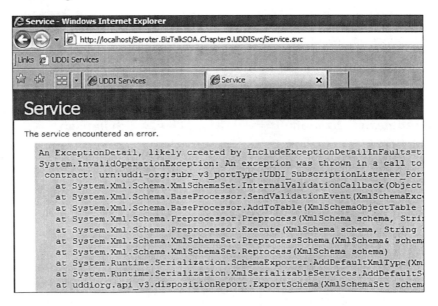

Clearly, that service's metadata is NOT in good shape. But, I'm not too worried about the service's own ability to serve up metadata because I just pointed to the public WSDL and established that as the source of metadata. This is done by setting the **externalMetadataBehavior** attribute on our service behavior.

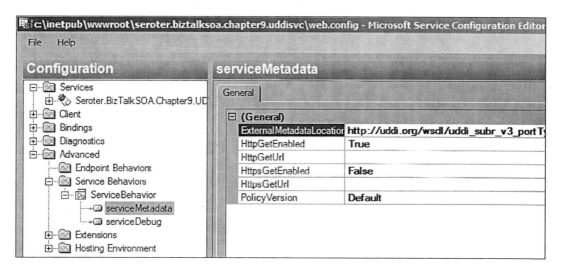

Now in order for us to use this service as a notification service, it actually needs to be registered in the UDDI directory itself. Within the same UDDI provider (**BizTalkSOA**), we add a new service and point it at this endpoint.

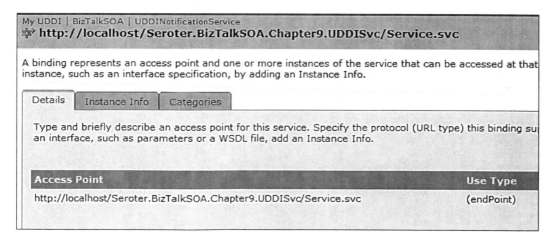

We're almost done setting up this service minus one last change. This listener service must specifically be categorized as a UDDI listener within the registry. This is done by switching to the **Instance Info** tab on the service configuration and searching for the correct tModel named **uddi-org:subscriptionListener_v3**.

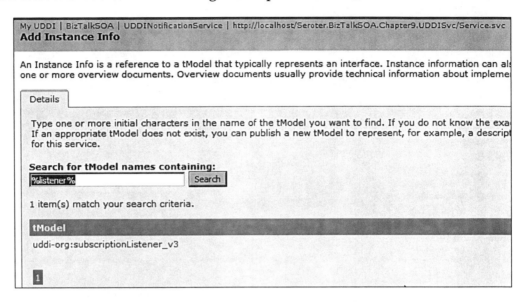

Select that particular tModel, and our configuration is complete. Now, we go to the **Subscribe** tab of the UDDI site where we define a new subscription. After clicking the **Add Subscription** button, choose the type of data entity we wish to write a subscription for.

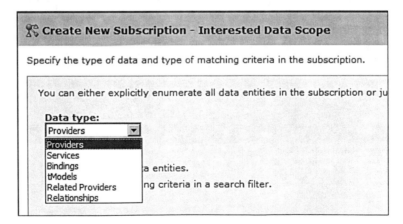

I've chosen **Services** and am next presented with a screen used to find the service we're specifically interested in subscribing to. A search for %**batch**% yields a single result pointing to our recently added **MasterBatchService**. After adding that service to the **Selected Element** list, we designate our notification mechanism for this subscription.

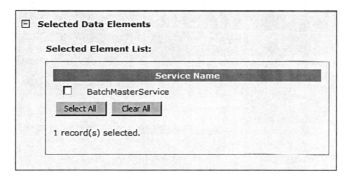

We select the **Enable Notification** checkbox and then select the binding associated with our subscription listener endpoint. In our case, it's the second choice presented below.

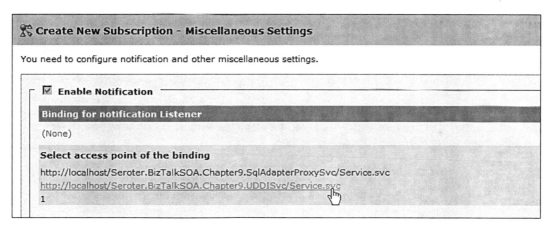

After selecting the appropriate service and choosing a notification interval (which determines how frequently the UDDI Service publishes changes) our subscription is complete. We should now see a subscription listed on the left-side tree, and be able to peruse our subscription settings.

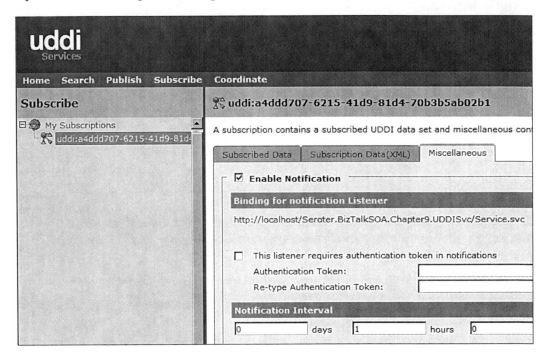

If we make a change to our service and execute the subscription (by either waiting the designated interval, or right-clicking the subscription and choosing **Execute**), we should see our listener service get executed.

Note that while I only showed changes being pushed out of UDDI via subscriptions, there is also a synchronous interface available for interrogating UDDI for changes on demand. Keep this in mind when deciding what changes you are interested in and if the information should be shared in an event-driven manner or simply on demand.

Summary

The UDDI V3 components included in BizTalk Server 2009 offer a set of services that are fully compliant with the UDDI standard. While there are dedicated vendors that offer very robust repositories alongside additional service governance solutions, if you are currently doing without an enterprise service repository, consider using UDDI Services.

In the next chapter, we take a look at the Enterprise Service Bus Guidance package that supports BizTalk Server 2009.

11

New SOA Capabilities in BizTalk Server 2009: ESB Guidance 2.0

Change starts when someone sees the next step.
-William Drayton

The final new SOA-friendly feature in BizTalk Server 2009 is the ESB Guidance package. This accelerator provides a diverse set of services and patterns that build upon a BizTalk foundation while making BizTalk a more loosely-coupled and flexible messaging engine. In this chapter, we will investigate ESB Guidance and walk through numerous scenarios that flex the core components.

What is ESB Guidance?

The ESB Guidance solution package rose from a desire to create an even more loosely-coupled, generic messaging model and toolset in BizTalk than already existed. ESB Guidance is not a product per se, as it has no official Microsoft support and should not be considered to be "ESB in a box" but rather, is an offering consisting of a set of services, components, and patterns which extend existing BizTalk capabilities.

Similar to BizTalk Server itself, you do not need to use the entirety of the solution, but instead you may pick and choose the components and services that solve a specific problem. You can apply the Transformation Service if you want to reuse BizTalk maps from external clients, or engage the Exception Management framework if you want a uniform way to publish, capture, and report on application exceptions.

The Itinerary processing services and components offer a compelling way to reduce the number of managed endpoints while enabling an easy way to model the path of a message through the service bus.

The ESB Guidance solution also integrates with existing SOA Governance platforms from SOA Software and AmberPoint to encourage integration of service management and repository usage.

Throughout the rest of this chapter, we'll look at some of the core aspects of ESB Guidance and build example solutions using the various components.

Available services

ESB Guidance 2.0 contains an impressive series of services that extract BizTalk functionality into a more abstract and reusable tier. These services include:

Service	Description
BizTalk Operations Service	Reveals runtime details about BizTalk hosts and applications. Can query the status of applications and ports and build processes or dashboards based on the information provided.
UDDI Service	Enables querying of UDDI repositories based on a variety of criteria.
Resolver Service	Used to look up ESB endpoints (be they UDDI, Business Rules Engine, and so on) and returns all known details about those endpoints.
Exception Handling Service	Accepts standard fault messages, enriches them, and publishes them to a central Portal for investigation, analysis, and resolution.
Transformation Service	Exposes the ability to execute BizTalk maps without going through the BizTalk messaging infrastructure.
Itinerary Services	Accepts messages and uses provided or resolved metadata to route the message through a series of services (such as orchestrations, transformations, transmissions) in either a synchronous or asynchronous manner.

The following examples make use of the Transformation Service, Resolver Service, Exception Handling Service and Itinerary Service.

Transformation Services

Let's first take a look at how to use the Transformation Service available from ESB Guidance 2.0. To start with, we'll design a new schema that represents data retrieved from a device which captures the status of a given batch.

Next we want a map which takes this `MaterialScannerOutput` structure and builds up a `BatchMaster` message. All of the unmapped fields have their values set to either empty (for strings) or 0 (for numbers).

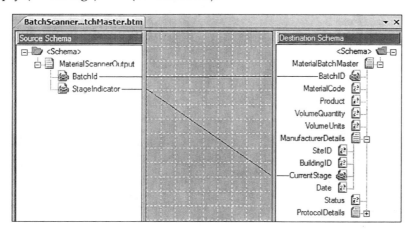

This is all that is needed from a BizTalk perspective. Build and deploy the project so that our assembly is updated in the GAC. Now, we turn our attention to the client application. In order to call the Transformation Service, we first need a service reference to the service located at `http://<server>/ESB.TransformServices.WCF/TransformationService.svc`. Once a service reference is established, the client code utilizes the generated proxy class to call the Transformation Service. The simplest way to call this service is by passing in a direct reference to the map you wish to execute. The code below demonstrates this particular technique:

```
private static void CallEsbGuidanceTransformServiceHardcode()
  {
Console.WriteLine("Calling ESB Guidance transform service");
TransformationServiceClient client =
    new TransformationServiceClient
       ("WSHttpBinding_ITransformationService");
  try
  {
  XmlDocument scannerDoc = new XmlDocument();
scannerDoc.LoadXml("<MaterialScannerOutput xmlns=\"http://Seroter.
    BizTalkSOA.Chapter9.EsbBits\"><BatchId>1</BatchId><StageIndicator>
    Completed</StageIndicator></MaterialScannerOutput>");
  string xmlString = scannerDoc.OuterXml;
```

```
   string map = "Seroter.BizTalkSOA.Chapter9.EsbBits.
BatchScannerOutput_To_MaterialBatchMaster, Seroter.BizTalkSOA.
Chapter9.EsbBits, Version=1.0.0.0, Culture=neutral,
PublicKeyToken=3a9902d460c201ec";
   string resultString = client.Transform(xmlString, map);
Console.WriteLine(resultString);
   client.Close();
   }
   catch (System.ServiceModel.CommunicationException) { client.Abort();
   }
   catch (System.TimeoutException) { client.Abort(); }
   catch (System.Exception) { client.Abort(); throw; }
Console.WriteLine("done");
Console.ReadLine();
   }
```

The result of this operation is as follows:

We passed one message type in, and indeed, got another one out. Note that this service does not depend on the BizTalk engine itself being up and running. It bypasses the BizTalk messaging layer and executes the maps directly from the relevant assemblies. Note that while this service does not rely on the BizTalk engine, it does require BizTalk Server itself to be installed on the same box where the transformation service runs. This is because the service needs the BizTalk assemblies (such as functoids) to successfully execute a map.

However, this is not an ideal execution scenario. Why should our service client need to possess this information and tightly couple themselves to an implementation detail? Instead, wouldn't we rather possess a token or key, which resolves the map assembly at runtime? As it turns out, this capability is what the "resolver service" offers us.

Resolver Services

The Resolver Service play an important role in the overarching ESB Guidance theme of loose coupling through the use of dynamic resolution techniques. ESB Guidance ships with a series of pre-built resolvers against common lookup repositories such as UDDI, WS-MEX, Business Rules Engine, and XPATH. It also supports the use of a "static" resolver which uses a hard-coded path to a particular resource (such as map, file path, service address).

Let's apply the Resolver Service to our previous mapping example. Instead of hard-coding a map assembly directive, we'd rather store this information and resolve it at runtime. One available repository for storage is the Microsoft Business Rules Engine that ships with BizTalk Server 2009. I've created a new rule policy named **Seroter.BizTalkSOA.Chapter9.Transform** and created a single rule called **SetScannerToMasterMap**. This rule utilizes an ESB Guidance-provided vocabulary that refers to the transport type (such as map assembly reference).

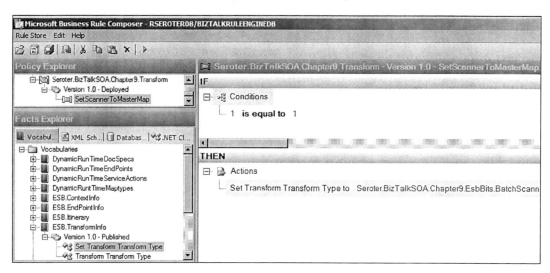

The Resolver Service executes this ruleset, and brings back the value that the Transform Service requires for completion. To use this Resolver Service, we add a service reference to our project and point it to: `http://<server>/ESB.ResolverServices.WCF/ResolverService.svc`

Start this example with code nearly identical to the last transformation exercise.

```
private static void CallEsbGuidanceTransformServiceResolve()
  {
Console.WriteLine("Calling ESB Guidance resolver service");

TransformationServiceClient client =
  new TransformationServiceClient
  ("WSHttpBinding_ITransformationService");
  try
  {
XmlDocument scannerDoc = new XmlDocument();
```

```
scannerDoc.LoadXml("<MaterialScannerOutput xmlns=\"http://Seroter.
   BizTalkSOA.Chapter9.EsbBits\"><BatchId>1</BatchId><StageIndicator>
   Completed</StageIndicator></MaterialScannerOutput>");
string xmlString = scannerDoc.OuterXml;
string map = "";
```

Instead of setting a map value here in code, we'll stand up the Resolver Service and query it for the appropriate information.

```
ResolverServiceClient rClient = new ResolverServiceClient
   ("ResolverEndpoint");
try
{
rClient.ClientCredentials.Windows.AllowedImpersonationLevel =
   System.Security.Principal.TokenImpersonationLevel.Impersonation;
string resolverString = @"BRE:\\policy=Seroter.BizTalkSOA.Chapter9.
   Transform;version=1.0;useMsg=";
Resolver[] resolverCollection = rClient.Resolve(resolverString);
foreach (Resolver resolver in resolverCollection)
{
if (resolver.Name == "Resolver.TransformType")
{
map = resolver.Value;
break;
}
}
rClient.Close();
}
catch (System.ServiceModel.CommunicationException){client.Abort();}
catch (System.TimeoutException) { client.Abort(); }
catch (System.Exception) { client.Abort(); throw; }
Console.WriteLine("Calling ESB Guidance transform service");
   string resultString = client.Transform(xmlString, map);
Console.WriteLine(resultString);
   client.Close();
   }
   catch (System.ServiceModel.CommunicationException){client.Abort();}
   catch (System.TimeoutException) { client.Abort(); }
   catch (System.Exception) { client.Abort(); throw; }
Console.WriteLine("done");
Console.ReadLine();
```

What I have here is a `resolverString` variable which uses the known BRE prefix and refers to a specific Business Rules Engine policy. Be aware that you may choose to omit the version number, and the Resolver will simply use the latest version of the deployed policy.

The result of the service is an array of values of which we cycle through until we find the property named `Resolver.TransformType`. We then proceed to pass our runtime-acquired value into the original Transformation Service.

```
string resultString = client.Transform(xmlString, map);
```

This is a much cleaner way to resolve transformation details and allow our application clients to survive small map-related bug fixes and updates without requiring a coding change.

Exception Services

The ESB Guidance toolkit includes a rich set of capabilities for exception management. What we'll focus on here is the exposed WCF service that allows external applications to publish their exception details to a central service where unified processing is applied.

Let's build a small example of this service in action. After adding a reference to the Exception Service (located at `http://<server>/ESB.ExceptionHandlingServices.WCF/ExceptionHandling.svc`), we add a bit of code to our client application which inflates an XML document, and intentionally causes a mathematical error.

```
XmlDocument scannerDoc = new XmlDocument();

//for beta release, had to explicitly wrap with "any"
scannerDoc.LoadXml("<any xmlns=\"http://www.w3.org/1999/xhtml\
"><MaterialScannerOutput xmlns=\"http://Seroter.BizTalkSOA.
Chapter9.EsbBits\"><BatchId>1</BatchId><StageIndicator>Completed</
StageIndicator></MaterialScannerOutput></any>");

 try
 {
   Console.WriteLine("Causing exception");
   int numberOne = 20;
   int numberTwo = 0;
    int numberThree = numberOne / numberTwo;
 }
```

I've done a `divide by zero` situation, which will raise an exception in my code. While we've all come across logging frameworks for capturing exceptions in a common way, the ESB Guidance Exception Service provides us access to the full power of BizTalk Server for routing exceptions and introducing workflow activities to accommodate resubmission of data.

We need to catch our error and pump up the ESB Guidance exception message (of type `FaultMessage`) which our service expects.

```
catch (Exception codeEx)
  {
Console.WriteLine("Calling ESB Guidance exception handling service");

ExceptionHandlingClient client =
  new ExceptionHandlingClient("WSHttpBinding_ITwoWayAsyncVoid");

  try
  {
//**create fault message
FaultMessage fault = newFaultMessage();

//**header details
  fault.Header = new FaultMessageHeader();
  fault.Header.Application = "BizTalkSOA";
  fault.Header.Description = "Calculation failed";
  fault.Header.ErrorType = "Math Error";
  fault.Header.FaultSeverity = 1;
  fault.Header.FaultCode = "00001";
  fault.Header.FailureCategory = "System";
  fault.Header.FaultDescription = "Fault Description";
  fault.Header.FaultGenerator = "Client Code";
  fault.Header.Scope = "CallEsbGuidanceExceptionService";
  fault.Header.ServiceInstanceID = System.Guid.NewGuid().ToString();
  fault.Header.ServiceName = "Exception Service";
  fault.Header.MachineName = System.Environment.MachineName;
  fault.Header.DateTime = DateTime.Now.ToString();
  fault.Header.ControlBit = "1";
  fault.Header.MessageID = System.Guid.NewGuid().ToString();
  fault.Header.ActivityIdentity = System.Environment.UserName;
  fault.Header.NACK = false;
```

Once the header values are in place (where the values are at your discretion and not pre-defined), we attach our exception details.

```
//**exception object details
    fault.ExceptionObject = new FaultMessageExceptionObject();
    fault.ExceptionObject.Message = codeEx.Message;
    fault.ExceptionObject.Source = codeEx.Source;
    fault.ExceptionObject.Type = codeEx.GetType().ToString();
    fault.ExceptionObject.TargetSite =
    codeEx.TargetSite.ToString();
    fault.ExceptionObject.StackTrace = codeEx.StackTrace;
    //the innerexception is null for this demonstration
    //fault.ExceptionObject.InnerExceptionMessage=string.empty;
    //codeEx.InnerException.Message;
```

In this case, all of the exception values are pulled directly from the .NET exception object thrown by my "divide by zero" code. Note that you could just as easily affix your own custom values here for business exceptions.

If this were a BizTalk message, or if you wanted to provide additional context about the message itself, the FaultMessage has a context property bag to house such details.

```
//**context properties
    FaultMessageMessageContextProperty[] context =
    newFaultMessageMessageContextProperty[1];
    context[0] = new FaultMessageMessageContextProperty();
    context[0].Name = "MaterialStage";
    context[0].Type = "Seroter.BizTalkSOA.Batch";
    context[0].Value = "Completed";
```

Next we create an array of the actual message(s) containing the data relevant to this exception.

```
//**message data
    FaultMessageMessageMessageData msgData =
    new FaultMessageMessageMessageData();
    XmlNode[] docField = new XmlNode[1];
    docField[0] = (XmlNode)scannerDoc;
    msgData.Any = docField;
```

Finally, we append those messages to an object containing additional details about the particular message instances.

```
//**message
    FaultMessageMessage[] messages =new FaultMessageMessage[1];
    messages[0] = new FaultMessageMessage();
    messages[0].ContentType = "text/xml";
    messages[0].InterchangeID = "InterchangeID1";
    messages[0].MessageID = "MessageID1";
    messages[0].MessageName = "MessageName1";
    messages[0].MessageType = "MessageType1";
    messages[0].MessageContext = context;
    messages[0].MessageData = msgData;
    messages[0].RoutingURL = "";

    fault.Messages = messages;

    client.SubmitFault(fault);
```

At last, we submit our actual fault message. While there are a lot of data points that comprise an ESB Guidance exception message, this should be seen as a benefit, not detraction. Whenever I'm stuck troubleshooting an error, I always appreciate more information over less. Plus, the availability of categorical information means that we have a diverse set of criteria on which to route the exception.

Now, we don't want to execute this code just yet. Where is this exception going to go once it reaches BizTalk Server? By default, there is a "catch all" send port (called **ALL.Exceptions**) installed with the ESB Guidance BizTalk application. This port subscribes to any `ErrorReports` that reach the `MessageBox`, or, any message with an ESB Guidance `FaultCode` in its context. It puts these messages into the ESB Guidance Exception Database where the provided interactive portal allows for viewing and reporting on these errors.

In our scenario, we want to catch these exceptions and print them to disk as InfoPath forms. This way, an IT professional can review the exception in an easy-to-read way. The ESB Guidance installation instructions tell us to create Windows "shares" for the provided InfoPath form located at `C:\Projects\microsoft.practices.esb\Source\Samples\Exception Handling\Source\ESB.ExceptionHandling.InfoPath.Reporting\Publish`. Once this is in place, visit the BizTalk Administration Console and add a reference to the **Microsoft.Practices.ESB** application from the **BizTalkSOA** application. We must do this so that the send port in our application is able use property schemas associated with the **Microsoft.Practices.ESB** application.

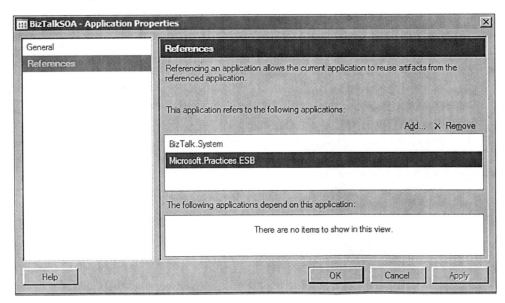

Next, create a new send port whose filter looks for the existence of an ESB fault.

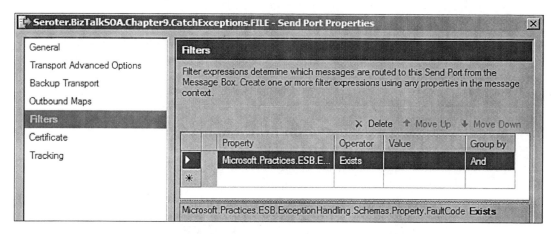

In order for this form to be discharged as an InfoPath form, we must add the appropriate processing instruction to the outbound message. The **ESBFaultProcessor** pipeline is a powerful tool for encoding exceptions from BizTalk messages, but we do not need to harness much of that power here. Instead, I've clicked the ellipse next to the pipeline and configured it by turning off the last two pipeline components (which control mapping and BAM integration) and added an InfoPath processing instruction to the **ESB Exception Encoder** pipeline component.

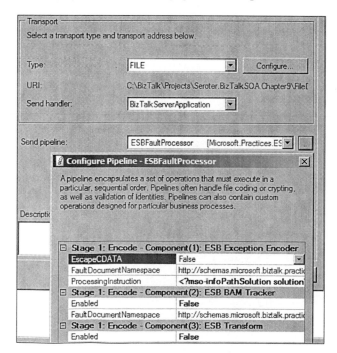

My InfoPath processing instruction is:

```
<?mso-infoPathSolution solutionVersion="1.0.0.361"
productVersion="12.0.0" PIVersion="1.0.0.0" href="file:///\\
localhost\Publish\Microsoft.Practices.ESB.ExceptionHandling.
InfoPath.Reporting.xsn" name="urn:schemas-microsoft-com:office:
infopath:Microsoft-Practices-ESB-ExceptionHandling-InfoPath-
Reporting:http---schemas-microsoft-biztalk-practices-esb-
com-exceptionhandling" language="en-us" ?><?mso-application
progid="InfoPath.Document"?>
```

If our client application is run and the exception is raised, we should see a message traverse the BizTalk bus and settle in on disk. After opening the form, we are first presented with the general exception details.

Next we are shown the low-level details of the exception itself.

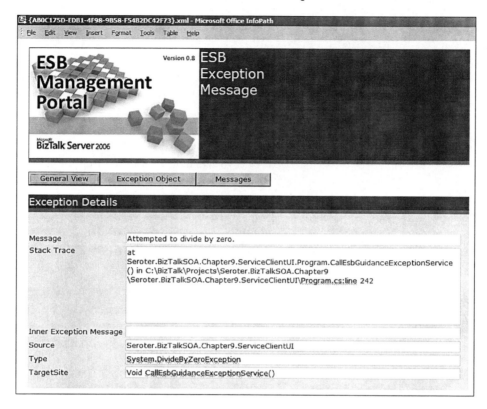

The very last option (**Messages**) allows us to view any of the messages that we attached to the exception alongside any context properties that came along for the ride.

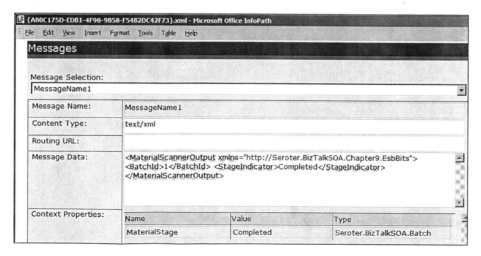

It would be quite easy to write multiple chapters solely about the ESB Guidance Exception Management components, so this serves only as an exercise to whet your appetite for more. While the Exception Service provides a valuable on-ramp for external parties to gather their exception processing in a single place, some of the nicest qualities of this library exist for internal BizTalk exception processing. While I did not cover that here, I highly encourage you to do some investigation and consider using it as a central exception framework in your BizTalk solutions.

Itinerary Services

Itinerary processing represents a critical part of the ESB Guidance package. An itinerary is a set of instructions which outline a sequence of services that the bus should perform on a given message. This capability is carried out through a set of WCF services, pipeline components and well-defined metadata schemas. These components work in concert to maintain state, track and advance the itinerary through each service, and perform resolution of transformations, endpoints, and orchestrations.

A key value of itineraries is that they attach to the message itself and do not require any deployment to the BizTalk environment. Instead, itineraries offer us a way to compose processing paths made up of existing (BizTalk) services while not incurring the cost of building, deploying, and maintaining tightly-coupled orchestrations.

A new aspect of the itinerary services introduced in ESB Guidance 2.0 is the Itinerary Designer hosted in Visual Studio.NET. In earlier releases, it was the task of the developer to either handcraft an XML itinerary and design time or compose the necessary itinerary members in code at runtime. Now, you right-click a Visual Studio. NET project and directly add an itinerary. There is a succinct set of design shapes that load up in the Visual Studio.NET toolbox and are available for arranging the itinerary.

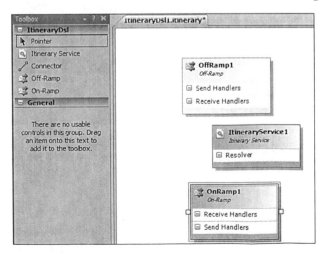

An **On-Ramp** is a component that receives messages onto the service bus. It is configured to receive either synchronous or asynchronous messages. Similarly, the **Off-Ramp** shape is a means for exiting the service bus in either a synchronous or asynchronous manner. The **Itinerary Service** shape is an all-purpose activity that enables either of the following two options:

1. Message-based routing or transformation.
2. Orchestration services such as transformation or routing.

The difference between the messaging and orchestration-based services is that messaging-based services get tightly coupled to an **Off-Ramp** or **On-Ramp** due to the fact that they get executed as part of a receive or send pipeline. Conversely, the orchestration-based services may be invoked at any part of an itinerary and are not associated with a particular endpoint.

Notice what is NOT part of itinerary design. First of all, there is no definition of the messages in an itinerary. That would introduce coupling and limit reuse, and the ability to use dynamic resolution makes explicit message definition unnecessary and unwanted. Secondly, see that there is no concept of control flow shapes. That again is not the purpose of an itinerary. The itinerary allows us to patch together a series of services that our message should pass through. Business logic needs to be part of the services themselves and not seep into the itinerary.

Each itinerary has an important set of model properties that are visible by clicking on any empty space in the design window. You can set the synchronous/asynchronous nature of the itinerary through the **Is Request Response** flag, provide a **Name** for the itinerary, and dictate how to export the itinerary. Once the model is done, you export it for clients to consume. By default, the **XML Itinerary Exporter** is selected. This exporter sends the XML itinerary to the location specified in the **Itinerary XML file** property. If you wish to allow for dynamic resolution and easier sharing, you should flip the exporter to the **Database Itinerary Exporter,** which stashes the XML itinerary (and accompanying metadata) into a database table.

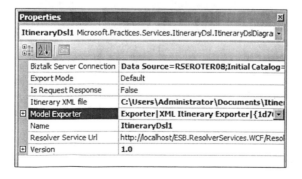

We have a short set of basics down, so how about we build a few scenarios that demonstrate an increasingly complex set of itineraries and consumption patterns.

Building a basic routing scenario

First, we will construct an example where we define a simple routing itinerary and execute it from the client application.

Before we do anything inside Visual Studio.NET, we first need to craft a dynamic send port that acts as the final step in our itinerary. From the BizTalk Administration Console, define a new, one-way dynamic port with a **PassThroughTransmit** pipeline. The most important part of this send port is the filter expression. Apply the following parameters:

Context property	Condition	Group by
Microsoft.Practices.ESB.Itinerary.Schemas. IsRequestResponse	== false	And
Microsoft.Practices.ESB.Itinerary.Schemas.ServiceName	== DistributeBatch	And
Microsoft.Practices.ESB.Itinerary.Schemas.ServiceState	== Pending	And
Microsoft.Practices.ESB.Itinerary.Schemas.ServiceType	== Messaging	

Once these values are in place, save the send port and return to Visual Studio.NET. To hold our itineraries, I created a new Visual Studio.NET class library project. Note that these files do not need to reside in an assembly (or any .NET project type for that matter), but it is a convenient place to store them.

After right-clicking the new project and adding a new Itinerary, I named the itinerary **BatchWithRouting.itinerary**. This itinerary has three shapes: On-Ramp, Itinerary Service, and Off-Ramp.

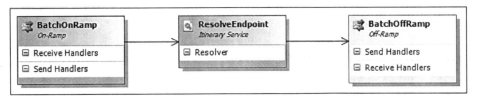

For the **BatchOnRamp** shape, we set the **Extender** property to **On-Ramp ESB Service Extension**. I don't need to create my own receive port to receive itinerary messages as one is already pre-built in the **Microsoft.Practices.ESB** application. Therefore, I set the **BatchOnRamp's** property named **BizTalk Application** to **Microsoft.Practices.ESB** and set the **Receive Port** property to **OnRamp.Itinerary**.

Click on the **BatchOffRamp** shape and set it to use the **Off-Ramp ESB Service Extension** extender. Our off-ramp should use the dynamic send port we just created, so set the **BizTalk Application** value to **BizTalkSOA** and choose the previously built port. Once we do this, a series of read-only attributes (e.g. **ServiceName**, **ServiceType**) are set based on the send port's subscription criteria.

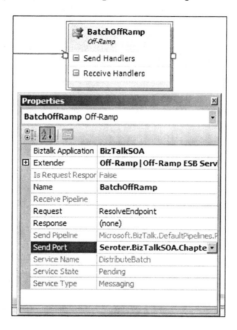

Finally, we must configure the **ResolveEndpoint** shape, which is responsible for setting the outbound transport and location of the off-ramp. Its **Itinerary Service Extender** property needs to be equal to **Off-Ramp Itinerary Service Extension**. The missing component here is an actual resolver, so right-click the **Resolver** section of the shape and add a new resolver. I set the **Resolver Implementation** to **Static Resolver Extension** with the intent of putting a physical endpoint directly into my itinerary. My **Transport Name** is equal to FILE and the **Transport Location** is set to a valid file path on my system.

When we attempt to save this itinerary, our property settings get evaluated and verified for correctness. We discussed the "export" capabilities of itineraries, and for this example, we are exporting to the file system. After confirming an acceptable location via the **Itinerary XML file** property, right-click anywhere in the model and select **Export Model**. If the export succeeds, you should see the itinerary in XML format.

```
C:\...\BatchWithRouting.xml    BatchWithRouting.itinerary
URL: C:\BizTalk\Projects\Seroter.BizTalkSOA.Chapter9\Itineraries\BatchWithRouting.xml

   <?xml version="1.0" encoding="utf-8" ?>
 - <Itinerary xmlns:xsi="http://www.w3.org/2001/XMLSchema-instance"
     xmlns:xsd="http://www.w3.org/2001/XMLSchema" uuid="" beginTime=""
     completeTime="" state="Pending" isRequestResponse="false" servicecount="1"
     xmlns="http://schemas.microsoft.biztalk.practices.esb.com/itinerary">
     <BizTalkSegment interchangeId="" epmRRCorrelationToken="" receiveInstanceId=""
       messageId="" xmlns="" />
     <ServiceInstance name="DistributeBatch" type="Messaging" state="Pending"
       position="0" isRequestResponse="false" xmlns="" />
   - <Services xmlns="">
       <Service uuid="8fdc8e69969546dab6ebf1a4e0b9ad56" beginTime=""
         completeTime="" name="DistributeBatch" type="Messaging" state="Pending"
         isRequestResponse="false" position="0" serviceInstanceId="" />
     </Services>
   - <ResolverGroups xmlns="">
       <Resolvers serviceId="DistributeBatch0"><![CDATA
         [STATIC:\\TransportType=FILE;TransportLocation=C:\BizTalk\Projects\Seroter.Bi
         \FileDrop\Seroter.BizTalkSOA.Chapter9.SendItineraryResult\BatchRoutingOutput.
         ></Resolvers>
     </ResolverGroups>
   </Itinerary>
```

At this point, we are ready to execute this itinerary from client code. Add a service reference to the asynchronous Itinerary Service located at http://<server>/ESB. ItineraryServices.WCF/ProcessItinerary.svc. The first activity in our code is to read the itinerary XML from disk and serialize it into a typed object.

```
private static void SubmitEsbGuidanceItineraryRouting()
  {
Console.WriteLine("Calling ESB Guidance itinerary service");

ProcessRequestClient client =
  new ProcessRequestClient("WSHttpBinding_ITwoWayAsyncVoid1");

  try
  {
//reference itinerary on disk
XmlDocument itineraryDoc = new XmlDocument();
  itineraryDoc.Load(@"C:\BizTalk\Projects\Seroter.BizTalkSOA.Chapter9\
    Itineraries\BatchWithRouting.xml");

  StringReader itineraryReader =
    new StringReader(itineraryDoc.DocumentElement.OuterXml);

//serialize XML into itinerary object
XmlSerializer ser = new XmlSerializer((typeof(Itinerary)),
  "http://schemas.microsoft.biztalk.practices.esb.com/itinerary");
  Itinerary basicItinerary = (Itinerary)ser.Deserialize
    (itineraryReader);
```

Our itinerary is properly parsed and loaded so we set a unique ID for this instance and send the itinerary to the service alongside the actual message payload.

```
//set unique ID
basicItinerary.uuid = Guid.NewGuid().ToString();

//inflate actual XML payload of request
XmlDocument batchScanResult = new XmlDocument();
                batchScanResult.LoadXml("<MaterialScannerOutput
xmlns=\"http://Seroter.BizTalkSOA.Chapter9.EsbBits\"><BatchId>BatchId_
0</BatchId><StageIndicator>StageIndicator_0</StageIndicator></
MaterialScannerOutput>");

client.SubmitRequest(basicItinerary, batchScanResult.OuterXml);
```

After this code is executed, we find a message on disk matching what was sent into the on-ramp service.

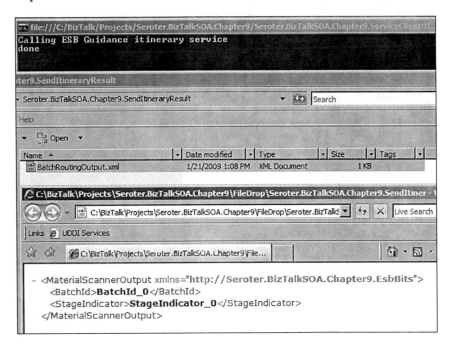

This was a very straightforward itinerary that didn't take advantage of many loose-coupling benefits of the ESB itinerary processing. How about we see how to dynamically load the target itinerary from client code, and add new services to the itinerary itself?

Building a routing scenario with transformation

In this example, we vary the previous itinerary slightly, but also show a new way to load up an itinerary at runtime for execution.

I've created a brand new itinerary named **BatchWithRoutingTransform** which has the exact same three shapes as the last itinerary, with one additional shape tacked on.

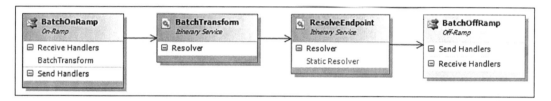

The **BatchTransform** shape is responsible for mapping the inbound content into a different format. The shape's **Itinerary Service Extender** is set to **Messaging Itinerary Service Extension**. These extensions are executed as part of a port's pipeline, so we will designate its container as the **BatchOnRamp** shape's receive handler. There are two known service types for a messaging-based itinerary service: routing and transformation. Since this shape is doing transformation, we must set the **Service Name** to **Microsoft.Practices.ESB.Services.Transform**. Do you remember earlier when we called the Transformation Service and resolved the map details at runtime through the Resolver Service? Guess what? We're going to reuse the work we did there.

Add a new resolver to the **BatchTransform** resolver collection and name it **BRE Resolver**. Its **Resolver Implementation** uses the **BRE Resolver Extension** as we will reuse the business rule policy created for the earlier transformation resolution. The available policies on our server are presented in the **Policy** property and I chose the **Seroter.BizTalkSOA.Chapter9.Transform** ruleset. To be confident that our resolver is configured correctly, we right-click the resolver and choose **Test Resolver Configuration**. This command actually executes the resolver and returns back the XML result of the query.

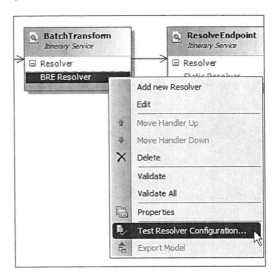

Our itinerary is complete and we are ready for export. Instead of exporting this itinerary to disk, let's instead put it into a database. Switch the **Model Exporter** property of the overall model from the default **XML Itinerary Exporter** to the sexier **Database Itinerary Exporter**. By stashing our itinerary in a database, we open up more opportunities for reuse and runtime resolution.

In the client code, we are going to yank this itinerary from the database instead of loading it physically from the file system. This is a much more flexible model that doesn't require the XML itinerary to be installed with the client or made available on a network file system.

```
XmlDocument itineraryDoc = new XmlDocument();

Console.WriteLine("Calling ESB Guidance resolver service");

ResolverServiceClient rClient = new ResolverServiceClient
    ("ResolverEndpoint");

    try
    {
```

```
    rClient.ClientCredentials.Windows.AllowedImpersonationLevel =
      System.Security.Principal.TokenImpersonationLevel.Impersonation;
    string resolverString = @"ITINERARY:\\name=BatchWithRoutingTransform;
      version=1.0";
  Resolver[] resolverCollection = rClient.Resolve(resolverString);

    rClient.Close();

    foreach (Resolver resolver in resolverCollection)
    {
    if (resolver.Name == "Resolver.Itinerary")
      {
    itineraryDoc.LoadXml(resolver.Value);
    break;
      }
    }
}
    catch (System.ServiceModel.CommunicationException) { rClient.
Abort(); }
    catch (System.TimeoutException) { rClient.Abort(); }
    catch (System.Exception) { rClient.Abort(); throw; }
```

So using nothing but the itinerary name, we've been able to resolve the full contents of the itinerary and loaded it into an XML document for later usage. The remainder of the code closely resembles the flow used in the previous exercise.

```
Console.WriteLine("Calling ESB Guidance itinerary service");

  ProcessRequestClient client =
    new ProcessRequestClient("WSHttpBinding_ITwoWayAsyncVoid1");

  try
  {
  StringReader itineraryReader =
    new StringReader(itineraryDoc.DocumentElement.OuterXml);

//serialize XML into itinerary object
XmlSerializer ser = new XmlSerializer((typeof(Itinerary)),
  "http://schemas.microsoft.biztalk.practices.esb.com/itinerary");
  Itinerary basicItinerary =
    (Itinerary)ser.Deserialize(itineraryReader);

//set unique ID
  basicItinerary.uuid = Guid.NewGuid().ToString();

//inflate actual XML payload of request
XmlDocument batchScanResult = new XmlDocument();
batchScanResult.LoadXml("<MaterialScannerOutput xmlns=
  \"http://Seroter.BizTalkSOA.Chapter9.EsbBits\"><BatchId>BatchId_0
    </BatchId><StageIndicator>StageIndicator_0</StageIndicator>
      </MaterialScannerOutput>");
```

```
client.SubmitRequest(basicItinerary, batchScanResult.OuterXml);
client.Close();
}
catch (System.ServiceModel.CommunicationException){client.Abort(); }
catch (System.TimeoutException) { client.Abort(); }
catch (System.Exception) { client.Abort(); throw; }
```

This time, we end up with a transformed file on disk which matches our
BatchMaster format.

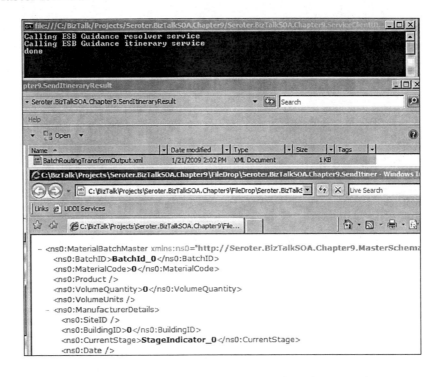

So now we know how to add services to itineraries that do more than just routing.
But what if we want to include a custom orchestration in our process? And how
about not dealing with itineraries AT ALL on the client side and leaving it up to the
server to attach these processing instructions?

Building a scenario with chained operations and orchestration

Let's put a few more pieces of this puzzle into place. In this use case, I want to query
a table using the WCF SQL Server Adapter and send those results to an orchestration
which in turn, maps the message, performs some logic, and returns a result back to
the original itinerary caller. Sounds like fun?

While building the first itinerary scenario, we constructed a one-way dynamic send port, which was responsible for sending the final messages of our itineraries. For this use case, we need a two-way dynamic send port that we are able to exploit to call the WCF SQL Server Adapter and route the response. Unlike our previously built send port, this two way port requires ESB pipeline components in the send and receive pipeline.

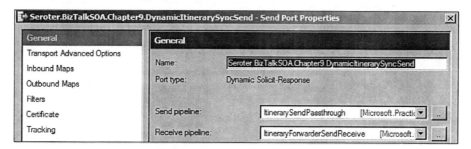

These pipelines ensure that the itinerary of the outbound message is stored and reattached to the message returning to the port. We also must add the appropriate filters to this port, which enable it to retrieve messages designated for it.

Context property	Condition	Group by
Microsoft.Practices.ESB.Itinerary.Schemas.IsRequestResponse	== false	And
Microsoft.Practices.ESB.Itinerary.Schemas.ServiceName	== BatchLookup	And
Microsoft.Practices.ESB.Itinerary.Schemas.ServiceState	== Pending	And
Microsoft.Practices.ESB.Itinerary.Schemas.ServiceType	== Messaging	

Return to our Visual Studio.NET project, which contains itineraries. Because we're doing a synchronous transaction, the first thing we have to do in our new itinerary is set the model property **Is Request Response** to **True**. This ensures that the inbound ESB Guidance receive pipeline sets the necessary Endpoint Manager correlation tokens that are required for the message to find its way back to proper receive port instance after the itinerary is completed.

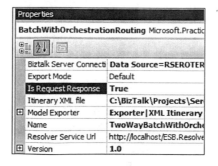

We start our drawing with an on-ramp shape and service shape. The on-ramp, named **BatchOnRamp** will be a synchronous on-ramp, so after setting the **Application** property to **Microsoft.Practices.ESB**, I chose the **OnRamp.Itinerary. Response** receive port.

The **MessageTransform** service shape uses the **Message Itinerary Service Extension** extender and its processing **Container** is the **BatchOnRamp** shape's receive handler. Its service type is **Microsoft.Practices.ESB.Services.Transform**. I added a static resolver to the transformation shape which applies the existing BizTalk map that takes a `BatchMaster` record and morphs it into the `BatchTableRequest` message.

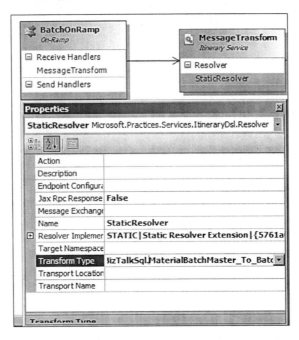

Now we need to provide the required transport details in order to invoke the WCF SQL Server Adapter from our upcoming dynamic send port. Add another service shape named **Enrichment Routing**, which also uses the **Message Itinerary Service Extension** extender and is attached to the on-ramp as its container. Unlike the previous shape, this one uses a **Service Name** of **Microsoft.Practices.ESB. Services.Routing** because it's responsible for setting up routing instructions (vs. performing transformation).

I've added a static resolver to this shape which is responsible for assigning required routing details. After setting the **Resolver Implementation** to **Static Resolver Extension**, I chose **WCF-Custom** as the **Transport Name**. This allows us to set the **Action** property, binding type (through the **Endpoint Configuration** property), and connection URI (via the **Transport Location** property).

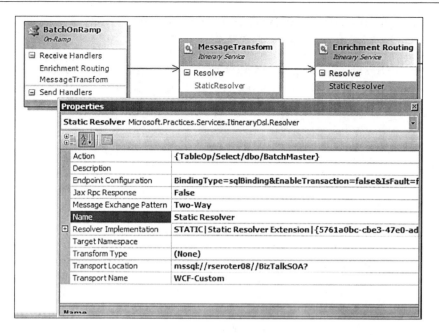

Next we add an off-ramp, which is responsible for calling the WCF SQL Server Adapter. This off-ramp, named **BatchLookupOffRamp**, uses the **Off-Ramp ESB Service Extension** extender and references the **BizTalkSOA** application and our new two-way dynamic send port.

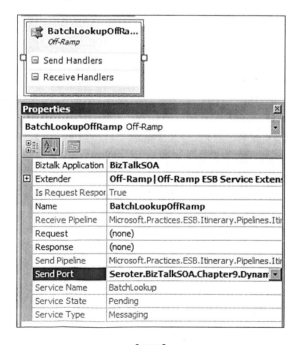

In order to invoke the **BatchLookupOffRamp**, we explicitly need a service shape assigned with an **Off-Ramp Itinerary Service Extension**. This shape, tied to the off-ramp shape, will advance the itinerary and establish the subscription for the dynamic port. This shape, named **InvokeOffRamp**, needs no resolvers, is associated with the **BatchLookupOffRamp's** Send Handler, and uses the **Off-Ramp Itinerary Service Extension**.

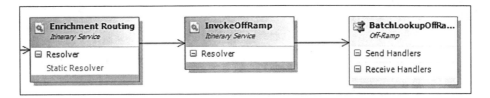

Another goal for this scenario is to call a custom orchestration, so let's take a break from itinerary design and build an orchestration that is capable of being plugged into this sequence of services. In a BizTalk project, create a new orchestration. Create orchestration messages for the `BatchSelectResponse` schema and `BatchMaster` schema. The topmost receive shape, similar to a send port, requires a set of filters that enable it to pick up our message at the correct point in the itinerary flow.

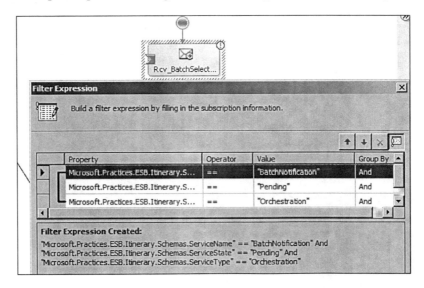

Notice that I've designated a service name particular to this orchestration. Before we progress further, add project references to the **Microsoft.Practices.ESB.Itinerary.dll** and **Microsoft.Practices.ESB.Itinerary.Schemas.dll**. These provide us with helper classes and property schemas we need to complete the orchestration. Once you have those references, add an orchestration variable of type **Microsoft.Practices. ESB.Itinerary.ItineraryStep**. Now in our orchestration designer, drag an expression shape and insert the code needed to determine what the current itinerary step is.

```
//get current step
itineraryStep = Microsoft.Practices.ESB.Itinerary.ItineraryHelper.
CurrentStep
(BatchSelectResponse_Input);
```

Now we construct our outbound message by transforming the result of the WCF SQL Server Adapter call into the canonical `BatchMaster` format. Create a new map which performs this transformation.

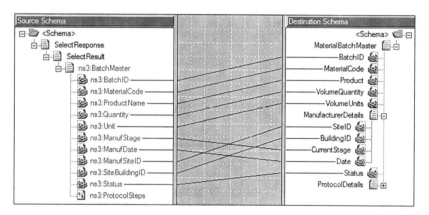

In our orchestration, after calling the **Transform** shape, we add an **Assignment** shape where we insert the necessary code to copy the context from the previous message and advance the itinerary.

```
//copy context so that ESB Guidance properties transfer over
BatchMaster_Output(*) = BatchSelectResponse_Input(*);
```

```
//advance itinerary to next step
Microsoft.Practices.ESB.Itinerary.ItineraryHelper.AdvanceItinerary(Bat
chMaster_Output, itineraryStep);
```

After adding a direct-bound orchestration receive port, our orchestration flow is complete.

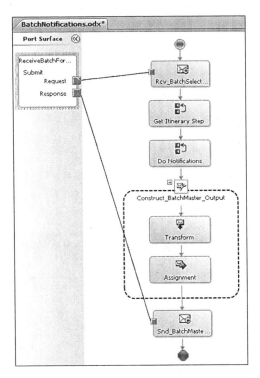

However, there is one step remaining prior to deploying this orchestration. We must ensure that critical context values from the outbound message are thrust into the promoted property bag so that the necessary itinerary routing can continue. The only way to ensure that this happens is to create correlation sets and initialize them on the way out of the orchestration. I have created two correlation types: one for all orchestration that are part of itinerary solutions, and another that is only required when the orchestration is part of a synchronous itinerary solution.

The first correlation set includes the following properties:

Property
BTS.OutboundTransportLocation
BTS.OutboundTransportType
Microsoft.Practices.ESB.Itinerary.Schemas.IsRequestResponse
Microsoft.Practices.ESB.Itinerary.Schemas.ServiceName
Microsoft.Practices.ESB.Itinerary.Schemas.ServiceState
Microsoft.Practices.ESB.Itinerary.Schemas.ServiceType

These properties must always be promoted on outbound messages. The second correlation type contains properties vital in associating the message with the receive port that originally received it and awaits a response.

Property
BTS.CorrelationToken
BTS.EpmRRCorrelationToken
BTS.IsRequestResponse
BTS.ReqRespTransmitPipelineID
BTS.RouteDirectToTP

Now that our correlation sets are added and associated with the outbound send shape, our orchestration should be deployed.

Back in our itinerary designer, drag a new service shape to the surface and name it **Custom Orchestration** and set its **Itinerary Service Extender** equal to **Orchestration Itinerary Service Extension**. Also, don't forget to flip the **Is Request Response** flag to **True** indicating that this orchestration behaves synchronously. After connecting it to our previous off-ramp, we want to select our new orchestration as the **Service Name**. But, when we look at the un-editable drop-down list, all we see are the Routing and Transform orchestration services. How do we get our new fellow in there?

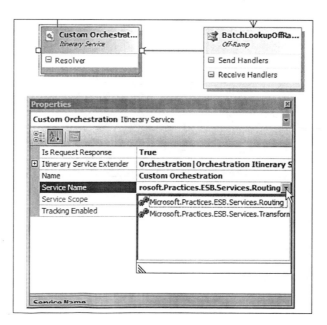

The trick is to open the **esb.config** file located at `C:\<installation directory>\esb.config`. Find the `<ItineraryServices>` node and add a new `<ItineraryService>` child with the details about our new orchestration. For instance, mine looks like this:

```
<itineraryServices>

  <itineraryService id="6a594d80-91f7-4e10-a203-b3c999b0f55e"
name="Microsoft.Practices.ESB.Services.Routing" type="Microsoft.
Practices.ESB.Itinerary.Services.RoutingService, Microsoft.Practices.
ESB.Itinerary.Services, Version=2.0.0.0, Culture=neutral, PublicKeyTok
en=31bf3856ad364e35" scope="Messaging"
        stage="AllReceive"/>

...

<!-- custom -->
  <itineraryService id="d6ac2709-da66-41c8-939f-db647e1b111"
name="BatchNotification" type="Seroter.BizTalkSOA.Chapter9.
EsbBits.BatchNotifications, Seroter.BizTalkSOA.Chapter9.EsbBits,
Version=1.0.0.0, Culture=neutral, PublicKeyToken=3a9902d460c201ec"
scope="Orchestration"
  stage="All" />
</itineraryServices>
```

Don't forget to assign a unique GUID for the identification attribute so that the engine doesn't get confused when loading your custom service. Once this configuration file is saved, we need to close down Visual Studio.NET and reopen it. Once you do, you should now have the option of choosing **BatchNotification** as your orchestrations service name.

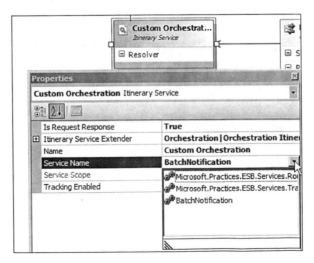

To complete our itinerary, we connect our custom (two-way) orchestration shape to the original on-ramp.

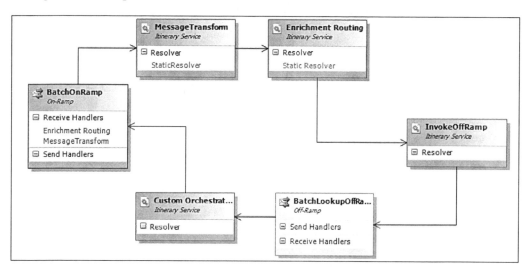

Save the model and export it to the database. As we discussed at the beginning of this use case, we want to avoid ANY client reference to an itinerary. All the client does is transmit a payload to an endpoint. So how does the itinerary get attached? In the **Microsoft.Practices.ESB** BizTalk application there is a receive location named **ESB.ItineraryServices.Generic.Response.WCF**. This is associated with the generic ESB Guidance on-ramp service which only takes the XML payload and no itinerary. Its receive pipeline, **ItinerarySelectReceive**, has a component that does itinerary resolution.

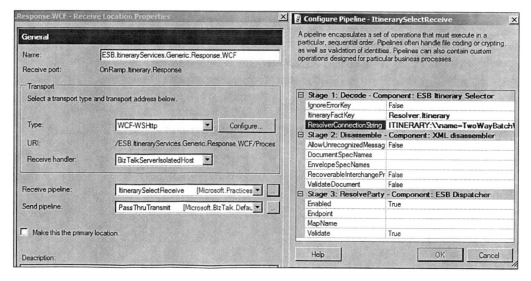

The resolver string entered here, `ITINERARY:\\name=TwoWayBatchWithOrchestr ationRouting;` implies that ANY message arriving at this endpoint will have this itinerary attached to it. Clearly, this isn't very loosely coupled or reusable. In the real world, you'd want to you use the BRI resolver (which uses the Business Rules Engine to look up the itinerary) or write a custom resolver that applies party resolution or other lookup techniques. But for our example, we'll keep it simple.

In our client code, we include a new service reference to the generic on-ramp service located at: `http://<server>/ESB.ItineraryServices.Generic.Response.WCF/ ProcessItinerary.svc`. Now we are able to execute the pleasantly uncomplicated code to call this endpoint.

```
private static void SubmitEsbGuidanceItinerarySync()
   {
Console.WriteLine("Calling ESB Guidance two way itinerary service");

//inflate actual XML payload of request
XmlDocument batchQuery = new XmlDocument();
   batchQuery.Load(@"C:\BizTalk\Projects\Seroter.BizTalkSOA.Chapter9\
     Instances\MaterialBatchMaster_XML_output - BatchIDOnly.xml");

   object resp = batchQuery.OuterXml;

ProcessRequestResponseClient client = new ProcessRequestResponseClient
   ("WSHttpBinding_ITwoWayAsync1");

   try
   {
   client.SubmitRequestResponse(ref resp);

   client.Close();
   }
   catch (System.ServiceModel.CommunicationException) { client.Abort(); }
   catch (System.TimeoutException) { client.Abort(); }
   catch (System.Exception) { client.Abort(); throw; }

XmlDocument responseBatchXml = new XmlDocument();
XmlElement root = responseBatchXml.CreateElement("root");
   foreach (XmlNode fragment in (IEnumerable)resp)
   {
   root.AppendChild(responseBatchXml.ImportNode(fragment, false));
   }

Console.WriteLine(root.InnerText);

Console.WriteLine("done");

Console.ReadLine();
   }
```

In this scenario, we successfully injected a synchronous service call as well as a custom orchestration process into our itinerary. At runtime, instead of requiring the client to understand the association between the message and its itinerary, we interfaced with the generic on-ramp service and left itinerary resolution to the server.

Summary

While one of the biggest reasons for organizations to upgrade to BizTalk Server 2009 is platform modernization, don't overlook these three critical pieces that are incorporated into the product. In the previous two chapters we saw the new, powerful WCF SQL Server adapter and in the last chapter we looked at the new UDDI service registry that ships with BizTalk Server 2009. In this chapter, we investigated how the ESB Guidance 2.0 package enables a more service-oriented approach through standalone services, dynamic resolution, and itinerary processing.

These are all exciting technologies that warrant more of your attention and future examination. Each of these offerings could justify a book of their own, so my only goal was to introduce you to each and hopefully boost your interest in them.

In the following final chapter, we take a look at the future of Microsoft's SOA platform and where things are going with BizTalk Server.

12
What's Next

Go forth to meet the shadowy Future without fear and with a manly heart.
-Henry Wadsworth Longfellow

Microsoft has not chosen to let their mature frameworks and existing product base act as their sole service strategy. Instead, Microsoft is entering a compelling period of new offerings that enables us to create, consume, and compose services in ways not previously possible. In this chapter, we'll briefly talk about three brand new technologies that are core to Microsoft's long-term application platform strategy. Then we'll talk about what the future holds for the BizTalk Server product. Finally, we'll close out our time together with a summary of the material we've covered in this book. Please note that all discussions of upcoming technologies will contain information that is subject to change prior to the formal release of the corresponding products.

"Dublin"

"Dublin" is the code name for a set of service extensions added to IIS 7.0 and Windows Server 2008. These extensions enable a rich set of management capabilities targeted at WCF and Windows Workflow (WF) applications. Specifically, this includes support for durable services and long-running WF workflows.

What problem does it solve?

Today, WF developers are forced to make all sorts of decisions and trade-offs when choosing a host for their workflow. While strides have been made, there is no clear, easy choice. Dublin offers a consistent WF host that provides automatic support for important WF concepts like persistence and messaging. Dublin also supplies administrators with a coherent way to view and interact with running and suspended workflows.

Speaking of administration, that's really where Dublin solves a problem with current WCF and WF hosting options. Today, there is no straightforward way to iterate all WCF services on a web site or get a consolidated view of service status. Dublin's IIS/WAS extensions give us a new way to monitor services and interact with WF workflows.

Dublin is being positioned as a core "application server" as opposed to BizTalk Server being an "integration server". If you are looking to build application workflows or don't need the infrastructure that BizTalk Server provides, then the combination of Dublin and WF offer you a significant value proposition: rapidly build (declarative) workflows that can be singularly deployed to an enterprise-scale application server. However, a solution consisting of Dublin + WCF + WF does not equate to a BizTalk-based deliverable. BizTalk provides a deep array of B2B services, a high-performing rules engine, Business Activity Monitoring, flexible exception handling, and powerful message-oriented routing, among other things. The introduction of Dublin as a WCF/WF host means that we can build even richer solutions that consist of exceptional service hosting and enterprise class messaging.

For WCF developers, Dublin introduces a more full-featured server to host our services. Whether it's using the messaging capability to do content-based routing, or finally introducing a richer management experience, Dublin makes it easier to deploy business services within the enterprise.

.NET Services

Windows Azure is the "cloud platform" offering from Microsoft that consists of developer services and infrastructure used to construct Internet-scale hosted applications. The .NET Services component of Windows Azure introduces cloud-based functionality which addresses connectivity, access control and workflow. The three core components (Service Bus, Access Control Service and Workflow Service) form an exciting and innovative way to securely move your organization into cloud computing with an intriguing set of features.

The Service Bus provides a robust infrastructure for connecting cloud users to services residing behind secure organizational walls. I can take a service that is not currently public Internet-addressable and expose it securely to the "message bus" in the cloud. This relay capability is loaded with message exchange pattern options ranging from one-way message to request/response all the way to broadcast scenarios. All of this is done with new WCF bindings, which means that little to no changes are required in the service code itself to accommodate these new cloud-based scenarios.

The Access Control Service provides a standards-based infrastructure for authentication and authorization in the cloud. Here you can define the parties and claim-mapping rules that are relevant to your specific application.

The Workflow Service is essentially Windows Workflow in the cloud. You get access to a specific set of cloud-friendly WF activities which are built to enable a workflow to exchange messages and exist in a long-running fashion. In addition to development tooling, the Workflow Service also provides an administrative interface where you can interact with workflow instances running in the cloud.

What problem does it solve?

The .NET Services solve problems inherent in cross-organization communication. The Service Bus enables us to easily share services that don't belong on the public Internet but still provide capabilities desired by strategic external partners. The diverse set of message exchange patterns means that we can participate in meaningful two-way conversations with other parties while using the Service Bus as a router that abstracts and protects the actual service endpoints.

The Access Control Service aids in the creation of truly federated identity solutions where identity stores tightly coupled to application logic or maintenance of a single registry of external partner credentials are giant headaches. This service can translate claims submitted from a varied set of inbound identity repositories and emit a single set of standard, trusted claims, which the application uses to authorize users. The key is that application developers can avoid writing custom authentication logic, querying multiple identity directories, or storing accounts and corresponding permissions. The Access Control Service decouples these applications from any one identity store and acts as the single intermediary.

Finally, we can use the Workflow Service to tie all these other services together. Consider the possibilities of having a stateful, long-running workflow that sits between business partners and uses the Service Bus to share messages and the Access Control Service as the security umbrella over the process.

"Oslo"

"Oslo" is the code name for the set of technologies that make up the new modelling platform from Microsoft. The Oslo suite is comprised of a repository which stores models and associated context, a modelling language (codenamed M) that describes the model information, and a tool (codenamed Quadrant) which provides a visual mechanism for interacting with models in the repository. In the Oslo world, a model represents anything from an application to a deployment landscape to a business process. Unlike UML, which is frequently used for describing systems, the Oslo models are meant to both represent abstract concepts and actually be the application itself.

What problem does it solve?

There is rarely a tight correlation between the design of a process and its implementation. Sure, a developer does their best to maintain the spirit of the business process or rule when they write their code, but there is no direct relationship between the modelled processes and the final solution. The ambitious goal of Oslo is to change the way that we design, build and manage applications. The "model" takes center stage as a critical part of any application. In the case of building an application workflow in Oslo, this model itself becomes an executable component so that changing the workflow means actually changing the model! By having a common way to define models that address a wide range of abstract and concrete entities, and a shared location to store them, Microsoft hopes to allow organizations to maintain better control and visibility of their application throughout its lifespan.

Future of BizTalk Server

There are aspects of Dublin, .NET Services, and Oslo that all sound eerily familiar to BizTalk developers. It's not surprising to see such valuable capabilities escape the confines of a single product (BizTalk) and become more readily available as platform-level services. Durable workflow and content-based routing? Check. Diverse message exchange patterns and workflow meant to integrate disparate parties? Check. Designing executable models in a consistent way? Check. But what does all this mean to BizTalk Server and its legion of customers moving forward?

In mid-2008, Microsoft reaffirmed its investment in the BizTalk platform by promising to maintain a distinct development team which is chartered with regular releases of the product. The proposed feature list for future versions of BizTalk Server includes low latency messaging, richer development tools, stronger B2B management, and consistent support for the latest and greatest platform technologies.

But what role does BizTalk play in this new world of capabilities offered by Microsoft? As it stands today (and for the foreseeable future), BizTalk Server is your best choice for reliable and available enterprise messaging between systems, B2B scenarios with EDI/AS2 and industry-compliant formats like SWIFT, and sophisticated visual tooling for designing and administering enterprise service solutions. I hesitate to mention "adapters" as a key differentiator given the trend of making technology and LOB system connectivity a commodity that is accessible at broad level. The value of BizTalk really comes from the number of relevant capabilities that are simply available out of the box and don't require us to try to design the infrastructure services we need to build reliable, scalable applications.

While there has been a logical move to take some of BizTalk's strongest ideas and make them accessible outside of the product, do not expect BizTalk to be cannibalized until all that remains is a flat file parser. An "integration server" (as Microsoft has begun to categorize BizTalk Server) isn't just about connecting disparate applications/services but rather it addresses a full set of non-functional requirements around fault handling, reliability, single sign on, event publishing and robust orchestration. While still a non-brainer for EAI and B2B scenarios, BizTalk Server still has a home as a service bus that enables an extensive set of use cases within your organization.

Summary

SOA is all about architecture, not products. The point of this book was to demonstrate real, concrete examples of the principles and patterns of SOA through the use of BizTalk Server 2009. Does using BizTalk Server instantly make you service-oriented? Of course not; no software can (or should) make that claim. Instead, it is up to you to internalize the core concepts of loose coupling, abstraction, encapsulation, interoperability, and reuse and aggressively apply them wherever it makes sense. Products like BizTalk Server are simply tools that allow you to apply your service-oriented principles in a software solution.

I hope that this book triggered new ideas in your mind and offered you innovative ways to tackle the problems that you currently face. With the tooling finally beginning to catch up to the promise of SOA, we are surely in for an exciting period of software design.

Index

B

basic routing scenario, building
  about 348-353
  BatchOffRamp shape 349
  BatchOnRamp property 349
  BatchOnRamp shape 349
  BatchWithRouting.itinerary 348
  Extender property 349
  Itinerary Service property 350
  Receive Port property 349
  Resolveendpoint shape, configuring 350
benefits, asynchronous communication
  event-driven, encouraging 158
  fewer operation dependencies 158
  long-running process support 158
  no client blocking 158
binding, service aspect 246
BizTalk adapter Pack 2.0
  about 278
  components, SQL Server adapter 278
  SQL Server adapter, features 278, 279
  WCF LOB 278
BizTalk Mapper
  about 26, 27
  functoids 26
BizTalk message type
  using 105
BizTalk messaging, configuring 28-30
BizTalk project
  prerequisites 19
  setting up 19-21
BizTalk schema
  about 21, 22
  creating 22-24
  property schema 25
BizTalk Scripting 104
BizTalk Server 2009. *See also* BizTalk Server
BizTalk Server
  about 9, 14
  acting, as service provider 184
  adapters 9
  architectural choice benefits 11
  architecture 15
  asynchronous communication, importance
    158

asynchronous services, using with WCF
    171-178
BasicHttpBinding 42
BizTalk Mapper 26, 27
BizTalk messaging, configuring 27-30
BizTalk project, setting up 19-21
BizTalk WCF adapters 56
business-to business (B2B) role 12
Business Process Automation (BPA) 12, 13
callbacks, receiving 184
composite transactions, executing 282-290
defining 14
dynamic ports 107
EAI 10
endpoint, versioning 253
ESB Guidance 333
features 277
future 372, 373
host 58
host, in-process host 58
host, isolated host 58
long-running orchestration, versioning 262
multiple tables, updating 281
NetMsmqBinding 43
NetNamedPipeBinding 43
NetTCPBinding 42
ochestration, working with 30, 31
orchestration 200
queuing logic 190
relation, with WCF 56
reusable schema 126
roles, reviewing 56
scalar query aspcct, adding 290, 291
schema, creating 21-24
schema, versioning 246
Schema Editor 133
service-oriented endpoint pattern 147
service-oriented schema pattern 120
solution, to problems 10-13
UDDI version 3 314, 325
versioning 243
WCF 33
WCF duplex bindings, using 185
WCF LOB 125
working 15, 16
WSHttpBinding 42

Thank you for buying
SOA Patterns with BizTalk Server 2009

About Packt Publishing

Packt, pronounced 'packed', published its first book "*Mastering phpMyAdmin for Effective MySQL Management*" in April 2004 and subsequently continued to specialize in publishing highly focused books on specific technologies and solutions.

Our books and publications share the experiences of your fellow IT professionals in adapting and customizing today's systems, applications, and frameworks. Our solution based books give you the knowledge and power to customize the software and technologies you're using to get the job done. Packt books are more specific and less general than the IT books you have seen in the past. Our unique business model allows us to bring you more focused information, giving you more of what you need to know, and less of what you don't.

Packt is a modern, yet unique publishing company, which focuses on producing quality, cutting-edge books for communities of developers, administrators, and newbies alike. For more information, please visit our website: www.packtpub.com.

Writing for Packt

We welcome all inquiries from people who are interested in authoring. Book proposals should be sent to author@packtpub.com. If your book idea is still at an early stage and you would like to discuss it first before writing a formal book proposal, contact us; one of our commissioning editors will get in touch with you.

We're not just looking for published authors; if you have strong technical skills but no writing experience, our experienced editors can help you develop a writing career, or simply get some additional reward for your expertise.

Business Process Execution Language for Web Services 2nd Edition

ISBN: 1-904811-81-7   Paperback: 350 pages

An Architects and Developers Guide to BPEL and BPEL4WS

1. Architecture, syntax, development and composition of Business Processes and Services using BPEL

2. Advanced BPEL features such as compensation, concurrency, links, scopes, events, dynamic partner links, and correlations

3. Oracle BPEL Process Manager and BPEL Designer Microsoft BizTalk Server as a BPEL server

Business Process Driven SOA using BPMN and BPEL

ISBN: 978-1-847191-46-5   Paperback: 328 pages

From Business Process Modeling to Orchestration and Service Oriented Architecture

1. Understand business process management and how it relates to SOA

2. Understand advanced business process modeling and management with BPMN and BPEL

3. Work with tools that support BPMN and BPEL (Oracle BPA Suite)

4. Transform BPMN to BPEL and execute business processes on the SOA platform

Please check **www.PacktPub.com** for information on our titles

WCF Multi-tier Services Development with LINQ

ISBN: 978-1-847196-62-0   Paperback: 365 pages

Build SOA applications on the Microsoft platform in this hands-on guide

1. Master WCF and LINQ concepts by completing practical examples and apply them to your real-world assignments

2. First book to combine WCF and LINQ in a multi-tier real-world WCF service

3. Ideal for beginners who want to build scalable, powerful, easy-to-maintain WCF services

4. Rich with example code, clear explanations, interesting examples, and practical advice – a truly hands-on book for C++ and C# developers

Business Process Management with JBoss jBPM

ISBN: 978-1-847192-36-3   Paperback: 300 pages

A Practical Guide for Business Analysts

1. Map your business processes in an efficient, standards-friendly way

2. Use the jBPM toolset to work with business process maps, create a customizable user interface for users to interact with the process, collect process execution data, and integrate with existing systems

3. Set up business rules, assign tasks, work with process variables, automate activities and decisions.

Please check **www.PacktPub.com** for information on our titles

Printed in the United States
220423BV00003B/36/P

9 781847 195005